THE LIFE

OF

THOMAS MORRIS:

PIONEER AND LONG A LEGISLATOR OF OHIO,

AND

U. S. SENATOR FROM 1833 TO 1839.

EDITED BY HIS SON,
B. F. MORRIS.

"His memory should be kept freshly living among the lovers of liberty and progress."
SALMON P. CHASE.

CINCINNATI:
PRINTED BY
MOORE, WILSTACH, KEYS & OVEREND.
1856.

Stereotyped and Printed by
WILLIAM OVEREND & CO.
CINCINNATI.

PREFACE.

This work comes before the public, with no ambitious pretensions. It is the compilation and record of the thoughts and acts of a plain and earnest man, narrated in a plain and honest style. It claims not, nor was it the aim of the Editor, to present a work of finished literary excellence; this would not have comported with him, whose thoughts occupy so large a share of these pages, nor with the taste or ability of the Editor. The simple purpose has been, to gather, and weave into a connected narrative, the memorials of the life of one, who was an active laborer in the fields of human toil and freedom, and who, in his day, and in his way, did something to augment the influences that are rising and swelling that great volume of power, which is to achieve the regeneration of humanity, and to inaugurate and establish the final and perpetual reign of freedom. Every contribution, however small, to this stream and tide of influence, is an increment added, and is essential to the combination and completion of the entire power. It is the rivulets that form the rivers and the great oceans of the earth.

The work will be chiefly prized, by the friends of freedom especially, as illustrating the manly heroism of one of the early laborers in the cause of liberty; and of the value and triumph of a persistent adherence to the principles of right, justice, and Constitutional freedom. The true treasures of a State consist in its true principles, and the men who have the courage to give them practical and universal application. Principles, as abstract ideas, or symbols of theory, are intangible and fruitless; they must have, if their nature and achievements are felt, on the varied interests of the State and Society, an outward development, and a radical, universal application. Men, can be men, in all the active elements of a true manhood, only when they are the embodiments and revelators of just and eternal principles. This is their mission, and on its execution depends, their usefulness and moral dignity.

The reader, if his patience will carry him through the pages of this work, will find that he, whose life and services it commemorates, was a man who had settled convictions of right and true principles; and who gave them an honest and steadfast application to his whole political life. For their defense and maintenance, he sacrificed the honors and preferments of office, choosing rather to be robed in the well woven garment of principle, than to possess and wear the insignia and tinsel baubles of office.

The work is an humble contribution to the political Anti-slavery literature of the country. The cause of freedom, in its active antagonism, with the system of slavery, has been prolific in this age, in the creation of a multitude of works, gay and grave, in which slavery has been exposed and freedom vindicated. The forum of the State, the Altars of religion, the Sanctum of the everteeming press, the genius of the Poet, and the fertile fancy of the Romancer, have produced their varied literary contributions to the great Anti-slavery cause of the country and the world. In these departments of intellectual effort, freedom, and the forming National literature of the country, have been richly augmented. This work, while claiming no pretension to an elevated literary standard, yet, in the manly thoughts, uttered through its pages by him, whose life it records, will be, we trust, no mean offering to the Anti-slavery literature of the country.

The work is also a correct historical exhibition of the progress and results of the important political contest, between freedom and slavery, during the age of our Republic, but especially during the last twenty-five years. Sentiments and acts, the indices of public opinion, are given, to enable the reader to have an intelligent and accurate view of the question, that now absorbs and agitates the nation; care has been taken to give historical facts as they are found in the public records and papers of the times in which they transpired, yet some errors may possibly be found. It was the feeling and purpose of the editor, "nothing to extenuate or set down aught in malice." He has been only a gleaner in the wide field of facts, that belong to the historic times, in which they were evolved, and has clothed them in the unvarnished language of truth. Greater amplification of the materials at hand might have been made.

The work, it is hoped, will not prove an unacceptable offering to the people of the great State of Ohio, whose early history and legislation are briefly sketched, and whose public servant, its subject was, longer, perhaps, than any other of the many distinguished men who were his compeers, in forming the character of the State, and giving to her, her present elevation of political power, wealth, and material prosperity. The work, National in its sentiments, is yet eminently a State work. The Subject, the Editor, the Publishing House, and the Events recorded in the work, all belong, mainly to the history and times of Ohio, and as such, are presented to the people of the Empire State of the West, and the country, to undergo their impartial scrutiny and judgment. To their judgment the work is now committed.

September, 1856.

CONTENTS.

CHAPTER XVII.

CHAPTER XVIII.

CHAPTER XIX.

CHAPTER XX.

CHAPTER XXI.

CHAPTER XXII.

INTRODUCTORY CHAPTER.

"HONOR to whom honor is due." The pioneers of freedom are worthy to be honored and immortalized in history. The unalterable friends of freedom, they lay the first offerings upon its altar, and devote, at the peril of their own political standing, and of life itself, their energies to its defense and progress. History presents noble testimonials of the struggles, and achievments of these proto-martyrs to freedom and the rights of man. Political confiscation, banishment from political parties, and blood flowing from the block, attest the faith, and the self-sacrificing devotion of these patriots. Such men ought not to die from the memory, or the history of their country. They do not die. "In this world they will have their judgment day, and their names which went down, temporarily, like a gallant banner, trodden in the dust, shall rise again, all glorious in the sight of the nation."

Emmet, the patriot, and martyr for the freedom of Ireland, said, "Let not my history be written during the present generation. The future will rectify the judgment of public opinion, and remove present prejudices; then posterity will do me justice, and vindicate my memory." Truth is certain of an ultimate triumph; and when that triumph shall come, their names and memories will live in grateful remembrance;

and before the world, "*their age shall be clearer than the noon-day; they shall shine forth, they shall be as the morning.*"

The present is a fitting time to present to the lovers of liberty, the life and services of one of the first co-laborers in the cause of human freedom, in its contest with the aggressions of American slavery. THOMAS MORRIS, of Ohio, in the councils of his country, State and National, was ever the honest, earnest, out-spoken, and fearless friend of freedom. In him Constitutional liberty, the rights of man, the cause of universal emancipation, and resistance to the slave power of the country, found a faithful sentinel, and an able advocate. He was among the first political martyrs in the great struggle between freedom and slavery. Having fresh Senatorial honors proffered by the Democratic party that honored him with a seat in the Senate of the United States, if he would be an apostate to conscience and freedom, he rejected them, as unworthy of such a sacrifice; and the party that had for nearly forty years honored him with political trusts and preferments, decreed his political crucifixion. He paid the penalty on the 4th of March, 1839, and retired from his seat as Senator in Congress, with the proud consciousness of political rectitude, and of unfaltering faithfulness to freedom and the true principles of the Constitution.

Seventeen years have passed away since his voice for freedom was heard in the halls of the National Congress, and twelve years since the grave held all that was mortal of Thomas Morris. The man dies, but his services and memory live. And the valuable services he rendered to freedom, when but few voices were heard in its defense, either in the country, or in Congress, will now be appreciated, approved, and gratefully remembered. His warnings and prophecies, uttered with a fearless independence, in reference to the purposes and aggressions of the slave power, seeking perpetual expansion and supremacy, have been fearfully fulfilled. The present avowed purpose of the slave power, to hold, if possible, the balance of political power in its own hands, and to give indefinite extension to the system of slavery, is but the true fulfillment of the predictions of Thomas Morris, uttered from high places of public trust. He foresaw the evil, and gave the alarm to the country.

A distinguished and early co-laborer in the cause of liberty, Salmon P. Chase, who for six years filled with distinguished ability the seat in the Senate of the United States, once occupied by Thomas Morris, and is now the able and accomplished Governor of Ohio, says of him: "I knew him well, and honored him greatly. He was far beyond the time he lived in. He first led me to see the character of the slave power, as an aristocracy, naturally in league with the money power; and the need of an earnest and consistent Democratic organization to counteract its pretensions. Few anti-slavery men of to-day, with all the light thrown on the subject, saw this matter as clearly as did he. His memory should be kept freshly living among the lovers of liberty and progress."

His life, services, and some of his speeches in the Senate of the United States, and in the Legislature of Ohio, together with various papers on the subject of American slavery, are now presented to the public. The work is undertaken and published from motives of filial affection, and patriotism; and from a desire to perpetuate the services of an honored ancestor, who was a friend to the oppressed, an able champion of freedom, an incorruptible patriot, an honest politician, and a moral hero. In its prominent features the work is anti-slavery; presenting the historical facts of the rise and progress of the sentiment of freedom, now so happily prevalent, to the ascendancy of which Thomas Morris gave no unimportant impulse. It is also a brief historical record of the early settlement, and legislation of Ohio, with which Mr. Morris was prominently and intimately identified.

The volume is dedicated to the Citizens of Ohio and the Freemen of the United States; in the humble hope that it will add an additional momentum to the resistless power of a growing public sentiment, that will overthrow the system of American slavery, and give freedom a complete and perpetual triumph over the American continent. In that triumph the name and services of Thomas Morris will not be forgotten, who declared, "against this foe of God and man, we have waged a perpetual war; and we will teach our children to lay their hands upon the altar of their country's liberty, and swear eternal enmity to slavery."

CHAPTER II.

The Morris Name—Ancestors of Thomas Morris—His Birth—Removal to Western Virginia—Their Character—Home Education—Library—Learned to Read at his Mother's knees—Anti-Slavery Incident of the Parents.

The name of Morris is prominent in English history, and is redolent with patriotism and piety. Some fell among the martyrs in the reign of "bloody Mary," and others have a place in the history of the Parliamentary struggles with Charles the First, and in the campaigns of Cromwell. Uniformly they were found on the side of freedom, and the name is extant with numerous and honorable representatives in England, Wales, Scotland, Ireland and America. In 1637, the first representative of the name came from England and settled in Massachusetts, from whom numerous and honorable descendants sprang; and the head of that first family bore the name of Thomas, the same as he whose life and services are presented in this volume.

The ancestral family from whom the subject of this memoir was descended, was from Wales. Isaac, the father of Thomas Morris, was born in 1740, in Berks county, Pennsylvania, and his mother, Ruth Henton, in 1750, and was the daughter of a Virginia planter. Nine sons and three daughters were the fruits of their marriage. Thomas was the fifth child, and was born on the 3d of January, 1776, the memorable year of American Independence. Soon after the birth of Thomas, his parents moved to the wilds of Western Virginia, and settled in Harrison county, near Clarksburgh. They were both members of the Baptist Church, and lived and died exemplary Christians. The father was a minister in that denomination, and during sixty years preached the Gospel, never failing in a single appointment, nor never took a dose of medicine. At his death, occurring at the ripe age of ninety-one, in 1830, there were three hundred descendants. His descendants, living and dead, now number about a thousand persons.

The mother forms the character and directs the destiny of the child. Thomas had a Christian mother, who gave him the first lessons in education, and trained him in the school of virtue and freedom. In those early days, the privileges of the common schools were rare, and hence the entire education of most families was received at home. This was so of the Morris children. It was the habit of their mother, whenever in her log cabin she sat down to sew or knit, to have one of her children by her side reading the Bible; for all of her children could read well before they were six years of age. The historical portions of the Bible were selected as the most interesting to the juvenile mind. This home education, the stool at the mother's knee, is the first round in the ladder of advancement. Here the young soul drinks in the first draught of wisdom, and is schooled in motives drawn from the fountain of perfect and eternal truth. Here the first aspirations for knowledge are formed, and the first inspirations for freedom and virtue are received. It was in the home school, and from a mother's lips, that Thomas Morris was trained to love truth and freedom. Here the elements of a character were planted which, becoming the radical convictions of his nature, made him, in the manhood of life, strong and fearless in the resistance of slavery and wrong.

The library of the Morris family consisted of three Bibles, four Testaments, and as many Hymn books and Spelling books, a Dictionary, Dillworth's School-Master's

Assistant, the Young Man's Companion, an Arithmetic and an Outline of Astronomy; Scott's Lessons on Elocution, part of Bunyan's and Baxter's writings, and twelve volumes of sermons. These were the only facilities that Thomas Morris had for his early education. Three months at a common school completed his scholastic education. His college was the mountain wilds of Virginia, and there he graduated with a diploma from nature, and a blessing from a Christian mother. He early developed strong natural powers of intellect, an eager thirst for knowledge, and a manly self-reliance. At fourteen, he made a full hand in the harvest field; at sixteen, he shouldered his musket to repel the aggressions of the Indians on the frontiers of Virginia and Pennsylvania; at seventeen, he served several months in Captain Levi Morgan's company of wood rangers, stationed in the wilderness, in what is now the eastern part of Ohio. He was endowed with a strong mind and a vigorous body, and the early training of his mother imbued him with the elements of a character marked with boldness, self-reliance and fearless independence.

An incident in the life of his parents will reflect honor on their anti-slavery sentiments, and show how early their children were taught, by precept and example, in the school of freedom. His mother, in girlhood, held frequent conversations with a number of native Africans, kidnapped and brought in slave-ships to Virginia, the slave-trade then being sanctioned by law. Her father was a slaveholder, and at his death left, by will, one female slave, all he had, to his wife during her lifetime. At her death, this slave, with her increase, was to be the patrimony of the two daughters. In 1798, the wife of Henton died, and eight "human chattles" was the inheritance of the two daughters. The executor of the will gave information of these facts, aud desired to convey to Morris and his wife their share of the slaves. The proposition was rejected as an outrage on their sense of justice, and they declared that they would do no act that would recognize the right of one man to make another man chattel property. It was a matter of regret to the Morris family that they did not receive them and give them the boon of freedom. This noble act of the parents of Thomas Morris was one of the home lessons he received in the school of freedom.

CHAPTER III.

Early History of Ohio—Settlement at Marietta—Ordinance of 1787—Settlement at Columbia—The early Pioneers—The first Baptist Church—Supply of Cincinnati with preaching—John Smith, Preacher, first United States Senator, implicated with Burr—Morris emigrates to Columbia—Employed by Smith—Hunts in the forest where Cincinnati stands—A Contrast.

In 1795, the territory now constituting the State of Ohio became the permanent home of Thomas Morris. The great North-western Territory, out of which the five States of Ohio, Indiana, Illinois, Michigan, and Wisconsin have been formed, was ceded by Virginia to the United States. In 1787, Congress passed an ordinance which consecrated forever this vast domain to the reign of freedom. Slavery was forever prohibited. The wisdom of that great act has been most signally vindicated in the present prosperity and greatness of the State of Ohio. In her material wealth, in her noble systems of education, in her agricultural and commercial prosperity, in her political power and influence, and in all that constitutes the best types of a Christian civilization, Ohio presents a noble monument of freedom, and the most unanswerable evidence of the wisdom of that policy that forbids the foot-prints of a slave to tread the soil of a free nation. This noble ordinance of freedom was, on the 4th of July, 1788, made the special topic of eulogy and thanksgiving by the emigrants who, on the 7th of April, 1788, made their settlement at Marietta, on the banks of the Ohio river. In the groves of nature, and in the midst of the enchanting scenery that surrounded them, breathing an air made fragrant with freedom, did the pioneer emigrants from New England celebrate the anniversary of their national independence, by an oration of thanksgiving to God for that ordinance that had forever consecrated the soil of Ohio to freedom.

In November, 1788, seven months subsequent to the settlement at Marietta, a colony of emigrants began another settlement at Columbia, Hamilton county, five miles above Cincinnati. Among others, these emigrants consisted of Goforth, Stites, Major Gano, Col. Spencer, Rev. John Smith, Francis Dunlavey, and John Reily. Judge Burnet, himself an early pioneer, and a distinguished actor in the history and legislation of Ohio, in his Notes on the North-western Territory, says of the settlers in Columbia: "They were all men of energy and enterprise, and were more numerous than either of the parties who commenced their settlements below them on the Ohio." The village of Columbia, it was thought, would become the great commercial town of the Miami country, and for many years maintained a vigorous rivalry with the rising settlements of Cincinnati and North Bend. Cincinnati, however, became the center of commerce and population, and so rapid has been her progress, that she now almost includes within her corporate limits Columbia, once her rival and superior.

The Indians were numerous and hostile, and hence it became necessary for the emigrants to erect a fort, called Fort Miami, for their protection, and which afforded to the families a place of safety and refuge. Farms were opened and agriculture prosecuted under a military police. While one part of the emigrants were working in the fields, another must be watching lest the Indians should attack them by surprise.

Several of the early emigrants were Baptist preachers, and one of the first acts was to organize a church, and to erect a house for the worship of God. The church was constituted on the last Saturday of March, 1790, by Rev. Stephen Gano, of Providence, Rhode Island. There were nine members who united in the constitution, viz.: Benjamin and Mary Davis, Isaac Ferris, John Ferris, Elizabeth Ferris, Jonah Reynolds, Amy Reynolds, John S. Gano and Thomas C. Wade. During the Spring of 1790, the frame edifice was opened for worship. It was built on a beautiful eminence, and stood, for a half century, a suggestive relic of pioneer faith and enterprise. Many years after, when the venerable building was passing into ruins, some one gave utterance to his feelings in a poem, of which the two following stanzas only remain:

"Near where the Ohio winds its lonely way,
Through fields and flowers, and herbage richly gay;
There on a green, luxuriant sloping sod,
In ruined mantles clad, stood the lone house of God.

A strange sensation thrilled across my breast,
As its drear aisles my wandering footsteps pressed;
Their sounds alone disturbed the pensive scene,
That spoke what it was then, and told what it had been."

At the dedication of this church, which was the second erected in Ohio, in order to be protected from the attacks of the Indians, the militia appeared armed for defense, and Col. Spencer, long a venerable and honored citizen of Cincinnati, addressed them at the close of the sermon, on the danger the congregation was in if attacked only by a half dozen Indians; and on subsequent Sabbaths, this congregation of pioneer worshipers were dispersed in great haste for fear of the Indians. Thus the institutions of Christianity and of civilization, were planted by the perils and privations of our noble and self-denying pioneers. This Baptist church had the true missionary spirit, and labored to diffuse the blessings of the Gospel into destitute regions. Cincinnati then needed the ministrations of a Gospel minister; and in April, 1790, the church formally passed a resolution "that in view of the entire destitution of preaching in Cincinnati, Bro. Smith, (afterward the celebrated John Smith, Senator of Ohio), be allowed to spend half his time in that place."

Rev. John Smith was the first regular pastor, and emigrated from Pennsylvania, in May, 1790. He was a remarkable man, possessed of varied talent, and a versatile genius. He was a successful merchant, an adroit politician, a sagacious legislator, and an able divine. A cotemporary, Judge Pollock, of Clermont county, said of him: "As an ox-driver, no man was his superior; at a log-rolling, or horse-racing, he was the foremost man; at the end of a handspike, few could outlift him. The Sabbath day would find him in the pulpit, an able advocate of the doctrines of Christianity and of the Baptist denomination. As a member of Congress, he stood among the great men of the nation."

In 1802, Ohio was admitted into the Union, and John Smith was elected one of her first Senators in Congress, which office he filled for one term. At the close of his Senatorial term, he became implicated with Aaron Burr in his treasonable project of forming a South-Western independent government. Smith, in 1807, resigned his Senatorship, fled from Ohio in disgrace, lost his great wealth, and ended his career in dishonor and poverty at Bayou Sara, Louisiana.

In 1795, Thomas Morris, a young and enterprising adventurer, nineteen years of age, from the mountains of Western Virginia, arrived in Columbia. He was immediately employed as a clerk in the store of Rev. John Smith, and became a great favorite with him. During this time his mind became deeply exercised on the subject of personal religion, and his feelings found utterance in in frequent poetic effusions, which are all lost. Rev. John Smith, and others, regarded these productions as of great merit for a youth of his age and limited education. For several years he continued in the employ of Smith, improving, as he could, his mind by reading, and preparing for a wider sphere of action.

The plat of ground on which the great commercial city of Cincinnati now stands, was frequently traversed by Morris. His feet threaded the forest, then in the wild magnificence of nature, and the crack of his rifle brought down many a wild turkey from the tops of lofty trees which covered the very spot on which now is erected and established that noble building and institution, the Young Men's Mercantile Library Association. How wonderful the change in fifty years! Now, commerce, arts, science, education, Christian institutions, and the highest forms of a refined social civilization, and a prosperous, industrial population of over two hundred thousand people, cover with their peaceful and noble triumphs, and their monuments of taste and civilization, and happiness, the same forest where young Morris was accustomed to shoot his wild game.

"Peace has her triumphs no less than war."

CHAPTER IV.

Marriage — Incident in the girlhood of his Wife — Their Descendants — Removes to Clermont County, in 1800 — Location in Bethel — An Anti-slavery Incident — Studies Law — Bar of Clermont — Quoting the Scriptures — Character as a Lawyer — Defends the Laboring Classes — Incident in a Court-house.

Among the first emigrants to Columbia, was the family of Benjamin Davis; originally from Lancaster county, Pennsylvania, but direct from Mason county, Kentucky. The ancestors of this family were from Wales, worthy and honored. The children of Benjamin and Mary Davis consisted of five sons and three daughters, of whom Răchel was the youngest. On the 19th of November, 1797, two years after he reached the Columbia settlement, Thomas Morris and Rachel Davis were married.

She was reared in the midst of the privations of a pioneer life, and was the fitting companion of him who was to endure the hardships of a new country, and to achieve his own fortunes and character. The pioneer women of the West, were efficient and faithful participators in the great work of laying the foundations of the new empire, and endured with patient heroism the dangers and privations of a back-woods life. An incident, in the girlhood of Rachel Davis, will illustrate the daring and self-independence of the early females of the West. In 1796, she and her sister made a visit to the old family residence, in Washington, Mason county, Kentucky. The distance from Columbia was forty-five miles, and through an unbroken wilderness, unmarked, except by a horse-path. The Indians were roaming in the forests, and travelers were in constant danger. Nothing daunted, these traveling girls started alone on their journey, on horse-back, and, without once alighting from their horses, safely accomplished their journey. A linen wallet with some shell corn in one end, and their dinner in the other, afforded refreshments for man and beast, at noon, when by the side of a running stream they stopped, poured the corn on the ground for their horses, and partook of their own refreshment on horseback.

The marriage life of Thomas Morris and Rachel his wife continued almost fifty years; she surviving her husband eight years, and dying at the age of seventy-four, on the 16th of January, 1853, near Cincinnati. They raised and educated eleven children, who lived to fill posts of usefulness and honor in society. The oldest son, after filling with ability for nearly twenty years the clerkship of the Supreme Court, and that of the Common Pleas, in Clermont county, represented, for four consecutive years, the Congressional District of Ohio, in the National Legislature, succeeding, in 1846, the distinguished and lamented Thomas L. Hamer; the second son held during twenty years, and during several administrations, the office of Post-Master, of Bethel, Ohio; the third son has been a minister of the gospel during the last seventeen years, in the New-School Presbyterian church; and the fourth son, a resident of Quincy, Illinois, engaged in the profession of law, has been for the past twenty years a prominent and active member of the Democratic party, and was honored with the office of Chief Commissioner of the Public Works of that State, and elected as a member of the Legislature, and is now a candidate for Congress.

There are now living about sixty descendants of Thomas and Rachel Morris, and scarcely one either dead or living, was openly infidel or irreligious. All the children were members of the Methodist or Presbyterian church, but two, and they firm in the faith of Christianity, and some who are dead were distinguished for their Christian character.

This fact is suggestive and instructive. The parents were themselves the children of Christian parents, and the mother for thirty years a member of the Baptist church. They taught their children to believe in Christianity, and to attend upon the institutions of the Gospel, and in their old age they had the pleasure of witnessing their descendants moral and religious. These results had their origin in the Log-Cabins of the West, where their own Christian parents taught them the great truths of the Bible, in early childhood.

In 1800, they removed from Columbia to Williamsburgh, Clermont county, Ohio, for many years the capitol of that county, and in 1804 they permanently located in Bethel, where they resided the most of their active life.

An incident, marking the anti-slavery sentiment of that time and village, must, here, have an honorable record. The proprietor of the village was Obed Donham, who laid it out in 1802. He was from Virginia, and a member of the Baptist church; and in donating two lots to the Baptist denomination, he put into the deed of conveyance the following record, viz.: "I also give two lots in said town, Nos. 80 and 180, for the use of the regular Baptist church, who do not hold slaves, nor commune at the Lord's Table with those who do practice such tyranny over their fellow creatures—for to build a house for the worship of Almighty God, and to bury the dead, and for no other use." Mr. Morris said, for this act, Mr. Donham deserved a marble monument. The removal of Thomas Morris to Clermont proved fortunate. His energies found an active field for development and effort, and he resolved to be a successful winner. Without friends, without pecuniary means, with a growing family, without a preceptor, and with few books, he commenced, in 1802, the study of law. Early and late he was at his legal books.

After the hard labors of the day were over, night found him at his studies reading Blackstone, not by the light of an astral lamp, nor yet by the common light of a tallow candle, for his poverty forbade this cheap convenience, but by the light afforded by hickory bark or a clapboard in his cabin, and often from a brick kiln which he was burning, for the support of his family.

Under these formidable difficulties, with a resolute purpose and an iron will, he pushed his onward way, and reached the goal before him. Completing two years of study, he was admitted to practice as an attorney and counsellor at law. He had not mistaken his profession or his powers. He soon took a leading position as a lawyer, and reputation and business rapidly accumulated.

The Bar of Clermont, for many years, was distinguished for its ability in its home and visiting lawyers. Benham, Fox, W. H. Harrison, jr., and others from Cincinnati; Corwin, from Warren; Hamer, from Brown; Martin Marshall, from Kentucky; and Fishback, now the patriarch of the legal profession in Clermont, men of great legal attainments and intellectual abilities, were the men who met at various courts, to measure weapons with each other. Morris was among the first of that circle of distinguished lawyers. Before a jury, there were none who surpassed him in power and effect. Engaged in almost every case in Court, he ever maintained an eminence equal to the highest, and was a successful winner in the field of legal honors.

As a lawyer, and a public speaker, he quoted more frequently than most public men, from the Bible, and those quotations, being apt and accurate, greatly added to the conclusiveness of his arguments before a jury. His readiness to employ the Scriptures to confirm his sentiments showed his familiarity with them, and his belief in their Divine authority.

In the Senate of the United States, when making a speech on the monetary interests of the country, and the evils resulting from the credit system, tending to the destruction of self-independence, he cited Bible authority, that "the borrower is servant to the lender." A co-Senator, Mr. Mangum, of North Carolina, with great earnestness, denied the truth of such a doctrine. Mr. Morris replied, that the authority was of Divine origin, and he submitted the question to the Senate, whether the Senator or the Bible was of the highest authority.

A successful lawyer for forty years, yet he never encouraged litigation. "It ought to be," said he, "our aim to prevent litigation, as far as practicable with the rules and ends of justice." His services as a lawyer were rendered as willingly and energetically to the poor as to the rich. Indeed he was generally on the side of the poor; if it had not been so, his ability as an advocate would have yielded him an immense fortune. With him the right was the great leading motive, and the effort to violate it stirred the strongest energies of his nature, and brought him down on his adversary with an irresistible power and force.

In a legal contest with Benham, an able lawyer, in which he, (Benham) wielded his sarcasm and eloquence against the citizens of villages, who, he affirmed, when they got a few mechanics and one or two professional men, put on airs of importance and dignity—Mr. Morris retorted with a power and eloquence that was felt by his distinguished opponent. He contrasted city gentlemen with the free, honest, and independent citizens in country villages, and made a most powerful defense of the noble position and honorable calling of mechanics and laboring men. The vindication and triumph were complete. Mr. Benham said afterward, that Morris was harder to vanquish than any lawyer he contended with.

In a case of great importance, before the Court of

Brown county, he desired a continuance of his case, a principal witness being absent, on account of high waters. The Court refused the motion; and Mr. Morris procured a horse, swam the stream, and with his witness behind him, returned and replunged again into the swollen stream, entered the Court, and gained his case.

These incidents are illustrative of his unconquerable energy, as well as of his ability as a lawyer. His success had a significant connection with his reading Blackstone, by the light of hickory bark, in his log-cabin.

CHAPTER V.

ELECTED to the Legislature—Early Legislative History of Ohio—Narrow escape of Freedom in the Convention—Character of the men who framed the Constitution—Judge Cutter—Character of the Legislators of Ohio, for the first thirty-five years—Mr. Morris's position as a Legislator.

IN 1806, Mr. Morris was elected a representative from Clermont county, and took his seat at Zanesville, then the capital of Ohio.

The early legislation of Ohio forms one of the brightest and most honorable historical chapters in her record. The legislators, to whom were entrusted the task of constructing the organic system of the civil government of Ohio, were men of practical wisdom, and of just and liberal views. Its territorial government was the creation of the living breath of freedom. The Ordinance of 1787 laid the chief corner stone in the structure of her greatness and prosperity; and the men who framed the State Constitution, and created her system of legislation, conformed their policy to this great charter of freedom. They consecrated the State to Religion, Education, and Freedom. The Bill of Rights declares, "That neither slavery nor involuntary servitude, except for crime, shall exist in the State; that religion, morality, and knowledge, being essentially necessary for good government, and the happiness of mankind, schools and the means of instruction shall forever be encouraged by legislative provision; and that all men are born equally free and independent, and have the right to life, liberty, and of pursuing and obtaining happiness and safety."

These enactments saved Ohio from the blight and curse of slavery. The slave power, however, early made a strong effort to gain a foothold on the virgin soil of Ohio. At the first session of the Territorial legislature which met, February 4th, 1799, in Cincinnati, petitions were presented by many Virginians, who owned lands in the Virginia Military Bounty District, west of the Scioto river, to settle, with their slaves, on their own lands. These petitions were rejected at once. *The legislature believed that the Ordinance of* 1787 *left them no option whatever, and they did not even entertain the petitions.*

A second effort was made, when the State Constitution was formed, to introduce and fix slavery upon the soil of Ohio. Presidential power was used then, as now, to give extension to the system. Jefferson was President; and Jeremiah Morrow, Ohio's first representative in Congress, when his duties called him to the seat of government, called on the President, who expressed to him his deep regret that slavery had not been allowed to enter the new State. The reason assigned was, that the extension of slavery over a large area tended to destroy it. A great error, as the history of American slavery mournfully confirms.

In the convention met to form the Constitution of Ohio, John W. Brown, from Hamilton county, chairman of the Committee on the Bill of Rights, presented a section declaring that, "No person shall be held in slavery, if a male, *after he is thirty-five years of age;* and if a female, after twenty-five years of age." This section was defeated by the heroic firmness of Ephraim Cutler, of Marietta. He framed the eighth section, containing the Bill of Rights, in which slavery was forever prohibited, and this section was incorporated into the Constitution. It was the opinion of Mr. Cutler, that the section allowing slavery, in a modified form, originated with President Jefferson; and Browne, in advocating this policy, said—

"What he had introduced was thought, by the greatest men in the nation, to be, if established in the Constitution, a great step toward the general emancipation of the slaves." Mr. Cutler, in view of the narrow escape freedom had, in this contest with slavery, made in his journal the following record: "Thus an overruling Providence, by His wisdom, makes use of the weak often to defeat the purpose of the great and wise; and to His name be the glory and praise."

Let Ohio ever honor and hold in grateful remembrance the services and memories of her first legislators, and those who in her subsequent history, with earnestness and ability, maintained the principles of freedom, which gave her birth, and by which she has risen to unexampled prosperity and greatness.

Judge Burnet says—"The delegates who framed the Constitution were, with but few exceptions, the most intelligent men in the counties." Jeremiah Morrow, the first representative in Congress, afterward senator and governor, a man who was ever faithful and honest, and who died, full of years and honors, in 1852; Dunlevy, an early pioneer to Columbia, a man of integrity and liberal education; John Reily, an honored citizen of Butler county; Tiffin and Worthington, from Ross, and Hungtingdon, from Trumbull, all of whom were Governors of the State; Cutler and Putnam, from Washington; and Gatch and Sargeant, from Clermont, were among the honored men who successfully labored, in the construction of the State Constitution and the early legislation of Ohio. Gatch and Sargeant were elected because they were anti-slavery men. They were both Virginians, and both were practical emancipators. General Harrison, the Territorial representative from Ohio, in Congress, in a public letter, written in 1820, when a candidate for Congress in Ohio, in which he was defending himself against the charge of pro-slavery sympathies, refers to his "venerable friend, Philip Gatch, who was a member of an abolition society in Virginia."

It is a debt of gratitude due from the great State of Ohio to honor the memories, and to perpetuate, in her historical annals, the services of those earliest legislators and founders of her fame and greatness; men who ornamented the State by their private virtues and public labors. In this catalogue of able men and upright legislators, who, from the date of the birth of Ohio, through the subsequent thirty years of her legislative history, aided in adjusting and perfecting the system of government, must be named—Jacob Burnet, John McLean, Ethan Allen Brown, Charles Hammond, Benjamin Tappan, John M. Goodenou, John C. Wright, Elisha Whittlesey, Samuel M. Vinton, Joshua Collet, Reuben Hitchcock, Allen Trimble, Duncan McArthur, Reuben Wood, James Cooly, Joseph Vance, and others. The present generation, says the author of the memoir of Judge Hitchcock, know but little of the treasures of knowledge and talent brought to Ohio by her energetic and enterprising pioneers. The present generation is inclined, most erroneously, to arrogate to itself superior abilities, in proportion to its greater facilities. On hearing a remark claiming this superiority, the reply of one of the survivors of that day was—"You are mistaken; I tell you there were giants at the West in those days." Nearly all of those, distinguished in the constitutional and legislative history of Ohio, have passed away, but they have left noble monuments of their wisdom and labors.

Thomas Morris was among the ablest and wisest of the legislators of Ohio, and identified during a long period with her legislative history, being a member of the General Assembly for twenty-four years, and connected with the politics of the State for fifty years.

CHAPTER VI.

His labors and influence as a Legislator—Against Liquor Licenses and Lotteries—Against Prohibiting the Emigration of Colored People to Ohio—Speech on the Rights of Conscience—On Abolishing Imprisonment for Debt—His Faith in the People—The People to elect all Officers—Jury Trials before Justices—Internal Improvements—Opposed to the Canal System of Ohio—Prophecy about Railroads—A Ride in a Canoe—A Contrast.

In the legislature of Ohio, he was a prominent and active participator. His abilities soon placed him among the first of the distinguished men who from year to year met in the legislative halls. No matter what party was in power, he was chairman of the most important committees, most generally the judiciary, and often appointed on special committees. His influence, in the judgment of cotemporaries, was always equal to any in the legislature.

As a legislator, he labored for the equal rights of all, and to conform the action of civil government to the true doctrines of democracy, and the principles of justice and Christian morality. He was opposed to all chartered monopolies, and to all legislation that gave one class civil privileges above another. His entire legislative history is free from selfish ambition, and in general accordance with the fundamental principles of right as revealed in the Bible, the only source of true national prosperity.

He believed the traffic in spiritous liquors, as a beverage, was a moral wrong, and on all occasions voted to restrain the evil, by putting the price of license up to the highest possible sum, so as to prohibit it altogether. He warmly enlisted in the great Temperance Enterprise, and gave it his influence and aid, as a legislator and a man, by precept and example.

He voted against all lotteries, a species of legislation not then uncommon in the older States. In 1827, a bill was introduced to aid Ohio in her system of canal improvements; the author of the bill affirming—"That it was good policy, while the lotteries of other States were draining specie from Ohio, the bill would have a tendency to bring some back. The city of New York," said he, "would buy ten or fifteen thousand dollars worth of tickets."

Mr. Morris, regarding it as immoral, and as compromising the honor of the State, moved its rejection. "I object to it on the score of morality and policy. Suppose the gentleman's speech is printed in New York, what a happy tendency it would have to procure assistance for the construction of our canal. Their opinion of our resources would be greatly increased, when they perceived we had to resort to the pitiful expediency of a lottery, to raise funds to carry on our system of internal improvements. It was encouraging a species of gambling." The bill was rejected by a large majority.

An effort was made during this session of legislature, to prohibit by penal legislation, the future immigration of blacks and mulattoes into Ohio. Faithful to the rights of man, he opposed the principles of the bill, as unjust, unconstitutional, and odious. It was rejected.

This session also witnessed a strong effort to legislate on the rights of conscience. A bill for the support of common schools contained a clause that "no teacher should teach any sectarian creed, catechism, confession of faith, etc., unless each person entitled to send to said school shall consent to the same; and any teacher violating the provisions of this act shall be fined."

Mr. Morris made an able speech against the bill, in which he advocated the great Protestant principle of the freedom of the rights of conscience in religion. That speech contains the following sound doctrines:

"I meet these extraordinary provisions, with the broad denial that we have any power whatever to legislate on this subject. The right of conscience is an inalienable right, for the exercise of which man is not accountable to man: he is accountable to no power short of that of his Creator. It is a religious right with which human laws have nothing to do. The right of belief is the right of the individual, not of the community. Yet we are, as legislators, about to say that if any individual, as a schoolmaster, shall undertake to teach what he believes to be just and right, he shall be subjected to a penalty inflicted by the judicial officers of the law, and this too under the plausible pretext of securing the rights of conscience. These rights of worship, these dictates of conscience are too pure, sublime and holy to be touched by human legislation. They do not need the support of government, and in all cases where the secular support of the government have attempted to support, direct, control, or in any manner interfere therewith, instead of causing these rights to grow and flourish, it has caused them to wither, decay and die. The right of my neighbor to worship his Creator as his conscience dictates, is a right which legislation ought not to interfere with. It is his person, his place of worship, his place as a citizen while engaged in that worship, and not his religious faith, that our law can or ought to protect.

In our country we have a great variety of religious sects. Presbyterians, Methodists, Baptists, Episcopalians, Quakers, Unitarians, and others, who have different creeds and confessions of faith; some believing in the Divine atonement, and others believing that the Saviour of men was only "the way, the truth and the life;" and yet, according to this bill, our children are to be taught none of these doctrines in our schools, without making the instructor liable to the penalty of this law. Suppose the pupil should have heard of the name of Jesus Christ, and should ask his instructor, who is Jesus Christ? and the answer should be in the language of Scripture, 'The Son of God, the everlasting Father, the Prince of Peace, God made manifest in the flesh;' who by his sufferings and death made an atonement for all men. This would be teaching sectarian principles within the meaning of this bill, because all do not believe in these fundamental doctrines of Christianity. Do the friends of this bill mean that the use of the Bible shall be prohibited in our schools? That book is held by all denominations to be their only creed or confession of faith, and yet, by the principles of this bill, under pretext of securing the rights of conscience, teachers shall be subject to a fine for instructing their pupils out of the Bible, whence all profess to get their religious creeds. It is constituting the officers of the law the umpire, to decide what is, or is not, sectarian principles, and subjecting the conscience of the teacher to the power of legislation. Even parental authority strays beyond its proper bounds, when it shall be exercised to prohibit the child who has arrived at the years of discretion, from the examination of each and every sectarian creed and religious doctrine that he may wish. It is his duty to interpose with parental advice, but not with coercive measures.

"It is said that the law for the support of common schools, as it now stands, will compel the sect of Christians called the Friends or Quakers, to aid in the support of schools to which they can not conscientiously send their children, and that this numerous and respectable body of Christians are worthy of legislative attention and care. As a legislator, I am not disposed to fasten my political car to the chariot of any particular Christian sect. I respect them all, and acknowledge with gratitude the beneficial effects of their labors upon the lives and conduct of men; but as a legislator, I say to them as Christians, professing any sectarian creed, form, catechism, article or confession of faith, I know you not; these are yours, and in the exercise thereof, according to the dictates of your own conscience, I will, as far as in my power as a legislator, provide that every one of you 'may sit under your own vine and fig-tree,' and none shall be suffered to make you afraid; but your doctrines and your faith must not be used as a cloak to screen you from obedience to the municipal laws of your country; nor can we give any of you a preference; you all must 'render to Cæsar the things that are Cæsar's.'

"As legislators, we have the right, and it is our duty to provide for the support and regulation of schools; but this right does not extend to any acts of legislation affecting creeds or articles of religious faith, but to cultivating the human intellect, preparing the young and rising generation to become useful members of society; and to the general diffusion of knowledge, so essentially necessary to a good government; a kind of State property we are bound to increase and cultivate with the most assiduous care, as a means of giving perpetuity to our political institutions.

"I am willing to leave the government of our district schools, in reference to the reading of creeds, forms, rules, articles or confessions of faith, to the good sound sense and sound discretion of the householders in each district. It is the only safe depository of that power. Virtue, public virtue, is the base upon which the superstructure of our government is raised and must stand, and this is found among the people in larger proportion than in the halls of legislation. Permit me to say to the Friends who ask for this special legislation, depart in peace. Your religion needs not the support of human legislation; the weapons of your warfare are not carnal; cultivate peace, harmony and good will toward all men; be obedient to the laws of your country, and those who are in authority over you; overcome evil with good; and by a holy life and an upright walk and conversation, your children, the objects of your care, will be influenced and guided by your bright example, and their tender minds will receive more lasting and desirable impressions than can be made by the teacher of your district schools, though he be armed with all the sectarian creeds which the ingenuity, the ambition or the pride of man has ever invented." The bill was rejected.

The statute book of Ohio, with many other States, was for years dishonored with a law that imprisoned a man for inability to pay his debts. This relic of barbarous legislation is now swept away by the progress of juster and more Christian views. For its extinction in Ohio, Mr. Morris labored with an earnest ability. On a bill for its abolishment, in the legislature, he made an able speech, from which the following extracts are made:

"The state of society at this day does not require the dogmas of superstition, the precepts of ignorance, nor the conveniences of despotism to compel the payment of debts. The force of moral sentiment, properly cultivated and rightly directed, would be far more effectual than all the bars and cells of your prisons. Abandon, then, this relic of oppression, this appeal to force for the collection of debts. When you do this, that moral principle, which has a thousand times more influence than your penal laws, will assume its place, and be safely relied on. From what principle do the great body of your citizens act in the payment of debts? From the fear of your prisons? No; from higher and more exalted motives; from a love of truth and probity, from a desire to preserve a good name, which is more precious than gold, and more available in life than all the wealth this world can afford. I hope, then, Ohio will put her hand in earnest, at this auspicious moment, to the good work. She is emphatically a free

State. Her Constitution declares that no slavery shall exist within her borders, otherwise than for the punishment of crime; yet the worst of all slavery, imprisonment for non-payment of debt, exists. Let it no longer disgrace our statute book."

As a legislator, he was not afraid to trust the people with all political power, and to transfer to them the election of every officer required in the administration of the government. In this great principle of a democratic government he was in advance of his cotemporaries. The doctrine is now popular, to make all offices, even judges of our courts, elected by the people. It was advocated by Mr. Morris nearly thirty years ago, in the legislature of Ohio

In 1828, he brought in a bill in the Senate, to allow juries before justices of the peace, and in its defense said, "It is objected to this bill that justices of the peace will be rendered almost as important as judges of the court. I fear this is the secret spring that moves all the other objections. This hankering after power, this desire to concentrate it in as few hands as possible, this kind of *judge worship*, is the most dangerous spirit abroad. It is not the ermine of the Bench that ought to attract our notice, but justice, substantial justice; and all the ends of justice would be as well gained before justices of the peace, if we would allow them juries, as in our courts of a higher grade."

"Justice has a higher and more perfect origin than human legislation. It can not be found in the dictum of judges, in the decrees of emperors, or in the maxims of lawyers. Its best and only legitimate standard is traced by the finger of the Creator in the moral nature of every man; and its motto is, 'do unto all men as you would have them to do unto you,' and the nearest we can approximate to justice is through the medium of a trial by jury. The trial by jury is our security for the liberties we enjoy, our protection and safety; and hence it is political wisdom and sound policy to extend its benefits to all possible cases.

In 1829, he brought in a bill, that judges should not charge juries as to matter of facts, but may sum up the evidence and declare the law, and on it he presented some important rules in the administration of justice. "That jurors are judges of the facts, and courts of the law, are obvious truths, and to keep each within its proper sphere is the duty of the legislature. It is a clear departure from duty in a judge, to undertake to explain and to instruct the jury as to the strength and applicability of the testimony. It is stepping beyond the limits of his own power, and an intrusion into that which the law has vested in a distinct, though component part of the court. In permitting the judge to forestall the opinion of jurors, as to the facts in the case, you deprive the citizen of the whole benefit intended to be secured by a trial by jury. You mock him with the shadow, while in truth you deny him the substance. Moreover, judges, though vested with authority, are still men, subject to all the frailties, partialities and prejudices of other men." He had no faith in the infallibility of courts.

He labored, as a legislator, to keep the taxes as low as the necessity of the government would permit, and opposed all extravagant expenditures of the public money. He held to the doctrine that legislation should be impartial, and if special favors were granted, the industrial classes should receive them. In 1812, he obtained the passage of a bill, "That each person who has a family shall be allowed to hold twelve sheep, also the wool, and the yarn cloth manufactured by such families, exempt from all executions for payment of debts. In 1828, he endeavored to obtain a law taxing all chartered institutions, and such manufactories as founderies, glass-houses, mills and distilleries, and exempt all houses in each county from taxation.

Ohio was the first western State to enter upon a system of internal improvements. Canals were the objects of State enterprise then, and in 1825, Ohio began the great work of the Ohio Canal, by which the waters of lake Erie and the Ohio river were to be united. Gov. De Witt Clinton, of New York, designated as the father of internal improvements, was officially invited to visit Ohio. He accepted the invitation, and on the 4th of July, 1825, the forty-ninth anniversary of American independence, in the midst of a vast multitude of enthusiastic citizens, he made an address, and formally inaugurated the canal system near Newark, Licking county. The Ohio and Erie canal was completed in 1831, is three hundred and nine miles long, and cost the State about five millions of dollars. Mr. Morris strenuously opposed the system, in opposition to almost all of the public men of the State. He declared his convictions of the impractical nature of such a system to develop the resources of the State, and which would involve a debt of many millions, which never could be paid off by the revenue from the canal. "I am an unbeliever," he said, "in the visions of future wealth from the profits of the canal system. It would render the State insolvent."

He made a prophecy which has been fully realized. "In twenty-five years," he said, "Ohio will be covered with a net-work system of railroads, and canals will be superseded." Ohio has now 2400 miles of road, traversing the State in every direction, augmenting her wealth a million fold. A confirmation of the prophecy and sagacity of Thomas Morris.

An incident will illustrate the wonderful progress of Ohio, and the present rapid transit over the area of the State, when compared with her condition twenty-five years ago. At an adjournment of the legislature, in March, 1827, heavy rains had made the ordinary mud roads from the capital impassible for the stage, then in common use. The streams were overflowing their banks, rendering a homeward return of the members almost impossible. Mr. Morris determined to conquer all obstacles. The Scioto river, on whose banks the capital of Ohio has stood for the past forty-five years, afforded an egress for some of the members. A canoe, or, in Western dialect, a dug-out, was made and put upon the rapid current of the swollen river, and Mr. Morris and Robert T. Lytle, an eloquent and able representative from Hamilton county, embarked with their baggage in this water-craft for home. A passage of some hundred miles brought them to Portsmouth, where the Scioto mingles its waters with the Ohio, and there, embarking on a small steamboat, they safely reached their homes, after a perilous journey of four days. The transit now, by railroad, from the capital to any part of Ohio, occupies but four hours.

CHAPTER VII.

POPULAR Education — Colleges and Common Schools — Advocate of the Common School System — Relation of Education to Government — Female Education — Commissioner of the School Fund — Taxation for School Purposes—Opposition to it—Looses his Election on account of it.

OHIO has been, in her legislative history, distinguished for her zeal and success in the cause of popular education. One of her organic laws was—"*That schools and the means of instruction shall forever be encouraged by legislative provision;* and to promote, as an object of primary importance, institutions for the diffusion of knowledge," through the medium of common schools, has been the great effort of the legislation of Ohio. Colleges and the higher grades of seminaries have received her fostering supervision. Congress, in 1803, donated two townships of land for collegiate purposes, and out of these have been erected two universities—the Ohio University, at Athens, and Miami University, at Oxford. These, as gifts from Congress, have been preserved and fostered, but have never received any special endowment from the State. The establishment of a system of common schools, by taxation, was the great end of the legislation of Ohio, in respect to education. This was rightly regarded as indispensable to the well-being and liberties of the State.

Mr. Morris, during his whole legislative history, was an ardent and able friend of the common schools, and voted for the largest accumulation of a fund devoted to this great object. His views are presented, in brief extracts, from his speeches on the subject.

"Our government," said he, in 1828, "is a beautiful

machinery made up not of parts, but of the whole body of the people. It requires, therefore, not the aid of a few, but the aid of all to keep it in motion. To do this, *every citizen* must understand all its parts and all its movements. He must possess knowledge, virtue, and intelligence; because, in the language of our own Constitution, they are essentially necessary to good government and the happiness of the people. To provide means for the instruction of all is, then, a duty that devolves on those who are called to administer the government. This is not only necessary to the safety and correct administration of the government, but for the happiness of the people. Let us, then, be faithful to this great duty, so that to the praise and honor of this generation, let the next say, that there is not one among them who is not able to read the Constitution of his country. This will preserve the Constitution more securely than walls of adamant or temples of brass. Let us not, either, overlook female education. The advancement of the female character, and the instruction and cultivation which woman receives, has always been justly viewed as evidence of the improved state of society where it exists. It is, therefore, an indispensable duty to provide for female education; for knowledge is the handmaid of virtue, prudence, and economy; and where female virtue, knowledge, and intelligence abound, man can never be degraded or a slave."

The salt lands in the Scioto Valley were, by Congress, given to Ohio for literary purposes. In 1826, an effort was made in the legislature to apply the proceeds of these lands to colleges. Mr. Morris said—"These lands were ours for literary purposes, the proceeds to be devoted to the common school fund. The grant of Congress is broad, and will admit the appropriation to be made for the improvement of the human mind. Sound policy dictates that we should apply them to the common school fund, since we have the right to do so. I must solemnly protest against applying them to colleges, in the present situation of the State. The *diffusion of knowledge among the people is first to be regarded.* We are told that colleges must be encouraged, in order to raise up lawyers and statesmen, and legislators. What is this but going a considerable part of the way toward constituting a Patrician class, from which, those who are to administer the government are only to be chosen. If this were an age of monkish ignorance, and it were necessary to protect a privileged order, then we should throw our means into a fund for their support. But this is not our situation. We have undertaken to diffuse knowledge among the people, and to the accomplishment of this object it is our duty to direct all our attention."

In his own county, he was active in his efforts to build up a fund for the support of common schools. He brought the funds, appropriated to Clermont, from the State treasury, and for several years, acted as Commissioner of the County School Funds. In bringing the School Fund into existence, he says, "I well knew that I was incurring great personal responsibility. Conscious of the rectitude of my intentions, and the purity of my motives, I feel much gratified that the day has arrived in which a disinterested tribunal, under the authority of law, can furnish evidence of my integrity in this whole matter. I have now fulfilled the task I imposed on myself, and which I have long had in view, to establish the means by which the entire youth of this county should receive a common school education. Having laid the foundation of a fund for that purpose, and given to it all the security, system, and order of which I was capable, I yield up my trust under the grateful conviction, that my agency, in establishing the School Fund of Clermont county, is among the best acts I have ever been able to perform for the citizens of the county."

Believing that popular education was the shield of free institutions, giving to the national structure, solidity and perpetuity, and developing the elements of national prosperity and greatness—Mr. Morris, in the legislature of Ohio, earnestly advocated taxation for school purposes. Taxation is to carry on the functions of civil government, and intelligence and virtue being essential to the operations and very existence of free governments, it is the first duty of a free people to tax themselves for the support of universal education. Colleges, seminaries, and common schools are nobler fruits of taxation than penitentiaries, jails and poor houses. If the former are not founded and fostered by taxation, the latter must be, for an uncultivated people must be a vicious people.

Among some portions of the American people formerly, there was an unwillingness to be taxed for the support of common schools. In Ohio, opposition to this taxation was manifested. "Fortunately," says John P. Foote, in his work on "The schools of Cincinnati," "men of intelligence, zeal, and industry, from different States, who knew the value of common schools, and their special necessity in a State with such an ultra Democratic Constitution, as was the first Constitution of Ohio—were fixed in their determination never to cease their efforts to obtain for the State a system of free schools, until it should be successful, and free schools be among the established institutions of the State. They succeeded in spite of much opposition, and more lukewarmness, and now the system is firmly fixed in the affections of the people of Ohio, and is considered by them as indispensable an element of their liberties, and guardian of our free institutions as the trial by jury, the freedom of the press, or the elective franchise."

As a legislator, Mr. Morris was among the most active and earnest in maintaining the doctrine of taxation for education, and in establishing and perfecting a system of common schools in Ohio. This measure was met with much opposition in his own county, and in one canvass, he lost his election for State Senator, mainly for his successful efforts in this matter.

Clermont county never had a more able, honest, and faithful public servant, and their appreciation of his ability and fidelity is demonstrated in his frequent re-elections. He represented the same constituency for twenty-four years, seventeen of them consecutively, a rare fact in the ceaseless changes to which public men are liable, under Democratic institutions.

CHAPTER VIII.

Impeachment of Judges—Morris appointed to conduct the Trial—A Select Committee on Vermont Resolutions in 1809—A Select Committee, in 1810, on the Measures of the General Government—Supports the War in 1812—South Carolina Nullification in 1832—Morris a Select Committee—His Resolutions—Letter of Judge McLean—Report on Colonization.

In 1808–9, the Legislature of Ohio preferred articles of impeachment against Calvin Pease and John Tod, two of the judges of Ohio, for an alleged unconstitutional interference with the powers and duties of justices of the peace, to whom jurisdiction in cases not exceeding twenty dollars, was given. This was decided unconstitutional by Judge Pease, of the District Court, and confirmed by Judges Huntington and Tod, a majority of the Supreme Court. This decision was made in view of the seventh amendment to the Constitution of the United States, which declares that "In suits at common law, where the value in controversy shall exceed twenty dollars, the right of trial by jury shall be preserved," and the eighth section of article eighth, which declares that "the right of trial by jury shall be inviolate." The substance of the impeachment charged that Judge Pease had, on various occasions, decided that the Court had full power to set aside, suspend and declare null and void any act of the State legislature, and that this had been done by the judge, in declaring null and void the act defining the duties of justices of peace. On this ground the impeachment was made by the House of Representatives, and the judges tried before the bar of the Senate. Thomas Morris was appointed to conduct the impeachment on the part of the

House ; and the historical record shows that he performed the duty with ability. In this prosecution, the legislature also procured the aid of Judge Baldwin, of Pittsburgh, a distinguished lawyer, and for many years one of the justices of the Supreme Court of the United States. After a protracted trial, the impeachment was not sustained, the Constitution requiring two-thirds of the Senate to sustain.

The ability with which Mr. Morris conducted this grave trial, as a lawyer and leader of the House of Representatives, secured for him, in 1809, his election as one of the Supreme Judges of Ohio, but by a subsequent act of the legislature, called the "Sweeping Acts," he was prevented from taking his seat.

In 1809–10, resolutions were sent from Vermont to the legislature of Ohio, proposing to amend the Constitution of the United States, so as to remove judges of the courts of the United States upon the address of a majority of the House of Representatives and two-thirds of the Senate. Mr. Morris was appointed a select committee on the Vermont resolutions, and reported that:

The General Assembly of the State of Ohio, viewing all public offices as belonging to the people, and they having a right to bestow them as they may deem proper; that the officers in every department of the government ought to be amenable to them for their conduct; and inasmuch as all government is established for the happiness and welfare of the people, therefore, when any public servant ceases to merit their approbation, they have at all times the right to withdraw their confidence, and bestow it on such others as they may deem fit. Therefore, our Senators in Congress are instructed, and the members of the House requested, to propose this amendment to the Constitution of the United States."

In 1810, Mr. Morris, appointed a Committee on the measures of the General Government, reported as follows:

"*Resolved, by the General Assembly of the State of Ohio,* That our political safety depends on our attachment to, and continuance in our federal relations with our sister States, and we pledge ourselves to the General Government to support the union of the States to the utmost of our power; and believing as we do, that the measures of the General Government are directed by sound policy, and with the welfare of all in view, we hesitate not to say, that Ohio will be found ever ready to support such measures as Congress may direct for securing our rights, sovereignty and independence."

Mr. Madison was then President, and war with Great Britain was anticipated, and was declared by Congress in 1812. Mr. Morris was a strenuous advocate of that war, and during its continuance was a member of the legislature of Ohio, and on committees which reported such resolutions as this, which the legislature adopted: "*Resolved*, That this General Assembly pledge themselves to their country, and with all their means and energies to aid in the vigorous prosecution of the present just and necessary war, until a safe and honorable peace can be obtained." Peace was concluded in 1815.

In 1832, South Carolina, aggrieved, as she declared, on account of oppressive tariff measures by the General Government, threatened a nullification of the law, and resistance to the authority of the General Government. President Jackson issued his proclamation, a very able State paper, warning them to desist from their treasonable course. Great political excitement and fears pervaded the country. The different States, by their legislatures passed resolutions generally approving the measures of the General Government. Ohio threw her influence on the side of the General Government. Mr. Morris, then a member of the Senate, was appointed a select committee, to whom was referred "the ordinance of the Convention of the people of South Carolina," and reported the following resolutions:

"*Resolved, by the General Assembly of the State of Ohio*, That we view with the deepest regret the unhappy movements and apparent determination of the State of South Carolina to nullify the laws of the General Government, made in conformity to the Constitution of the United States.

"*Resolved*, That the Federal Union exists in a solid compact entered into by the voluntary consent of each and every State; and that therefore no State can claim the right to secede from or violate that compact; and however grievous may be the supposed or real burthens of the State, the only legitimate remedy is in the wise and faithful exercise of the elective franchise, and the solemn responsibility of the public agents.

"*Resolved*, That the doctrine that a State has the power to nullify a law of the General Government, is revolutionary in its character, and is, in its nature, calculated to overthrow the great temple of American liberty; and that such a course can not absolve that allegiance which the people owe to the supremacy of the laws.

"*Resolved*, That in levying and collecting duties, imposts and excises, while the general good should be the primary object, a special regard should be had to the end; that the interest and prosperity of every section of the country should be equally consulted, and its burdens proportionably distributed.

"*Resolved*, That the first object of the American people should be to cherish the most ardent attachment to the Constitution and laws of the Union; and, as a first and paramount object of a free people, we should use every laudable means to preserve the Union of these States.

"*Resolved*, That we will support the General Government in all its Constitutional measures to maintain peace and harmony between the several States, and preserve the honor and integrity of the Union."

During the agitation of this subject in the legislature of Ohio, John McLean, then and now an able and upright Judge of the Supreme Court of the United States, whose private life and civic services have ornamented the history of Ohio and the nation, wrote to Mr. Morris the following patriotic letter. It shows the feeling that pervaded the minds of public men at that crisis.

WASHINGTON, 23d January, 1833.

DEAR SIR—I have not yet seen any expression of our legislature respecting the movements of South Carolina, and the steps taken by the President to counteract those movements. It is not my intention or wish to indicate any opinion upon the subject, further than to say—if you should act, I hope you will recommend forbearance on the part of the Federal Government. I do not mean by this, that there should be no action on the part of the General Government; but I wish to see the law take its ordinary course, without any extraordinary preparation to enforce it; and I should deprecate the employment of force, except to give effect to the laws, by aiding the proper officers of the courts in the service of their process. This will give time to our erring fellow citizens of South Carolina to reflect on their course, and this, I should hope, would bring them to a sense of their duty.

The Proclamation has had the effect in the South, which I had no doubt from the first, it would have, to exasperate the people of South Carolina, and greatly strengthen their cause in Virginia and the other Southern States. The late message will, I fear, increase this feeling. Do not understand me as questioning the motives which led to these measures, or as excusing, in any degree, the consequences which have followed them. Both measures should have produced very different effects; but we must, in anticipating results, consider men as they are, not as they should be.

General Jackson has great popularity in the South, and on this ground alone, I do not see how any one can regret his re-election. But there is danger of too much action. I have more fears from this, than from the unconstitutional edicts of South Carolina. Strongly as I feel opposed to their principles, I had rather see the tariff-law suspended in that State, for a season, than that one drop of blood should be spilt. From this suspension no lasting injury could result to the Union, and the instruments who had obstructed the law would be eventually held responsible to the country, and to individuals who had suffered damage; but if the Federal forces should meet in conflict those of South Carolina, I shall despair of ever seeing harmony restored. A case may occur in which a resort to physical force may be necessary against a part of our fellow citizens, but nothing short of the revolution of the country should justify such a procedure.

Suppose, during the late war, an army had been marched against Massachusetts and the Hartford Convention, what would have been the consequences? The Union would have been dissolved. Of this no one can doubt, who took a part in the political action of that day. Mild measures were pursued, and no extraordinary action of the Government was directed against any of the refractory States. Time was given for reflection, and public sentiment applied the necessary correction.

A bill is now before the Senate, which, if it shall become a law in its present shape, I fear may produce much mischief. If we shall be urged on by feelings of resentment, and in the exercise of extraordinary powers attempt to crush the State of South Carolina, there will be an end of our Government in a short time. I tremble at the gulf which lies before us. Shall this glorious heritage which is the admiration of the world, and our greatest pride, be destroyed? I assure you, our government is in danger, and we should all contribute our best efforts to preserve it. With great respect, yours,

JOHN McLEAN.

HON. T. MORRIS.

REPORT ON COLONIZATION.

During the session of the legislature, in 1831–2, numerous petitions were presented, asking appropriations for the purpose of colonizing the free people of color in Ohio, in the Republic of Liberia, on the coast of Africa. Mr. Morris was appointed a select committee on that subject, and reported the preamble and resolutions here inserted. The colonization scheme may accomplish a good work in the illumination and regeneration of Africa, but as a remedy for the evils of American slavery, is visionary. Emancipation on the soil of the United States, or perpetual slavery, is the only alternative. Mr. Morris, in his efforts against slavery and the slave power of the country, during the latter years of his life, neither attacked nor defended the colonization scheme.

Mr. Morris, from the Committee appointed for that purpose, reported the following

PREAMBLE AND RESOLUTIONS,

ON THE SUBJECT OF THE COLONIZATION SOCIETY.

Although we believe the existence of slavery in these United States is a moral evil, as well as a national calamity, and we recognize to its fullest extent the doctrine that all men are created EQUAL, "That they are endowed by their Creator with certain inalienable rights; that among these are life, LIBERTY AND THE PURSUIT OF HAPPINESS," and that it is the duty of every citizen of the United States to aid, as far as his situation will reasonably permit, in extending these inestimable blessings to the colored population of our country. This General Assembly can not for a moment entertain the belief that slavery, which is undoubtedly our greatest national sin, has been the consequence of any particular State regulation, or that it ought to be viewed as a local, and not a general misfortune; the curse is upon us all, and it is now vain and useless to inquire by what means it was first introduced. The States, in the adoption of the federal compact, recognize slavery among the existing order of things, by declaring that Congress should not prohibit the migration to, or importation of, any person into any of the States then existing, as they should think proper, prior to the year 1808; and also by further declaring that no person held to service or labor in any State, under the laws thereof, should, by escaping into any other State, be discharged from such service or labor, in consequence of any law or regulation therein; but should be delivered up on the claim of the party to whom such labor or service was due.

Although Ohio is emphatically a free State, whose territory and climate have never been contaminated by the withering influence of slavery; nor has the cultivation or improvement of her soil been extorted from the unwilling hand of the laborer—yet we disclaim all right to interfere between the slave and his owner in a political view of the subject, nor will we inquire into the policy or justice of the laws of our sister States, which acknowledge the existence of slavery. It is sufficient for the citizens of Ohio to know that any portion of the human family are suffering from the existence of slavery or any other cause, to induce them to lend their aid as far as the dictates of prudence and humanity shall require, without stopping to examine whether they are under any legal or Constitutional obligation to do so.

This General Assembly are not insensible to the horror and heart-rending scenes that must ensue from servile war waged by the colored population of our country, and should it by any possibility prove successful in the slave-holding States, that the peace of our own firesides, and the repose of our citizens would soon be assailed by the fell destroyer. Such war could admit of no prelude, it would not be a war of conquest, but of extermination of one or the other race, including all ages, sexes and conditions. This General Assembly believe that no man, who reflects seriously on the subject, can entertain the idea that domestic slavery, in this country, under the influence of our free institutions, can be perpetual; but that the time is not far in advance when it must terminate, either by the terrible scourge of insurrection, or by the wisdom, justice and liberality of our people.

To preserve this favored land from the punishment which justice demands for this, her National sin, Providence in the Colonization Society, has opened to us a door of hope. To the oppressed it is the pillar of fire and the cloud that leads to the land of their fathers; and it has begun the good work in our own land, and laid the foundation of a system which, if its operations could be commensurate to the object, would not only free our country from the alarming crisis to which she seems fast hastening, but would also restore to the indubitable rights of man and the country of their fathers, the long oppressed sons of Africa. And we believe that not only justice, duty and the honor of our people, demand that we should lend a helping hand to assist that society in the great undertaking; but that the safety and prosperity of our country, imperiously require that the government of the United States should take the subject under their consideration, and afford such additional aid as may be in its power.

It is hoped and sincerely believed, that the opinion of this General Assembly, on the difficult and important question of freeing our country from its colored population, will not be considered as obtrusive, but received with the same spirit of affection and regard with which it is offered.

All must be aware of the need of an early attention to this matter, and that time will be necessary for its completion; and although we have been aroused to reflection by scenes shocking to humanity, yet it is a melancholy pleasure that it has been at a time well suited to the benevolent exertions of our fellow citizens. Our country is at peace with foreign powers, and her resources commensurate with the object to be attained.

It is, therefore, seriously recommended to this people, as well as the government of the United States, whether it is not worthy of the attention of Congress, as well as the different State legislatures, to extend their care and fostering hand to the benevolent efforts of the Colonization Society, by affording pecuniary supplies and the means of transportation, to all free persons of color who are willing to emigrate to Liberia. This would not only be an act of naked justice to this long oppressed race of men, but seems to be required as the only means of preventing the shedding of human blood, and as a necessary measure for the security of ourselves and our posterity.

Resolved, therefore, That the benevolent exertions of the American Colonization Society are entitled to the approbation of the government and people of the United States; and that our Senators and Representatives are requested to use their influence to bring this question to the attention of Congress, and to prevail upon that body to adopt such measures as may be within their Constitutional powers, for the removal of the colored population from the several States in the Union, and their settlement in Liberia.

Resolved, That should Congress doubt their power to make appropriations of money from the national treasury for that purpose, it is recommended that the Constitution of the United States be so amended as to give such power.

Resolved, That we recommend to the citizens of this State to form Colonization Societies in their different settlements and neighborhoods, and make such yearly contributions as may reasonably be within their power in aid of the parent society

Resolved, That the Governor pay out of his contingent fund the sum of one thousand dollars, to aid the Colonization Society to remove to Liberia any persons of color now residents of this State, and who shall apply to the Governor and obtain his certificate for that purpose, until the amount shall be expended according to the rules and regulations of the Society.

Resolved, That it is hereby recommended to the colored male population residing in this State, to meet in their respective settlements or neighborhoods, and choose one or more of their number to meet in convention at Columbus, on the fourth day of July next, for the purpose of selecting some person of color to go to Liberia, to examine the country, and to report to them on his return, its advantages or disadvantages as a place of settlement for the colored people, with such other facts as he may be instructed to inquire into by the Colonization Society; and should such person be so selected as shall be approved by the Governor, his expenses shall be paid out of the Governor's contingent fund; and that such person proceed to Liberia and return, under the order and protection of the American Colonization Society.

CHAPTER IX.

His Radical Democracy—Learned from the Bible and the Teachers in the Democratic School—Not a Bigoted Partisan—Earnest Advocate of the Doctrines of True Democracy—His Popularity—Tendered the Nomination of United States Senator in 1826—Elected Senator in Congress in 1832—His Election Greeted with Enthusiasm—Letter of Judge Reuben Wood—Resolution against the United States Bank—Letter from Washington City.

THE political creed of Thomas Morris was radically Democratic. True Democracy is the creation of a true Christianity, and shields the rights and interests of every man. "It is a sentiment not to be appalled, corrupted, nor compromised. It knows no baseness ; it cowers to no danger; it oppresses no weakness. Fearless, generous and humane, it rebukes arrogance, cherishes honor, and sympathizes with the humble. It is a sentiment of freedom, of equal rights, of equal obligations. It is the law of nature and of the Bible pervading the law of the land." In the application of its doctrines, and in its progress and achievements, it will consecrate forever to freedom, the soil of every country, and "unbind every burden, preach deliverance to every captive, and let the oppressed of all nations go free."

It was with the true Democracy that Thomas Morris was in principle, in every impulse and effort of his life identified. He received his first lessons in the home-school of his mother, and in youth and manhood, from those who were regarded as the oracles and apostles of Democracy. He was a disciple in the Jeffersonian school of politics. In 1829, he said "in the election of Mr. Jefferson, we have the first evidence of the power of that vital principle of liberty contained in the Constitution of the United States. Under his administration the great principles of civil and Constitutional liberty produced their desired effect. The administration of Jefferson will be viewed as the true republican standard for the government of the United States in ages to come."

His hatred to slavery was intensified from the lessons of Jefferson. "Who taught me," said he, in the Senate of the United States, "to hate slavery and every other oppression? Jefferson, the great and good Jefferson! yes, Virginia Senators, it was your own Jefferson, Virginia's favorite son, who did more for the natural liberty of mankind, and the civil liberty of his country, than any man who ever lived in our country—it was he who taught me to hate slavery; it was in his school I was brought up. If I am, sir, an Abolitionist, Jefferson made me one; and I only regret that the disciple should be so far behind the master both in doctrine and practice."

His love of, and devotion to true Democracy was a passion of his soul, rooted and grounded in his nature. "He was called a partisan; but he only seemed so to his political opponents. His fearless independence, and his fidelity to the moral and political convictions of his nature, rendered him constitutionally incapable of working in the traces of party. It was only when they sustained the principles which he believed and loved, that he sympathized with them and advocated their measures. There was an independent, straightforward determination to go for his principles, which allowed no compromise with his opponents, and no communion with temporizing friends." "I follow party," said he, "where the Constitution and principle lead, and where men attempt to take their place, I halt. I choose to rely on the Constitution and that *moral principle*, which ought to govern the actions of men in all situations and under all circumstances."

"His plain, direct, honest and passionate advocacy of the principles of the Democratic school, impressed them upon the minds of the people and prepared them to sustain the measures of his party. For a length of time he seemed to be the presiding genius of the Democratic party in Ohio. Against him were aimed the shafts of the opposition, and upon him were the eyes of the Democracy as the great champion of their cause. But it was in the Senate of the United States that Thomas Morris proved himself, not a man for his party, but a man for his country. Disdaining to wear the shackles of a party, and indignant that the leaders of the Democracy should yield their necks to the yoke of the slaveholding oligarchy, he stood in the august Senate of the United States, the single champion of universal freedom to man."

His able and fearless devotion to the doctrines of true Democracy made him popular with the people. In 1826, the Democratic party tendered him the nomination of United States Senator, in opposition to Judge Burnet, but the party being in the minority, he declined. In 1832, on the 15th day of December, the Democracy again put him in nomination, and he was elected Senator in Congress, for six years. The fall previous, he was put in nomination by the Democratic party, in his district, for Representative in Congress, but owing to a division in the party, by an independent Democratic candidate, he was defeated, in a popular vote of 6276 by 156.

His election as Senator, was hailed by the Democratic party in Ohio, with hearty and general approbation. The organ of the party at the Capitol of the State said: "To the republican cause of Ohio, it is cheering to reflect that a gentleman of his known firmness, high order of talents and great experience, has weathered the political storm, and succeeded in an election to a station where his ability and faithfulness will find ample scope for future usefulness to his country."

Another leading Democratic organ declared on his election, that "Mr. Morris is the only Senator Ohio has had for a long time, who firmly held the pure Democratic faith, of a strict construction of the Constitution of the United States, and open war against all peculiar privileges and monopolies."

Reuben Wood, a distinguished Democrat, honored with the governorship, and Supreme Judge, of Ohio, and long the personal and political friend of Mr. Morris, on his election to the Senatorship, wrote: "Permit me to say, and I do not intend it as a common-place remark, that I most sincerely congratulate, not only yourself, but the Democratic party, on your re-election to fill the highest, most responsible, and at this peculiar crisis—the most difficult and important office in the gift of the Legislature. The Democracy of Ohio, may safely rely on being faithfully and fearlessly represented in the Senate of the United States; and my sincere wishes are, that the Democracy of the State, hereafter, may keep that ascendancy which it has cost so much strife and exertion to obtain, and, at a future period, again will be willing to reward you with the continuance of its approbation and confidence."

At that period, subsequent to his election, on the 8th of January, 1832, the Democratic party held their State Convention. In that convention, Mr. Morris offered a strong resolution against the Bank of the United States, which, after a stormy debate, was adopted. A prominent member of the party, then holding a high office at Washington, wrote, after the adjournment of the convention, to Mr. Morris, as follows: "I do not hesitate to say, that you merit the gratitude and the patronage of the whole Democratic party of the country, for your prompt, active, decisive and truly republican course in that convention of Ohio, on that trying and critical occasion; and for which you ought to receive the thanks of the party, and the patronage and favor of the Government. It places Ohio in the front rank of the Democracy of the country, and redeems her character from the imputation of being governed by the influence of a Monied Monopoly, or the arrogance of a domineering aristocracy. And it also shows that the old Democratic party of the State, can not trust to the counsels of *forward*, indiscreet young men, without experience, who present themselves as leaders."

CHAPTER XX.

TAKES his seat in the Senate—Slavery—Anti-slavery Sentiment of the Revolution — Opinions of Madison—Jefferson — Patrick Henry—John Jay — Washington — Franklin — Lafayette — Abolition Societies, in 1787—Thanks of Congress to an Abolition Society—Reaction in Public Sentiment—Slavery, the Ruling Power—The Causes of Reaction

MR. MORRIS took his seat in the Senate of the United States, on the opening of the session, in December, 1833. During his Senatorial service, he became identified with the growing anti-slavery movements against the extension and the aggressions of the slave power; it will be proper, therefore, to review, briefly, the history and struggles of freedom, in opposition to slavery, and to record the sentiments of the patriots and statesmen of the Revolution, on this engrossing national subject.

It was the aim of the great and good men, who inaugurated and established the civil government and political institutions of the United States, as declared in the Constitution they formed—"To establish justice, promote the general welfare, and secure the blessings of liberty." The rights of man, and the principle of universal freedom, had a public and solemn enunciation, in the Declaration of Independence, wherein it was stated—"That all men are created free and equal, and endowed by their Creator with certain inalienable rights, among which are, life, liberty, and the pursuit of happiness." Freedom, and not slavery, was the object for which the patriots and statesmen of the Revolution drew the sword, and labored to extend and establish. They found the system of slavery in existence; but they contemplated, not its expansion, but its speedy extinction. The Constitutional records of the country not only prove this to have been their great purpose and most ardent wish; but their repeated declarations testify, that freedom was National and slavery Sectional, and to yield soon to the spread of universal liberty. This record is worthy to be read, and freshly remembered, by every American citizen; to be taught to every American child, till the sentiment of freedom shall be the ruling sentiment of the nation. Let these declarations have a new record, and a re-hearing on these pages.

Madison, the father of the Constitution—"Thought it wrong to admit in the Constitution the idea that there could be property in man." "I object to the word slave appearing in a Constitution which I trust is to be the charter of freedom to unborn millions; nor would I willingly perpetuate the memory of the fact that slavery ever existed in our country. It is a great evil, and under the Providence of God, I look forward to some scheme of emancipation which shall free us from it. Do not, therefore, let us appear as if we regarded it perpetual, by using in our free Constitution an odious word opposed to every sentiment of liberty."

Jefferson, the great apostle of Democracy, declared—"The way I hope, is preparing under the auspices of heaven, for a total emancipation. The hour of emancipation is advancing in the march of time. This enterprise is for the young, for those who can follow it up, and bear it through to its consummation. It shall have all my prayers, and these are the only weapons of an old man. What execrations should the statesman be loaded with, who permitting one half the citizens thus to trample on the rights of the other, transforms the one into despots and the other into enemies, destroying the morals of one part, and the *amor patriæ* of the other. And can the liberties of a nation be thought secured, when we have removed the only firm basis, a conviction in the minds of the people, that their liberties are the gift of God. Indeed I tremble for my country when I reflect that God is just; and that justice can not sleep forever. The Almighty has no attribute that can take sides with us in such a contest."

Patrick Henry, the impassioned orator of the Revolution, affirmed — "Slavery is detested; we feel its fatal effects; we deplore it with all the pity of humanity. It would rejoice my very soul that every one of my fellow beings was emancipated. I believe the time will come when an opportunity will be offered to abolish this lamentable evil."

Judge Wilson, of Pennsylvania, said—"I consider the power given to this Constitution to prohibit the importation of slaves, as laying the foundation for banishing slavery out of the country. If there was no other lovely feature in the Constitution but this one, it would diffuse a beauty over its whole countenance. In the lapse of a few years, Congress will have power, (by an amendment of the Constitution), to exterminate slavery from within our borders."

John Jay, the first accomplished Chief Justice of the Supreme Court of the United States, and who aided in the formation of the Constitution, said: "The word slaves was avoided, probably, on account of the existing toleration of slavery, and its discordancy with the principles of the Revolution, and from a consciousness of its being repugnant to some of the positions in the Declaration of Independence."

Judge Tucker, an able civilian of Virginia, said to the legislature of his State: "Should we not at the time of the Revolution have loosed their chains and broken their fetters? or if the difficulties and dangers of such an experiment prohibited the attempt during the Revolution, is it not our duty to embrace this moment of Constitutional health and vigor, to effect so desirable an object, and to remove from us a stigma with which our enemies will never cease to upbraid us, nor our consciences to reproach us? The right of one man over another, to hold him in slavery, is neither founded in nature nor in sound policy. Slavery is perfectly incompatible with government. Shall we then neglect a duty which every consideration, moral, religious, political or selfish recommends?"

Mr. Parker, of Virginia, in the first Congress held under the present Constitution, said: "He hoped Congress would do all in their power to restore human nature to its inherent privileges, and if possible wipe out the stigma under which America labored. The inconsistency of our principles, with which we are justly charged, should be done away, that we may show by our actions the pure beneficence of the doctrine which we held out to the world in our Declaration of Independence."

Washington, the Father of his country, said: "I never mean, unless some particular circumstances should compel me to it, to possess another slave by purchase, it being among my first desires to see some plan adopted in this country, by which slavery may be abolished by law. Slavery might and ought to be abolished by legislative authority, and so far as my suffrage would go, it shall not be found wanting." He, at his death, freed all his slaves. Washington wrote to Lafayette, when the latter set all his slaves free in Cayenne: "Would to God, a like spirit might diffuse itself generally into the minds of the people of this country. The slaves ought, by degrees, to be set free, and that, too, by legislative authority."

Lafayette, the friend of America, and the co-patriot of Washington, who poured out his wealth like water, and led an army from France, to aid in achieving our independence, said: "I never would have drawn my sword in the cause of America, if I could have conceived that thereby I was founding a land of slavery."

Benjamin Franklin, the patriot, the philosopher and the philanthropist, closed his long and useful life by acting as President of an Abolition Society, formed on the 14th of April, 1775, and re-organized in 1788, when this venerable man accepted the Presidency, Dr. Rush acting as Secretary. These men, and their co-laborers in the cause of emancipation, sent to Congress the following

MEMORIAL:

From a persuasion that equal liberty was originally the portion, and is now the birth-right of all men, and influenced by the strongest ties of humanity, and the principles of our Institutions, your memorialists consider themselves bound to use all justifiable measures to loosen the bands of slavery, and promote a general enjoyment of the blessings of freedom. Under these impressions, they earnestly entreat your serious attention to the subject of slavery; that you will be pleased to countenance the restoration of liberty to those unhappy men, who alone in this land of freedom, are degraded into perpetual bondage, and who, amid the general joy of surrounding freemen, are groaning in servile subjection; that you will devise means for removing this inconsistency from the character of the American people; that you will promote mercy and justice toward this distressed race; and that you will step to the verge of the power vested in you for discouraging every species of traffic in the persons of our fellow-men.

BENJAMIN FRANKLIN, President.

PHILADELPHIA, Feb. 3, 1790.

Societies, having the abolition of slavery in view, were formed in a number of other States, including Virginia and Maryland; and in 1794, a General Convention of delegates from all the Abolition Societies in the United States was held in Philadelphia, to consult measures for the overthrow of slavery; and this General Convention met annually for twelve years. To the first Convention, Dr. Rush was a delegate, and Chairman of a Committee to draft an Address to the people of the United States, which contained the following views and condemnation of slavery:

"Many reasons concur in persuading us to abolish domestic slavery in our country.

"It is inconsistent with the safety of the liberties of the United States.

"Freedom and slavery can not long exist together. An unlimited power over the time, labor and posterity of our fellow creatures, necessarily unfits men for discharging the public and private duties of citizens of a Republic.

"It is inconsistent with sound policy, in exposing the States which permit it, to all those evils which insurrections and the most resentful war have introduced into one of the richest islands in the West Indies.

"It is unfriendly to the present exertions of the inhabitants of Europe in favor of liberty. What people will advocate freedom with a zeal proportioned to its blessings, while they view the purest Republic in the world tolerating in its bosom a body of slaves?

"In vain has the tyranny of kings been rejected while we permit in our country a domestic despotism, which involves in its nature most of the vices and miseries that we have endeavored to avoid.

"It is degrading to our rank as men in the scale of being. Let us use our reason and social affections for the purposes for which they were given, or cease to boast a pre-eminence over animals that are unpolluted with our crimes.

"But higher motives to justice and humanity toward our fellow creatures remain yet to be mentioned.

"Domestic slavery is repugnant to the principles of Christianity. It prostrates every benevolent and just principle of action in the human heart. It is rebellion against the authority of a common Father. It is a practical denial of the extent and efficacy of the death of a common Saviour. It is a usurpation of the prerogatives of the great Sovereign of the universe, who has solemnly claimed an exclusive property in the souls of men.

"But if this view of the enormity of domestic slavery should not affect us, there is one consideration more which ought to alarm and impress us, especially at the present juncture.

"It is a violation of a Divine precept of universal justice, which has in no case escaped with impunity."

Congress gave countenance and encouragement to these Abolition Societies, formed in various States of the Union, and as late as 1809, the Speaker of the House of Representatives, by a resolution, was directed to return a letter of thanks to an Abolition Convention, for a gift of Clarkson's history of slavery, which was ordered to be placed in the Congressional library.

The patriot and statesman, the philanthropist and Christian, the politician and divine, the guardians of public liberty and morality, were all united to exterminate this moral and political evil from the Republic. They deemed it a duty to saturate their schools, colleges, churches, legislatures and domestic circles, with the belief that slavery was a national crime, offensive to God, and destructive to the safety, happiness and prosperity of the people."

Mr. Leigh, of Virginia, in 1832, said—"I thought, till very lately, it was known to everybody, that during the Revolution, and for many years after, the abolition of slavery was a favorite topic with many of our ablest statesmen."

This too, was the religious sentiment of the Revolution, and of subsequent eras.

The Presbyterian church declared, in 1787, 1793, 1795, 1815, and in 1818, that—"Slavery was a gross violation of the most sacred and precious rights of human nature; utterly inconsistent with the law of God; totally irreconcilable with the spirit and principles of the Gospel of Christ; and that it is manifestly the duty of all Christians to use their honest, earnest and unwearied endeavors, *as speedily as possible*, to efface this blot on our holy religion, and to obtain the complete abolition of slavery throughout Christendom, and if possible, throughout the world."

This historical record shows the thorough anti-slavery sentiments and action of the founders of our political Institutions and the framers of the Constitution. Not one of those liberty loving men dreamed of its extension; not one but prayed for and anticipated its speedy extinction.

Before a generation had passed away, the sentiment of freedom began to grow less potential, and the spirit of slavery more aggressive and dominant.

During eighty years of national existence and progress, American slavery becomes the ruling power of the country. Its aggressions have triumphed over the free purposes and principles of the Constitution and of national patriotism. It has ignored the doctrines of the Declaration of Independence, and scoffed at that great charter of human rights. It has made slavery National and freedom Sectional. It has trampled on solemn compacts, and opened to the power of slavery immense territories, which have been for a generation, by a solemn act of legislation, consecrated to freedom, in which thirteen empires, as large as the great State of Ohio, may be formed. It has added five new Slave States to the Union. It has under its power more than one-half of the geographical domain of the Nation. It has originated wars for the purpose of giving expansion and perpetuation to the system.

It has controlled the Legislation of Congress, and indirectly of Free States, and avowed its purpose, as declared, by its Southern champions, " to give laws to the Government." It has practically denied the Constitutional right of Petition, and treated American citizens, who have petitioned for a redress from the evils of slavery, with contempt. It stifled, and prohibited for years, in the popular branch of the Government, free discussion on the subject of slavery. In the Convention of great political parties, slavery has decreed, who should, or who should not be President. In the executive, legislative and judicial departments of the Government, it has had the supremacy, and their emoluments. It has made political Anti-Slavery a ground for civil disfranchisement, social proscription and murderous persecution. It has corrupted the public conscience of the nation, and revolutionized public sentiment. It has subsidized the Press of the North to a considerable extent, both political and religious, into an advocacy of its arrogant claims. Christianity has been *perverted* and *converted* to its defense and perpetuation. The Pulpit and the Bible have been brought to its sanction and its declared Divine authority. Ecclesiastical bodies have been rent in twain by its unhallowed pretensions; and every fountain of influence, political, social, educational, and religious, have felt its corrupting power throughout the nation and Government.

The cause of this sad revolution in public sentiment, and the action of the people and Government, are mournful and manifold; and is one of the most humiliating chapters in American history. Whence this treachery to freedom? this apostacy from the sentiment, so prevalent in the first and pure ages of the Republic? It has come, mainly from two sources, the love of money and the love of Power; Avarice, and Ambition, the two dominant passions of the human heart. Material wealth has been too much the controlling interest and purpose of the American people. The discovery was made that cotton, in the planting regions of the South, would become the source of future wealth, and cultivated by slave labor; and hence, Cotton became "King," the ruling element in the monied and political power of the country. This great power pervaded the commercial interests of the North as well as of the South, and, in the course of time, brought the free North into subserviency to the policy of the South. The commercial, the social, and the religious interests of the North, were afraid of giving offense to the South, by the agitation of slavery, and hence acquiesced in its arrogant aggressions, and became the apologists and defenders of American Slavery.

Political power, also had a great influence in the revolution of public sentiment, and the action of the Government in favor of slavery. The balance of power has always been with the South, and under the progress and achievements of free institutions and free labor, this power was being transferred to the North. The South, so long accustomed to rule, made the strongest efforts to retain their ascendancy in the Government, and to perpetuate their political power. In this effort they uniformly succeeded in causing the free North to bow in subjection to their claims, so that in almost every Presidential election they obtained a President, and with him the whole political power of the Government, to favor the pretensions of the slave-power.

These two great interests controlled and directed the public sentiment of the country, and brought under their dominion, the principles and institutions of the

North. The Press, the Pulpit, religious and secular Literature, Churches, Ecclesiastical Bodies, Humane and Christian Societies, great Publishing Houses, Social affinities, Political parties, and State Legislation, became directly, or indirectly, auxiliary in corrupting the public conscience and public sentiment, and thus revolutionizing the action of the Government, and the popular influence of the country, so that the battle was turned in favor of Slavery and against Freedom.

This ascendancy too, of the slave power, has been kept and continued in defiance of equal justice and true Democracy. The population, the commerce, the enterprise, the wealth, the prosperity, the finical support of the Government, the means for the diffusion of Christianity and education, are greatly in favor of the North. Freedom—in all the elements of national prosperity and greatness, in all that constitutes a State—has greatly outrivaled slavery, as all the statistics of the country abundantly confirm.

The Census of 1850 gives 347,525 slave-holders; of these, 68,820 own but a single slave; 105,683 each own under five slaves; 80,765 had each less than ten slaves—making 255,268 who each owned less than ten slaves. This number taken from 347,525, the whole number of slaveholders, leaves but 92,257 who are the owners of ten slaves or more; and these have practically controlled the Government, and brought the Northern States—with all their superior wealth, enterprise, intelligence, and their five-fold population—into subserviency to the slave interest.

CHAPTER XI.

Agitation — Three Eras of Slavery Agitation — Revolutionary Era — Missouri Era—Present Era—Mr. Morris takes his Seat as Senator, in the beginning of the Present Era—Slavery and the Slave-Trade in the District of Columbia — Petitions to Congress — John Quincy Adams Threatened with Expulsion—Gag Resolutions of the House—Action in the Senate—Pro-Slavery Senators—Mr. Morris's Firmness—Resolution of the Senate — The Senate a Battle-Ground between Freedom and Slavery — Prediction of Mr. Morris — Senator Seward — Mr. Morris's Speech on the Right of Petition.

Agitation is the source of light and progress, securing the triumph of truth and freedom, and the downfall of error and despotism. The Providence of God has no clearer confirmation and no nobler vindication, than in the ceaseless agitation to which slavery has been subjected during the last quarter of a century. Freedom, after a season of inaction, roused itself to resist the aggressions of slavery, and to turn once more the action of Government to its original purpose of securing and expanding the blessings of freedom, and to denationalize slavery. All efforts to prevent agitation, but increased its intensity and thoroughness. To silence the voice of freedom, political conventions in their platforms, decreed the doctrine of non-intervention and entire silence; legislatures in free States, interdicted its discussion; great ecclesiastical denominations held it as heresy, to canvass the claims of slavery, or to utter anathemas against it; the press secular and religious, made the subject contraband in its columns; commerce and social influence labored to prevent its examination and exposure; and all possible efforts were combined to keep slavery from the searching ordeal of light and discussion. These efforts however, were unsuccessful. Freedom was too powerful for slavery; and in defiance of political, commercial and religious edicts, agitation increased till it became the absorbing subject of discussion and action of the American people and Government.

Three distinct eras mark the agitation of slavery. The First was, when the Constitution of the United States was formed, continuing till about 1808, the year in which the slave-trade ceased by law; the Second, when the State of Missouri sought admission into the Union with a Constitution establishing slavery, which produced a profound excitement throughout the country, and which was quieted by the Act of Compromise, which gave to freedom all the National Territory north of thirty-six degrees and thirty minutes; the Third began about 1832, and has been ever since, waxing deeper and stronger.

Thomas Morris took his seat in the Senate of the United States at the commencement of the Third Era of the political agitation of slavery, in which he bore a distinguished part till his death.

Petitions to abolish the slave trade in the District of Columbia, were sent to Congress as early as 1814. The traffic in human beings, shamelessly prosecuted in the Capitol of a Free Republic, and in view of the assembled legislators of the nation and the Representatives from Foreign countries, was deemed, even by the inhabitants of the District, a National reproach. Judge Morrill, of the Circuit Court of the United States, in charging the Grand Jury, declared: "That the frequency with which the streets of Washington city had been crowded with manacled captives, sometimes on the Sabbath, could not fail to shock the feelings of all humane persons." In the same year, 1816, John Randolph, made a motion that a Committee in Congress be appointed, which was carried, to report "what measures were necessary to put a stop to the slave trade in the District."

In 1828, more than one thousand inhabitants of the District, petitioned Congress to abolish the slave trade. In 1829, the Grand Jury of the District sent a report to Congress in which they prayed, "That provisions might be made to prevent slave dealers, from making the cities of the District, Depots for the imprisonment of the slaves they collected. It is believed the whole community would be gratified by the interference of Congress for the suppression and the exclusion of this disgusting traffic from the District."

In 1830, the Washington *Spectator*, echoing the public sentiment in an article on the Slave Trade in the Capitol, told the American people "That at the very time when the procession, which contained the President (Jackson) of the United States and his Cabinet, were marching in triumph to the Capitol, a procession of colored human beings, *handcuffed in pairs*, were driven in another direction to a slave ship, where, with others, they were to embark and be conveyed to the South. Where is the O'Connell that will plead for the emancipation of the District of Columbia."

These were the sentiments of the great body of the people in the Free States; and availing themselves of their Constitutional right to petition Congress for a redress of grievances, they sent, during the Senatorial term of Mr. Morris, numerous petitions, praying for the suppression of the Slave traffic, and the abolishment of slavery in the District of Columbia.

When these petitions were presented to the House of Representatives, the slave power was indignant, and Mr. Speight of North Carolina, said: "Nothing but respect for the Speaker, as an officer of the House, and his character, prevented him from rushing to the table and tearing the petition to pieces." "I warn these petitioners said another, Mr. Hammond, of South Carolina, "ignorant, infatuated barbarians as they are, that if chance shall throw any of them into our hands, they may expect a felon's death."

John Quincy Adams, Ex-President of the United States, and, subsequently for ten years, member of Congress from Massachusetts, presented a petition to abolish slavery in the District. Mr. Thompson of South Carolina, rose, and threatened him with expulsion from the House, and an indictment before the Grand Jury. "He may yet be amenable to the Grand Jury, and we may yet see an *incendiary* brought to justice." To prevent agitation on the subject of slavery, and to intimidate the freemen of the North from sending their petitions to Congress, the House, on the 26th of May, 1836, passed the following resolution:

" *Resolved,* That all petitions, memorials, resolutions, and propositions, relating in any way, or to any extent whatever to the subject of slavery, shall, without being read, printed, or referred, be laid on the table, and that no further action whatever shall be had thereon." The preamble declared the object to be, "That all agitation on the subject of slavery should be finally arrested, for the purpose of restoring tranquillity to the public mind."

The same spirit and purpose reigned in the Senate. On the 7th of January, 1836, Mr. Morris presented several petitions from the citizens of Ohio, asking the abolition of slavery in the District of Columbia. Mr. Calhoun, of South Carolina, rose and said: "It was not within the power of Congress to legislate on the subject; that one half of the Union was deeply slandered in these petitions; that receiving them would continue agitation; that agitation was what the South feared, because it would compel the Southern press to discuss slavery in the very presence of the Slaves, who would be induced to believe that there was a powerful party at the North ready to assist them; I object to receiving these petitions because they were sundering the ties that bound this Union together."

Mr. King, of Alabama, afterward Vice President of the United States, said: "He believed those miserable fanatics would yet become enlightened, and the spell of their delusion be dispelled."

Mr. Leigh, of Virginia, said: "The conduct of these petitioners was injurious, offensive, and calculated to produce agitation in our social relations, and to jeopardize the Union. Dr. Channing, of Boston, in 1836, published his views of American slavery; in reference to that Book Mr. Leigh declared, "That he never read any paper that filled him with deeper sorrow. It had done more to weaken the brotherly love of our Northern brethren than the whole exertions of the despicable company of abolitionists put together. It had no sympathy for the whites of his own race."

Mr. Preston, of South Carolina, said—"The Government should say to the South, that we can't receive the petitions of hot-headed and cold-hearted fanatics, who are waging a war of extermination against us. We ask, that Congress will distinctly and positively interfere between us and these fanatics. Let an Abolitionist come within the borders of South Carolina; if we can catch him we will try him, and notwithstanding all the interference of all the governments on earth, including the Federal Government, we will hang him."

Mr. Strange, of North Carolina, said—"I most confidently believe that the institution of slavery is favorable to the highest development of the freemen who live within its influence; that it promotes the growth of all the nobler and generous qualities of our nature in every bosom, except perhaps, that of the slave himself. The current of fanaticism which has crossed the Atlantic, has swept away in its course, one of our sovereign States, and how many more were doomed to follow, God only knew. Every agitation on the subject of slavery, weakens the moral force in our favor, and breaks down the moral barriers that now serve to protect and secure us. We have everything to lose, and nothing to gain by agitation and discussion."

Mr. Lumpkins, of Georgia, said—"Every lover of this Union should cease to agitate this question. The interference of the Abolitionists and their supporters with the domestic concerns of the South, is daily becoming more offensive. If abolitionists went to Georgia, they would be caught."

These were the uttered declarations of Southern Senators, when anti-slavery petitions were presented. Senators from the free States were as fierce in their denunciations.

Mr. Buchanan, from Pennsylvania, said—"These fanatics have been scattering fire-brands, arrows, and death, throughout the Southern States. Their motives may be honest, but their zeal is without knowledge. They render the condition of the slave miserable, with vague notions of freedom never to be realized. They are desperate fanatics."

Mr. Wall, of New Jersey, said—"Let us put an end to this exciting subject; let us by a prompt decision, carry balm to the wounded feelings of the slave-holding States; let not this Hall become a place for the discussion of Abolition."

Mr. Wright, of New York, said—"Refuse the right to petition on the broad principles, as relating to the subject of slavery, and these malignant agitators will seize upon the act to draw to themselves and their cause public sympathy. They were dangerous and wicked agitators of the North. Mr. Channing's Work on Slavery, had shown him ignorant of the opinion and feelings of the great mass of the citizens of the non-slaveholding States. The spirit in which it was written, as grossly abused the Northern feelings as its language did Southern morals."

Mr. Pierce, of New Hampshire, now President of the United States, said—"I regard the schemes of the Abolitionists as mad and fanatical."

In the midst of such an array of opposition, Mr. Morris, as a Senator from the free State of Ohio, earnestly and ably defended the Constitutional rights of his countrymen. A few extracts from his various speeches in defense of the right of petition, and the character of those who had petitioned Congress on the subject of slavery, are here presented:

"The subject-matter of these petitions were clearly within the power of Congress, and one upon which this body could act, whenever in their opinion it was necessary for such action to be had. He was well convinced that the petitioners entertained the same opinion with himself on the subject, and that they had in good faith, sent their petitions to Congress; and with equal good faith, it was the duty of Congress to provide means by which slavery and the slave-trade should be abolished in this District. The question now is, have these petitioners a right to be heard by this body, who possess primary, complete, and exclusive legislation upon this subject? This right is secured to them in the most ample manner, by the provisions of the Constitution itself. That instrument deprives Congress of all power to make any law, to abridge this right; the Constitution recognizing the right as inherent, and original, and does not in the slightest degree, permit Congress to interfere with it as a right. Upon this Constitutional provision the petitioners have placed themselves, as upon a rock which can not be moved; but in the exercise of this right, he was willing to admit, that the petitioners ought to observe that decorum which is necessary to the very existence of society.

"It is objected in this case, that the petitioners reflect in the language of their petitions, most unwarrantably on sovereign States, as well as on individual citizens of those States. He said—if the right of petition was deemed of so much importance as to be declared by the Constitution, a right which Congress should not abridge; with what propriety then, shall one branch of Congress undertake to declare, that petitions shall not be received, on the ground, that the object which the petitioners seek to obtain is not in the power of Congress to grant; or that the words used by the petitioners, are such as ought not to be heard?

"He would ask gentlemen, if this was not abridging the right of petition; for, if Congress could prescribe the matter and form in which petitions should be presented, there was at once an end to the right of petitioning. He could see no difference in principle, in prescribing the manner in which an act should be done, and in preventing it altogether. The petitions now presented, pray the action of Congress on a subject, over which Congress alone, has the power of legislation. They have expressed themselves in this matter, in such language as they judged proper for the occasion; this is their inherent right. The liberty of speech is theirs, without restraint, and they are subject for its abuse, only to the laws. Let us take care then, how we tread on this ground, lest in our attempts to make petitions palatable to ourselves, we do not abridge the sacred right of petitioning. In this belief he found assurance, that the petitions would be received, and the motion of the honorable Senator fail. It was not necessary, that he should express his views of the evil effects that would follow a contrary course." The feelings, said Mr. Morris, which prompted these petitions were the deepest rooted of any in the human breast; they were excited by a high sense of *religious duty*, and no human power could ever induce them to abandon what they believed themselves thus bound to perform. They had been termed miserable fanatics, vile incendiaries, and charged with an intention to dissolve the Union. These views were very erroneous. They were upright, conscientious, patriotic citizens, and they had a right to be heard. And to receive the petitions and immediately move their rejection, was tantamount to refusing to receive them. It was keeping the word of promise to the ear, and breaking it to their hope. If the right of petition fail us, will it not prove that the whole fabric of the Constitution is rotten, and not worth our care? I fervently hope, that the tear of some recording angel may yet be dropped on the words of shame and dishonor, and blot them out forever."

The Senate passed a resolution, that receiving a petition on the subject of slavery, should be negatived after it was read, thus striking down the great Constitutional right of Petition. This act, decreed and executed bythe Slave power, ever in the ascendancy in the Senate of the United States, and the repeal of the Missouri Compromise Act, in March, 1854, were but the fulfillment of a prediction made by Mr. Morris, on the floor of the Senate, in 1836. "I am clearly of the opinion said he, that if the liberties of the people of this country are ever destroyed, it will be by the act of an American Congress; and the first scene in the grand drama will take place in this Body."

Senator Seward of New York, on the triumph of slavery over freedom, in the act repealing the Missouri Compromise, uttered the same sentiment: "Successful resistance to this Act was never to be made in this Hall. The Senate floor is an old battle-ground, on which have been fought many contests, and always, at least since 1820, with fortune adverse to the cause of equal and universal freedom."

On the 10th of January, 1839, Mr. Morris made a special

speech on the subject of the right of Petition, which is here inserted. It is a Constitutional and able discussion of the whole subject. It is as follows:

SPEECH OF MR. MORRIS.

JANUARY 10, 1838.

Mr. Morris, on presenting the petition of sundry citizens of Brown County, Ohio, said he had received a petition with the request to present the same separately and alone; it contained the words Slavery and Slave Trade, and those words but once repeated; he feared, however, that it would fall under the practice of the Senate, and meet the same fate that other petitions containing the same words had done; that he would, however, avail himself of the opportunity, in support of the motion he was about to make, to submit a few remarks to the Senate, and which motion he should make in courtesy to the Senate, and not as a right existing in the body to require it. He had before him the Constitution and Rules of the Senate, both of which would sustain him in the course which strict duty would require him to take on the present occasion. He would first distinctly state, that he and those who thought with him on this subject, waged no war upon the laws and institutions of any State; the overgrown and unsatisfied power with which they were contending, had attacked them within their own borders. It was in self-defense, in defense of all that was valuable to honorable minds, that they were now compelled to act. It was in defense of political liberty, and the important and inherent right of petition, that they felt themselves pressed forward in this contest. And the first question he would consider was, who have the right of petition? Does it belong to the many, or to the few? has it any want of exclusiveness in its nature to prevent its equal enjoyment by ALL? Will the legislative bodies of the country (and he spoke with reference to the States as well as this

Government,) create an aristocracy of rights as they had an aristocracy of wealth? Shall the right of petition be tested by color, or by property? Either would be a gross assumption of power, and a palpable violation of right. He considered any human being capable of acquiring property, and upon whose person the laws could operate, and was susceptible of feeling and suffering, entitled to the full and unrestricted exercise of this right. A contrary doctrine he held to be not only odious, tyrannical and despotic in its nature, but in direct derogation of the fundamental principles of our Government. Yet this pretended right of judging, by legislative Assemblies, who shall petition, is finding advocates. Its exercise is an assumption of power having neither reason, truth nor common sense for its support.

No one has any just right to say, who among our people shall enjoy that right, or for what he shall petition. This unjust claim, he feared, was spreading its baneful and blasting influence through the country, and if newspaper information was to be relied on, was made a solemn question of debate in the Legislature of his own State. Men of talents, worth and respectability, had questioned the right of the colored man to present his petition through the hands of a member, on the ground that he was by the Constitution deprived of the right to vote, and of course, could not instruct the General Assembly, or any of its members. He deplored that such doctrine had found support in any State; and he had read with feelings of deep mortification and regret, of its advocacy in Ohio. So strange and so absurd did the objection appear to his mind, that he immediately applied to some of his brother Senators here, from the slave States, to know if it was the practice in the General Assemblies of their States, to refuse petitions from free persons of color, for the redress of any grievance under which they might suppose they labored, and he was assured such was not the case; but that persons of this description were allowed to petition as other citizens, and their petitions were received as a matter of right. And he asked to be corrected if wrong in his position. Indeed, one gentleman had said to him, "Why, sir, we allow our slaves to persuade us that they ought to be free." These, sir, are noble sentiments, and honorable feelings, worthy of the land of Jefferson, in the day when his hand was penning the Declaration of Independence. A contrary doctrine however, is now held and advocated by a class of small politicians, who, like insects have sprung from the corrupt and agitated waters of party spirit and drill; mere summer flies, who buzz round the circle of power, and draw a precarious and short lived existence from the putrid mass of prejudice, which interest has created, to keep the colored race in bondage. Politicians who would make the lacerated back of the trembling slave a hobby to ride into office, if no other would suit their purpose as well. He had no language to express his feelings with regard to such men, and the doctrine they held, and it was better perhaps he should not; but he would say, that it must be a most mean and contemptible Government which would subject a man to the operation of its laws, tax his property for its support, and then refuse to hear his petition. Such practice would be a refinement of despotism, of which modern Europe could not boast. Yet in some of our free States, this doctrine is advocated, and that too by many who profess to be republicans. It was a Republicanism beyond his conception, and one he did not understand—that we should tax a man for the support of government, and then because he is black or yellow, has a curly head, a flat nose, or thick lips, a petition from him shall not be received by the Legislature. Government could not, in his opinion, be guilty of an act of greater tyranny and more gross injustice than this. The philosophy and patriotism of the advocates of such doctrines, begin and end in the assertion, that a negro has no Constitutional right to petition, because he has not the right of voting at elections; and because he has no political rights, they deny him natural rights. What a bright thought is this; and what morality and philanthropy must dwell in the heart which conceived an idea cruel beyond description, and presumptuous beyond belief. The negro is not only permitted, but invited to approach his Maker by petition, and implore deliverance from existing evils while his fellow man, who has power over him, refuses to hear his petition, and in the meantime, raises a contribution from his property and labor, to pay the fees of the official station which he fills. Not having the right of representation, as a necessary consequence of paying taxes, is a sore grievance; but taxing, where the right of petition is denied, is gross injustice, and high-handed despotism. Well has it been said, that—

"Man, vain man,—
Drest in a little brief authority,
Plays such fantastic tricks before high heaven,
As makes e'en Angels weep."

Sir, said Mr. Morris, the advocates of such doctrines as I have mentioned, are in my belief, lovers of negro slavery, in its worst form; tyrants in heart, and enemies to the human race. This monstrous doctrine, he feared, most abounded in the free States; but he trusted its mushroom growth would be of short duration. It was a public prop injudiciously applied by public hands, to sustain the tottering institution of slavery. He remarked that the Senate, must not suppose from what he had said, that he was about to present a petition from any of the colored people. No! this was not the case. The petition was from free, white citizens of his own State, residents of the county of Brown, many of whom he knew personally, and could bear witness to their respectability and patriotism. They were persons of piety and intelligence; not fanatics or incendiaries, but men who loved their country; and what they would that others should do unto them, they were willing to do unto others; and though some of the signers were ladies, he considered that as giving the petition additional force.

The petitioners do not ask you to abolish slavery in the District of Columbia; they do not ask you to prohibit the slave-trade between the different States and Territories of the Union; they do not protest against the admission of Texas into the Union; they do not ask that additional slave States be kept out of our Confederacy; no, Sir! they have asked and prayed to you against these things, until deferred hope has made the heart sick. The petitioners only state as their opinion, that the existence of slavery in the District of Columbia is a great national sin; that, like the blood of Abel, it is calling loudly from the ground watered by its tears, to Heaven, the only place of its hope, for vengeance upon our beloved country, which vengeance they deprecate. And they earnestly pray that this Honorable Body will repeal all Acts of Congress in any way favoring slavery in the District; and they feel quite sure that it will not be contended that Congress have not the power to repeal their own laws. Mr. Morris said, he was well satisfied what would be the fate of these petitions, from the settled practice of the Senate on like former occasions. Their petitions, like those which prayed for the abolition of slavery itself, would not be received in this boasted temple of liberty, but would be thrown back by those who minister at the altar, into the face of the petitioners, as an unclean thing, forbidden by the Constitution and laws of the country. Not discouraged by these anticipations, he would, as he had formerly said, himself move the reception of the petition; but he protested against the power of the Senate to require such motion to be made, either by virtue of their own Rules or the Constitution, as a preliminary one before a petition could be received. The twenty fourth Rule of the Senate, which he would read, declares, that—"Every petition, or memorial, or other paper, shall be referred, of course, without putting a question for that purpose, unless the reference (not the reception) is objected to by a member, at the time such petition is presented. And before any petition or memorial be received or read at the Clerk's table, whether the same be introduced by the President or a member, a brief statement of the contents shall verbally be made by the introducer." He contended that this Rule of the Senate, was decidedly against the practice of requiring a motion to receive a petition, to be made, and then laying that motion on the table, in order to rid ourselves of the petition altogether. The first part of the Rule requires that a petition shall be referred as a matter of course, unless objections are made to the reference; and before those objections can be made, the petition must have been received and in possession of the Senate; otherwise the order of reference is nugatory and vain, and the very exception to receiving a petition, that its contents must be first stated by the introducer, excludes, upon every fair principle of construction, the idea that any other question can be made as to its reception, but a refusal on the part of the introducer to state briefly its contents.

An exception to the general rule, is always considered as evidence that the operation of the Rule is not to be impeded in any other manner but that prescribed by the single exception made a part of it. He considered, that to raise a question of reception to petitions of the kind he was about to present, was a new practice, and then to lay that motion on the table, and never permit it to be taken up and put to the vote, was a device for a special purpose, a false coin, to be put off as valuable, against the rights of the negro only; for never to his knowledge, had it been attempted against a petition for the relief of white persons. For their rights, it was not yet considered a lawful tender; but the time might soon come when it would be said here, that the laboring class of the white race, ought not to enjoy or exercise political privileges, but be placed on the same footing as the free colored race; indeed, this doctrine was already boldly advanced out of doors, by the aristocracy of the country, whether from the North or the South. He contended that the very proposition not to receive a petition, was in itself a dangerous tendency, destructive of the privileges of the people, and in derogation of their Constitutional rights. It was his opinion, that there was no power in the Senate to refuse to receive a petition; no matter what the prayer or the language was, it must be received before any judgment or order could be taken on it; the petition could then be rejected at once, thrown upon or under the table, or leave given to withdraw it, as the Senate might judge proper. He said, he had the authority of the House of Representatives to sustain him in his position, and he believed, of every State Legislature in the Union. The House, as he understood, had decided that it was bound to receive petitions, but had laid them on the table, without being read, referred, debated, or printed. But in not admitting petitions to be received, by making the acceptance a question, and then laying that question on the table, he believed the Senate of the United States, in this practice, stands alone. If glory was derived from its exercise, it was a glory whose whole brilliancy shone upon the dark side of slavery only.

It would be remembered that, but a few days since, a citizen of Philadelphia presented his petition, stating that he had discovered a means by which he could cause it to rain when and where he pleased, upon any given spot, from five to a thousand miles square, and by that means could keep the Ohio river always navigable, from Pittsburgh to its outlet, and praying Congress to aid him in his new and valuable enterprise. The Senate thought, and rightly too, that their power was confined to objects on the earth, and could not be exercised to control the elements above and around us, and that the object of the petitioner was not within their power; but yet, they did not refuse to receive this petition but read it and laid the same on the table.

A despotic or monarchial government he admitted, might, with some degree of propriety, some kind of plausibility, refuse to receive a petition from their subjects, because they hold that their power is derived from the Deity, and not from the people; and that they have the right of judging what the people need, as all the privileges they enjoy are derived, not from the laws of nature, but from the bounty of the Crown. But with us, the reverse of this is the foundation of our Government. The governing principle here is, that all power is inherent in the people, and all just Governments are founded upon their authority. It follows, therefore, that petitions from them ought to be considered in the light of instructions or orders, which their constituted agents are bound to obey.

But, there is another still higher and more important objection to the course pursued by the Senate, with regard to petitions of the character of that which he was called on to present. It is the practice, after a motion to receive such petitions is made, and the yeas and nays on the question are desired by one-fifth of the members present, to prevent that question being put to the vote by a subsequent motion, to lay the former motion on the table. He did not consider the Senate bound to take the vote immediately after the yeas and nays had been ordered, but they were bound to put the question and take the vote, in the ordinary course of business, and during the session. The Constitution, he considered as express on this point, that the obligation could not be dispensed with, without a palpable violation of its letter as well as its spirit. The words of the Constitution are, "And the yeas and nays of the members of either House, on any question, SHALL, at the desire of one-fifth of those present, be entered on the Journal." He thought that any rule or practice of the Senate, by which this positive requirement of the Constitution, when called for by the requisite number, is denied, evaded, or put off, during the session, was a palpable violation of the Constitution, and could conceive of no one more open and dangerous. Constitutions, laws, and rules, are framed for the protection of minorities,—for the weak and helpless. Majorities can, for the time being, take care of themselves; but majorities to-day may be minorities to-morrow, and need the same protection; hence the necessity of always adhering to correct principles.

To men not versed in political management, one would suppose this provision of the Constitution would have the same meaning, and that too, a certain and definite one, not to be altered by rule or evaded by policy. He feared it was the dark and murky cloud of slavery which obscured this provision of the Constitution, and prevented it from being clearly seen: when slavery is before our eyes, we seem incapable of seeing any other object. Gentlemen, he hoped, would not, on this question, continue in a like situation with that notable Indian woman, who declared that her husband was always before her eyes, and prevented her from seeing any other man.

His complaint was, not that the right of the small minority, in which he commonly found himself on questions of this kind, was unconstitutionally taken away—No! it was the rights of the people; not of his own constituents alone, but of the whole country. It surely is desirable that the votes of the members on important questions, should be known, and evidence by record, furnished of the fact how each member voted. This is the right and privilege of the country, a right which they have placed in one-fifth of the *members present*, to demand for them, and which demand, they have said, the remaining members SHALL obey.

He, then, in their name, demanded as a right, of the minority, that the yeas and nays on a motion to receive a petition on the subject of slavery, when desired by the competent number, be entered on the Journal. There was no policy or favor connected with the demand. It was a sheer, naked right, and to prevent its enjoyment, by the power of a majority, was a plain, palpable, and open violation of one of the clearest provisions of the Constitution. He said it was no frivolous objection on his part made to delay the business or weary the Senate. The question was of too high and important a character to be met and trifled with by technicalities. He never indulged in such pastimes; but he did consider it a question of vital importance to the country, to know how the members of the Senate would vote on the distinct question of receiving a petition to abolish slavery in the District of Columbia. He thought it highly improper, if not undignified, to evade this question, by laying it on the table. To him it was no new doctrine to contend for the rights of the people and the minority, on a question of this kind. The Constitution of his own State used the same language as the Constitution of the United States, on this subject, but placed the power in the hands of two members only. Attempts have been made in the Senate of his own State, when he had the honor to be a member of that body, to evade a question, by a side motion, after the yeas and nays had been called for by two members. He resisted it for the same reason which induced him to resist the motion now. He was then sustained by the Chair, and on an appeal was triumphantly sustained by the Senate.

It was hard for him to reconcile the practice of laying a motion on the table, never to be taken up, after the yeas and nays had been ordered, with another practice of the Senate, which would not permit even the mover of a proposition to withdraw it, after a like call had been ordered; but he left it for the gentlemen who had the power of the majority in their hands, to reconcile their inconsistencies here, and justify their practice to the country and posterity.

It was a miserable expedient to cover over our footsteps in our march against the temple of the Constitution. The present, it was true, was an isolated case. It stood alone; no other combination of power and strength had, before this, been able to accomplish so much. The slaveholding power alone, was now found sufficient to close the eyes, and still the voice of the country, *while its dark cloud is o'er-spreading the whole land.* He felt gratified, when now his official labors were ceasing, that, for himself and for his country, he had the opportunity to make his most solemn protest against the whole proceedings of Congress, with regard to petitions on the subject of slavery.

He would say to the friends of humanity, of justice, of the Constitution and laws, *be not discouraged.* Though the deadly mildew of slavery has destroyed the tender vine, yet shall its branches again shoot forth. The light in the Temple of Liberty is not yet quite extinguished; though your members are few, and yourselves at present, a despised class; yet your cause is just, strong and powerful; with the shield of faith, and the armor of right and hope, rush to the rescue, and prevent the now flickering flame from being totally extinguished. *A nation, a world is coming to your aid, and your final triumph is as certain as that, "seed time and harvest, cold and heat, summer and winter, day and night, shall not cease."*

Pray, Mr. President, who are those who, if petitions to abolish slavery are presented, or if Congress should attempt to consider the proceedings of one of the sovereign States on this subject, *threaten to dissolve the Union?* Is it we, who come before you as humble **petitioners?**

No, sir, we use no such language; nor do we for a moment, harbor such a thought, whatever may be our fate. Dissolve the Union! destroy the relations and amity now existing between these States! What State will first lift its fratricidal hands in this unholy work? What man, like Cain, would murder his brother? They are not, Sir, to be found among those with whom I act, who are the friends of liberty and law.

No, Sir! we throw back the charge upon those who are endeavoring to deprive us of our unquestionable rights. Is it from the deep fountain of the heart they speak, when they talk of dissolving the Union? To deny to any the right of petition, he thought, was a thrust aimed at one of the Union's strongest ligaments; but he trusted the vital principle of the Constitution was sufficient to restore it to its wonted vigor, from injurious assaults like this. This, Sir, is a disagreeable subject for discussion. He had always held, that to utter such sentiments, either in public or in private, that the Union would, for any cause whatever, be dissolved, was in bad taste. Gentlemen. he was sure, were mistaken, if they thought that by threats of this kind, the people could be induced to surrender an iota of their Constitutional rights. The safety and perpetual continuance of the Union, he considered, mainly depended on the preservation and full enjoyment of all those rights in their pristine purity.

For himself, he was not disposed to falter in his course, or fail to perform his duty, here or elsewhere, on the ground that if he did so, others threatened to rush upon crime. He wanted further to say, to the Senate and to the country, that though himself, and those with whom he thought on this subject, were disposed to bear and suffer much; yet they, as well as others, could think and could feel; and if that ill-fated hour should ever come when, *in defense of their dearest rights, it was found necessary, they could, and would, also act.*

CHAPTER XII.

INCREASED AGITATION — Numbers of Petitioners — Confessions of Senators — Calhoun's Resolutions — Counter-Resolutions, by Morris — His Remarks — Record in his Memorandum Book of this Struggle in the Senate.

THE session of Congress of 1837–8 was marked with a deeper and more extended agitation of Slavery, both in the country and in Congress. The vexed question, like an ever present apparition, would return and demand a re-hearing. To restore tranquillity appeared to be beyond the magical wand of Senatorial Wisdom. The great sea of public commotions, and agitations, rolled higher and deeper. The public mind and conscience of the nation had quickened and deepened, and went up with increased power to the tribunal of our national legislature. The session of Congress for 1834–5 received and rejected 34,000 petitioners; the session of 1835–6, 110,000; and the session of 1837–8, witnessed 300,000 American citizens petitioning Congress on the subject of Slavery.

It was in view of this increasing agitation, and augmenting power of freedom, that Mr. Morris, in a tone of triumph, asked his co-Senators, "Is abolitionism dead, or is it just awaking into life? Is the right of petition forgotten, or is it increasing in strength and force? Let me bring back the minds of Senators from their delightful visions of the death of abolition to sober realities and solemn facts. I have now lying before me the names of thousands of living witnesses, that slavery has not conquered liberty; that abolitionists (for so all these petitioners are called) are not all dead. But suppose abolitionism is dead, is liberty also dead, and slavery triumphant? Is liberty of speech, of the press, and the right of petition also dead? True, it is strangled here, but Senators will find themselves in great error, if they suppose it is also strangled in the country. It is a living principle which slavery can not extinguish."

Southern Senators were compelled to confess the same fact:

Mr. Clay said; "it was manifest that the subject of slavery in the District of Columbia, was extending itself in the public mind, and daily engaging more and more of the public attention."

Mr. Preston said: "The fire is wider, and is spreading wider and wider; the fire is not put out, but is kindled worse and worse."

Mr. Calhoun said: "Abolitionism was interwoven with the political condition of the North, and it runs, and must run into their struggles for State ascendency. It was impossible to prevent its having a control over the political parties of the North. Abolition efforts would begin with the lowest grades of society, but it would go up and spread. However much he and others were opposed to its doctrines, it would one day spread so as to drive him from public life, or compel him to yield to its dictates."

To counteract and arrest these efforts against slavery, Mr. Calhoun applied all his great abilities as a statesman. In December, 1837, he presented the following resolutions:

Resolved, That in the adoption of the Federal Constitution, the States adopting the same acted, severally, as free, independent, and sovereign States; and that each by itself, by its own voluntary assent, entered the Union with the view to its increased security against all dangers, *domestic*, as well as foreign, and the more perfect and secure enjoyment of its advantages, natural, political and social.

Resolved, That in delegating a portion of their powers

to be exercised by the Federal Government, the States retained, severally, the exclusive and sole right over their own domestic institutions and police, and are alone responsible for them, and that any intermeddling of any one, or more States, or a combination of their citizens, with the domestic institutions and police of the others, on any ground, or any pretext whatever, political, moral, or religious, with a view to their alteration, or subversion, is an assumption of superiority not warranted by the Constitution; insulting to the States interfered with; tending to endanger their domestic peace and tranquillity; subversive of the objects for which the Constitution was framed, and by necessary consequences, tending to weaken and destroy the Union itself.

Resolved, That this Government was instituted and adopted by the several States of the Union, as a common agent in order to carry into effect the powers which they had delegated by the Constitution for their mutual security and prosperity; and that in the fulfillment of this high and sacred trust this Government is bound so to exercise its powers as to give, as far as may be practicable, increased stability and security to the domestic institutions of the States, that compose the Union; and that it is the solemn duty of the Government, to resist all attempts by one portion of the Union to use it as an instrument to attack the domestic institutions of another, or to weaken or destroy such institutions, instead of strengthening and upholding them, as in duty bound to do.

Resolved, That domestic slavery, as it exists in the Southern and Western States of the Union, composes an important part of their domestic institutions, inherited from their ancestors, and existing at the adoption of the Constitution, by which it is recognized, as constituting an essential element in the distributions of its powers among the States; and that no change of opinion, or feeling, on the part of the other States of the Union, in relation to it, can justify them or their citizens in open and systematic attacks thereon, with a view to its overthrow; and that all such attacks, are in manifest violation of the mutual and solemn pledges to protect and defend each other, given by the States, respectively, on entering into the Constitutional compact, which formed the Union, and as such is a manifest breach of faith, and a violation of the most solemn obligations, moral and religious.

Resolved, That the intermeddling of any State or States, or their citizens, to abolish slavery in this District, or any of the Territories, on the ground, or under the pretext, that is immoral or sinful; or the passage of any act or measure of Congress, with that view—would be a direct and dangerous attack on the Constitution of all slave-holding States.

Resolved, That the Union of these States rests on an equality of rights and advantages among its members; and that whatever tends to destroy that equality, tends to destroy the Union itself; and that it is the solemn duty of all, and more especially of this body which represents the States in their corporate capacity, to resist all attempts to discriminate between the States, in extending the benefits of the Government to the several portions of the Union, and that to refuse to extend to the Southern and Western States, any advantage which would tend to strengthen or render them more secure, or increase their limits or population by the annexation of new Territory or States, on the assumption or under the pretext that the institution of slavery, as it exists among them, is immoral, or sinful, or otherwise obnoxious, would be contrary to that equality of rights and advantages which the Constitution was intended to secure alike to all the members of the Union, and would, in effect, disfranchise the slave-holding States, withholding from them the advantages, while it subjected them to the burdens of the Government.

These resolutions threw the Constitution, and the Legislation of Congress, and the sanctions of religion to the support and perpetuity of slavery. Mr. Morris presented counter resolutions, as follows:

"*Resolved*, That in the formation of the Federal Constitution, the States acted in their sovereign capacities; but the adoption of the same was by the people of the several States, by their agents, specially elected for that purpose; and the people of the several States, by their own free and voluntary consent, entered into the compact of union proposed in the Constitution, with the view to form a more perfect union, establish justice, ensure domestic tranquillity, provide for the common defense, promote the general welfare, and secure the blessings of liberty to themselves and their posterity; and that the means of attaining all those important objects are fully provided for in the grants of power contained in the Constitution itself.

Resolved, That the people of the several States, in delegating a portion of their power to the Federal Government, which they had formerly exercised by their own legislatures, severally retained the exclusive and sole right over their domestic institutions, which they had not, by the Constitution granted to the Federal Government; and they reserved to individuals, and to the States in their sovereign character, the full liberty of speech and to the press, to discuss the domestic institutions of any of the States, whether political, moral, or religious; and that it would be the exercise of unauthorized power on the part of this Government, or of any of the States, to attempt to restrain the same; and that any endeavor to do so would be insulting to the people and the States so interfered with; for each State alone has the power to punish individuals for the abuse of this liberty within their own jurisdiction; and whenever one State shall attempt to make criminal, acts done by citizens in another State, which are lawful in the State where done, the necessary consequence would be to weaken the bonds of our Union.

Resolved, That this Government was adopted by the people of the several States of this Union as a common agent, to carry into effect the powers which they had delegated by the Constitution; and in fulfillment of this high and sacred trust, this Government is bound so to exercise its powers as not to interfere with the reserved rights of the States over their own domestic institutions; and it is the duty of this Government to refrain from any attempt, however remote, to operate on the liberty of speech and the press, as secured to the citizens of each State by the Constitution and laws thereof. That the United States are bound to secure to each State a republican form of Government, and to protect each of them against invasion or domestic violence, and for no other purpose can Congress interfere with the internal police of a State.

Resolved, That domestic slavery, as it exists in the southern and western States, is a moral and political evil, and that its existence, at the time of the adoption of the Constitution, is not recognized by that instrument as an essential element in the exercise of its powers over the several States, and no change of feeling on the part of any of the States can justify them or their citizens in open and systematic attacks on the right of petition, the freedom of speech, or the liberty of the press, with a view to silence either, on any subject whatever; and that all such attacks are manifest violations of the mutual and solemn pledge to protect and defend each other, and as such are a manifest breach of faith, and a violation of the most solemn obligations, political, moral and religious.

Resolved, That it is the indisputable right of any State, or any citizen thereof, as well as an indispensable duty, to endeavor, by all legal and Constitutional means, to abolish whatever is immoral and sinful, and that Congress alone possesses the power to abolish slavery and the slave trade in this District or any of the Territories of the United States; and the right of petition, of speech, and of the press, to accomplish this object, is not to be questioned, and that an act of Congress on this subject would be within its Constitutional powers.

Resolved, That the Union of these States rests upon the virtue and intelligence of the citizens in supporting the Constitution of the United States, and not upon any supposed advantages it may afford to any particular State; and that it is the solemn duty of all, more especially of this body, which represents the States in their sovereign capacity, to resist all attempts to discriminate between the States; and that it would be unwise, unjust and contrary to the Constitution, to annex any new Territory, or State, to this confederacy, with a view to the advantage of any State, or its peculiar domestic institutions; that such an attempt would be contrary to that equality of rights which one object of the Constitution was to secure alike to all the States; and if done to favor the slaveholding States, for the purpose of giving to those States a preponderance in this Government, would in effect be to establish slavery in all the States.

Resolved, That to regulate commerce among the several States is an express power granted by the Constitution to the Congress of the United States. That, in the exercise of this power, Congress may rightfully prohibit any article, though made property by the laws of a State, from being used in such commerce, if the same would be detrimental to the general welfare.

Resolved, That Congress have possessed the power since 1808 to prohibit the importation of persons into any State as articles of commerce or merchandise.

Resolved, That the political condition of the people within the District of Columbia is subject to State regulation; and that Congress, in the exercise of its legislative powers over the District, is bound by the will of its constituents in the same manner as when legislating for the people of the United States generally.

Resolved, That this Government was founded and has been sustained by the force of public opinion, and that the free and full exercise of that opinion is absolutely necessary for its healthy action; and that any system which will not bear the test of public examination is at war with its fundamental principles; and that any proceedings on the part of those who administer the Government of the States, or any of the States, or any citizens thereof, which is intended or calculated to make disreputable the free and full exercise of the thoughts and opinions of any portion of our citizens, on any subject connected with the political or religious institutions of our country, whether expressed by petition to Congress, or otherwise, by attaching to the character of such institutions odious and reproachful names and epithets, strikes at the very foundation of all our civil institutions, as well as our personal safety, poisons the very foundation of public justice, and excites mobs and other unlawful assemblies to deeds of violence and blood. That our only safety is in tolerating error of opinion, while reason is left free to combat it.

When they were read, Mr. Calhoun exclaimed—"Yes! here was displayed the *absolute creed* of the Abolitionists, fully developed. It was a fair specimen of their doctrine in full color.

Mr. Morris remarked, in reply:

"The Senator from South Carolina, in offering his resolutions, had thrown the *glove*, and with expressions of triumph, asserted that none in the Senate, in his opinion, could vote against his views. He, however, *dared to enter the lists single handed, and engage with him*. The resolutions in themselves, were to his mind, broad, sweeping, and denunciatory. What was the object of these resolutions? Was it not that a free discussion on an important question should not only be discountenanced, but silenced by a vote of that Body? They were partial in their bearing, speaking on one side, and not on another. He did not, for one, believe that Southern rights existed antagonist to those of any other portion of the Union. Why talk of Southern interests, and of Southern feelings? Such sentiments might lead to geographical distinctions, but could never lead to the peace and happiness of the whole country.

He professed himself a State-rights' man, and had as high devotion to the Union as any one; but he did not agree with the views of the Senator, that this Republic was a Confederacy of separate and independent States. He considered the Constitution as adopted and ratified by the united voice of the people.

What does the Senator from South Carolina mean, by interfering with domestic policy? Would that Senator contend, that if the citizens of the free States talked of slavery in the abstract, as a *sin* — a great moral, social, and political evil — that they should have their rights abridged? Freedom of speech, of the press, and of the sacred right of petition, were all sought to be put down at one fell swoop. If we could not meet together and discuss subjects, and compare conditions with others, for evil or for good, we should, instead of progressing in our high national destiny, retrograde, and become cyphers. Was such a state of things contemplated by the framers of the Constitution? He should think not.

Mr. Morris intended to offer his resolutions as amendments; he would not now do so, but would press them on the notice of the Senate hereafter. He conceived the resolutions of the Senator from South Carolina, as liable to the strongest objections, and as warring against the dearest rights and privileges of freemen. The Memorial from the Legislature of Vermont, had said that slavery was considered a moral and political evil, and asked that it might be abolished in the District of Columbia; and had not that State a right to ask such a measure at the hands of Congress, if it thought such a step would tend to the national honor and prosperity?

He was not to be intimidated, or driven from the course he thought it his duty to pursue. He knew what he was about, and understood his own course; and he would be here, as well as elsewhere, free and unshackled, and exempt from all party restraints, as an American citizen ought to be, and express fully and freely his opinion on every subject before this Body.

In the arguments here on the liberty of speech, changes were continually rung on the Union. Now it was a question whether the resolutions themselves, of the Senator from South Carolina, had not a strong squinting toward a dissolution of the Union. It was not for him to say, that they were intended to produce that effect; but the country would scrutinize them. If they were not intended to operate against the liberty of speech and of the press, they would have that effect. If that right is put down by the laws of the country, I must submit to those laws.

He was responsible alone, to the State in which he lived for the abuse of this privilege, and not to this Government. They would not attempt to pass another gag-law; though the gag-law was a sheet of white paper, compared with these resolutions. Why attempt thus to silence speech and the press without a law? Let the same thing be done by law, and then see whether the people had become so base as to permit these privileges to be taken from them. All the world could give was less than chaff, compared with the liberty of speech.

In this contest, he well knew with whom he had to

engage; he knew the prejudices that were against him, and that his best friends would differ from him. *He had wholly counted the cost, and resolved to meet every difficulty, and do his duty.* No objection had been made to the doctrine of his resolutions; but it was to be put down by the imputation that it was intended to embarrass. The truth, Sir, often embarrassed those who were in error. It was their misfortune. When war was made on the freedom of speech, of the press, and the right of petition, these inalienable rights must and would be defended. They were "Heaven's best gift to man."

In order to save religion from the reproach of sustaining the system of slavery, he moved that the terms, "moral and religious," be stricken out from the Resolutions of Mr. Calhoun; which was largely voted down; and after some slight alterations, the Senate passed the Resolutions of Mr. Calhoun, by a very large majority.

The day on which Mr. Morris struggled so earnestly against these Resolutions, was the anniversary of his birth-day. Returning from the Senate Chamber to his room, he made the following record in his memorandum-book:

WASHINGTON, January 3d, 1838.

I am this day sixty-two years of age. Forty years ago, the 19th of November last, I was married; and am now about fifteen hundred miles from my wife, who is now at her daughter's, in the State of Illinois. We have raised eleven children, eight of whom are still living. We began the world poor and friendless, and have struggled through life with much difficulty. I am now a Senator in Congress from the State of Ohio, and have this day, in a small minority, been defending the liberty of speech, of the press, and of the right of petition. Resolutions have been introduced declaring, that we have no right—either political, moral, or religious—to discuss the institutions of any State, with a view to effect a change in those institutions. The object is to prevent the discussion of slavery in any of the States; but the Resolutions strike at all discussion. I regard these Resolutions as the most daring attempt against American liberty, that has yet been brought forward in Congress, since the foundation of the Republic, and as such I oppose them.

In these remarks and resolutions, the reader can not fail to see the stern inflexibility of principle, and granite firmness of a moral hero. He stood alone in that august body, in defense of the dearest rights of his countrymen, and in his noble position presents a spectacle of the moral sublime. How, too, are his prophetic words fulfilled! The nation has, indeed, inspired by the voice of freedom, rushed to the rescue; giving unmistakable evidences, that the cause which Mr. Morris so nobly sustained in the Senate of the United States, and elsewhere, will soon issue in a glorious victory.

CHAPTER XIII.

A MEMORABLE day in Mr. Morris's History — Mr. Clay's great Speech against Abolitionists and Slavery Agitation — Mr. Morris's great speech in answer to it. A Southern Senator said Mr. Morris deserved expulsion — Reception through the country — A Contrast — Death of Calhoun — Clay — Webster — Morris — Eternal nature of Truth.

THE 9th of February, 1839, was a memorable day in the political life of Thomas Morris, and in the history of the Senate of the United States. On that day he laid the corner-stone in the monument of his fame and character, in a great speech, replete with the principles of freedom, and uttered under the inspiration of their truth and importance. It was an occasion of unusual interest. All efforts to prevent agitation on slavery had failed. The voice of freedom, ever instinct with life, would be heard, and that voice, still rang loud and clear in both halls of the National Legislature. Agitators would agitate, and the public councils of the nation must be the arena for the battle between freedom and slavery.

Henry Clay, on the 7th of February, 1839, with all his fascinating eloquence, eminent abilities, and great political influence, made a great speech to counteract and arrest the public agitation of slavery. He presented "a memorial from a large number of the inhabitants of the District of Columbia, remonstrating against the interference of other parts of the country, on the subject of slavery in the District, and against any action on the part of Congress to comply with the objects of the anti-slavery petitions."

In that effort, Mr. Clay admitted the numbers, and

growing influence of the Abolitionists ; "they had ceased to employ the instruments of reason and persuasion, and had made their cause political, and their appeal to the ballot-box ; he deprecated the slave question to be carried into the arena of politics; he believed that neither of the two great parties, had a design to mingle it in the politics of the country ; it was inexpedient, if not unconstitutional to abolish slavery in the District of Columbia ; it was the purpose of the Abolitionists to operate on slavery in the States; they presented exaggerated pictures of the slave system to the country ; that there were insuperable obsticles to emancipation ; that twelve hundred millions of dollars were invested in human beings in the slave States; that through an uninterrupted period of two centuries, under every form of legislation it had been held, that that is property which the law declares to be property ; that the emancipation of the slaves would probably excite a servile war, and be attended with great evils to the free laborers of the North ; that the abolition of slavery must be left to the workings of Providence, in the future of the next hundred years; that its agitation produced great and manifold evils ; that the liberties of the slaves, if it were possible, could only be established, by violating the incontestable rights of the States, subverting the Union, and beneath the ruins of the Union, would be buried sooner or later, the liberty of both races. He therefore adjured the clergy, and entreated his white country-men, and all the inhabitants of the free States, to rebuke and discountenance measures, that must lead to the most calamitous consequences, the ink shed in signing memorials might prove a prelude to the shedding of the blood of their brethren."

"I am no friend to slavery," said Mr. Clay. "The searcher of hearts knows that every pulsation of my heart beats high and strong for civil liberty." "If I could" said this great orator, in the hall of Congress, in a colonization speech, "be the instrument in eradicating this deepest stain upon the character of our country, and removing the cause of reproach on account of it by foreign nations—if I could be instrumental in ridding this foul blot from that State which gave me birth, or that not less beloved State which kindly adopted me as her son, I would not exchange the proud satisfaction which I should enjoy, for all the triumph ever decreed to the most successful conqueror."

"What would they, who reproach us, have done? If they would repress all tendencies toward liberty, they must go back to the era of our liberty and independence, and muzzle the cannon which thunders its annual joyous return. They must revive the slave trade with all its train of atrocities. They must suppress the workings of British philanthrophy, seeking to ameliorate the condition of the unfortunate West India slaves. They must arrest the cause of South American deliverance from thraldom.

"They must blow out all the moral lights around us, and extinguish the greatest torch of all which America presents to a benighted world, pointing the way to their rights, to their liberties and their happiness; and when they have achieved all their purposes, their work will then be incomplete. They must penetrate the human soul, and eradicate the light of reason and liberty. *Then and not until then*, when universal darkness and despair prevails, can you perpetuate slavery, and repress all sympathies, and all human and benevolent effort among freemen in behalf of the unhappy portion of our race who are doomed to bondage."

How strangely these stirring words of the orator, uttered Jan. 20th, 1827, contrast with his sentiments, and doctrines proclaimed in the Senate of the United States, February 7th, 1839, when he made an extraordinary effort to repress all sympathies among freemen, for the eradication of what he called the "deepest stain," and "foul blot" upon the character of the nation.

Who then answered and confronted this distinguished orator and politician? Let the question be answered, in the language of Dr. W. H. Brisbane, a South Carolinian, a practical emancipator, and a tried friend of freedom.

"There were veterans in that Senate chamber whose talents and learning and mighty genius had long distinguished them as giants in debate, and who were recognized among the nations of the earth, as the sages of American statesmanship. There was Buchanan of Pennsylvania, the representative of the key-stone of the arch that sustains this united Republic; his very personal appearance the just index of his capacious mind, expressed senatorial dignity. His locks were silvered by more than three score years, the greater part of which he had spent in the legislative councils of the nation. There too, was the Senator of the Empire State, the calm, the courteous, the ingenious, the logical reasoner, Silas Wright, the leader of the administration party in the Senate. There was that mighty expounder of Constitutional law, the representative of the old cradle of liberty, the renowned Webster, whose lofty brow developed the organs of a mind that no other man has metaphysical science enough to analyze.

Buchanan and Wright were distinguished by that talismanic title, "Democrat," with which they could command the ears, the heads, the hearts of the people. Webster bore that no less potent title, made noble by Revolutionary scenes and the hallowed name of Washington. He was a Whig.

But no Whig was there to defend the principles for which the fathers of the Republic risked their lives, their fortunes, and their sacred honor, and in the faith of which they breathed their last prayer for their country. Nor was it the Democratic sage, Buchanan; nor was it Silas Wright, the premier of the Democratic government, whose voice was then heard reverberating through that chamber and its galleries, denouncing that accursed sentiment, that whatever the law makes property is property, though it be the bones, and sinews, and blood, and souls of men. Alas! when the illustrious western orator uttered this ignoble thought, and, Lucifer-like, fell from his empyrean hights, where he had shone a brilliant star among the brightest constellations of South American and Grecian memory, even in this debasement of himself, Northern statesmen "prostrate fell before him reverent." And the great Webster himself worshiped in silent meditation the master spirits of that Senate House, the proud Kentuckian and haughty Carolinian, as they grasped hands over the body of the prostrate slave. All, all, did obeisance, except *one*, whom neither the orator's silvery voice could charm nor his thunders intimidate. That one was Ohio's Senator. He dared to speak while tyrant Senators frowned upon him.

Read that speech, and you know Thomas Morris. His life, his soul, is embodied in it. There is his modesty, and there is his boldness. There is his generosity and there is his faithfulness. There is his uncompromising adherence to principle, his love of truth, his hatred of slavery, his devotion to Liberty. There is his mental power, his eagle vision, his patriotic ardor, his philanthropic heart;

> 'The firm patriot there,
> Who made the welfare of mankind his care.'"

SPEECH OF SENATOR MORRIS.

Mr. President—I rise to present for the consideration of the Senate, numerous petitions signed by, not only citizens of my own State, but citizens of several other States—New York, Pennsylvania, Michigan, Illinois, and Indiana. These petitioners, amounting in number to several thousand, have thought proper to make me their organ, in communicating to Congress their opinions and wishes on subjects which, to them, appear of the highest importance. These petitions, Sir, are on the subject of slavery; the slave-trade as carried on within and from this District; the slave-trade between the different States of this Confederacy; between this country and Texas, and against the admission of that country into the Union; and also against that of any other State, whose Constitution and laws recognize or permit slavery. I take this opportunity to present all these petitions together, having detained some of them for a considerable time in my hands, in order that as small a portion of the attention of the Senate might be taken up on their account, as would be consistent with a strict regard to the rights of the petitioners. And I now present them, under the most peculiar circumstances that have ever, probably, transpired in this or any other country. I present them on the heel of the petitions which have been presented by the Senator from Kentucky (Mr. Clay), signed by the inhabitants of this District, praying that Congress would not receive petitions on the subject of slavery in the District, from any body of men or citizens, but themselves. This is something new; it is one of the devices of the slave power, and most extraordinary in itself. These petitions I am bound in duty to present — a duty which I cheerfully perform, for I consider it not only a duty but an honor. The respectable names which these petitions bear, and being against a practice which I as deeply deprecate and deplore as they can possibly do, yet I well know the fate of these petitions; and I also know the time, place, and disadvantage under which I present them. In availing myself of this opportunity to explain my own views on this agitating topic, and to explain and justify the character and proceedings of these petitioners, it must be obvious to all that I am surrounded with no ordinary discouragements. The strong prejudice which is evinced by the petitioners of the District, the unwillingness of the Senate to hear, the power which is arrayed against me on this occasion, as well as in opposition to those whose rights I am anxious to maintain; opposed by the very Lions of debate in this Body, who are cheered on by an applauding gallery and surrounding interests, is enough to produce dismay in one far more able and eloquent than the *lone* and humble individual who now addresses you.

What, Sir, can there be to induce me to appear on this public arena, opposed by such powerful odds? Nothing, Sir, nothing but a strong sense of duty, and a deep conviction that the cause I advocate is just; that the petitioners whom I represent are honest, upright, intelligent and respectable citizens; men who love their country, who are anxious to promote its best interests, and who are actuated by the purest patriotism, as well as the deepest philanthropy and benevolence. In representing such men, and in such a cause, though by the most feeble means, one would suppose that, on the floor of the Senate of the United States, order and a decent respect to the opinions of others, would prevail. From the causes which I have mentioned, I can hardly hope for this. I expect to proceed through scenes which ill become this Hall; but nothing shall deter me from a full and faithful discharge of my duty on this important occasion. Permit me, Sir, to remind gentlemen that I have been now six years a member of this Body. I have seldom, perhaps too seldom, in the opinion of many of my constituents, pressed myself upon the notice of the Senate, and taken up their time in useless and windy debate. I question very much if I have occupied the time of the Senate during the six years, as some gentlemen have during six weeks, or even six days. I hope therefore, that I shall not be thought obtrusive, or charged with taking up time with abolition petitions. I hope, Mr. President, to hear no more about agitating this slave question here. Who has begun the agitation now? The Senator from Kentucky (Mr. Clay). Who has responded to that agitation, and congratulated the Senate and the country on its results? The Senator from South Carolina (Mr. Calhoun). And pray, Sir, under what circumstances is this agitation begun? Let it be remembered, let us collect the facts from the records on your table, that when I, as a member of this Body, but a few days since offered a resolution as the foundation of proceedings on these petitions, gentlemen, as if operated on by an electric shock, sprung from their seat and objected to its introduction. And when you, Sir, decided that it was the right of every member to introduce such motion or resolution as he pleased, being responsible to his constituents and this Body for the abuse of this right, gentlemen seemed to wonder that the Senate had no power to prevent the action of one of its members in cases like this, and the poor privilege of having the resolution printed, by order of the Senate, was denied.

Let the Senator from South Carolina before me, remember that, at the last session, when he offered resolutions on the subject of slavery, they were not only received without objection, but printed, voted on, and decided; and let the Senator from Kentucky reflect, that the petition which he offered against our right, was also received and ordered to be printed without a single dissenting voice; and I call on the Senate and the country to remember, that the resolutions which I have offered on the same subject, have not only been refused the printing, but have been laid on the table without being debated or referred. Posterity, which shall read the proceedings of this time, may well wonder what power could induce the Senate of the United States to proceed in such a strange and contradictory manner. Permit me to tell the country now what this power behind the throne, greater than the throne itself, is. It is the power of SLAVERY. It is a power, according to the calculation of the Senator from Kentucky, which owns twelve hundred millions of dollars in human beings as property; and if money is power, this power is not to be conceived or calculated; a power which claims human property more than double the amount which the whole money of the world could purchase. What can stand before this power? Truth, everlasting truth, will yet overthrow it. This power is aiming to govern the country, its Constitutions and laws; but it is not certain of success, tremendous as it is, without foreign or other aid. Let it be borne in mind that the Bank power, some years since, during what has been called the panic session, had influence sufficient in this body, and upon this floor, to prevent the reception of petitions against the action of the Senate on their resolutions of censure against the President. The country took instant alarm, and the political complexion of this body was changed as soon as possible. The same power though double in means and in strength, is now doing the same thing. This is the array of power that is even now attempting such an unwarrantable course in this country; and the people are also now moving against the Slave, as they formerly did against the Bank power. It, too, begins to tremble for its safety. What is to be done? Why, petitions are received and ordered to be printed, against the right of petitions which are not received, and the whole power of debate is thrown into the scale with the slave-holding power. But all will not do; these two powers must now be united: an amalgamation of the black power of the South with the white power of the North must take place, as either, separately, can not succeed in the destruction of the liberty of speech and the press, and the right of petition. Let me tell gentlemen, that both united will never succeed; as I said on a former day, God forbid that they should ever rule this country! I have seen this billing and cooing between these different interests for some time past; I informed my private friends of the political party with which I have heretofore acted, during the first week of this session, that these powers were forming a union to overthrow the present administration; and I warned them of the folly and mischief they were doing in their abuse of those who were opposed to slavery. All doubts are now terminated. The display made by the Senator from Kentucky, (Mr. Clay,) and his denunciations of these petitioners as abolitionists, and the hearty response and cordial embrace which his efforts met from the Senator from South Carolina, (Mr. Calhoun,) clearly shows that new moves have taken place on the political chessboard, and new coalitions are formed, new compromises and new bargains, settling and disposing of the rights of the country for the advantage of political aspirants.

The gentleman from South Carolina, (Mr. Calhoun,) seemed, at the conclusion of the argument made by the Senator from Kentucky, to be filled not only with delight but with ecstasy. He told us, that about twelve months since HE had offered a resolution which turned the tide in favor of the great principle of State rights, and says he is highly pleased with the course taken by the Kentucky Senator. All is now safe by the acts of that Senator. The South is now consolidated as one man; it was a great epoch in our history, but we have now passed it; it is the beginning of a moral revolution; slavery, so far from being a political evil, is a great blessing; both races have been improved by it; and that abolition is now DEAD, and will soon be forgotten. So far the Senator from South Carolina, as I understood him.

But, sir, is this really the case? Is the South united

as one man, and is the Senator from Kentucky the great center of attraction? What a lesson to the friends of the present Administration, who have been throwing themselves into the arms of the Southern slave-power for support! The black enchantment I hope is now at an end — the dream dissolved, and we awake into open day. No longer is there any uncertainty or any doubt on this subject. But is the great epoch passed? Is it not rather just beginning? Is abolitionism DEAD — or is it just awaking into life? Is the right of petition strangled and forgotten — or is it increasing in strength and force? These are serious questions for the gentleman's consideration, that may damp the ardor of his joy, if examined with an impartial mind, and looked at with an unprejudiced eye. Sir, when these pæans were sung over the death of abolitionists, and, of course, their right to liberty of speech and the press — at least in fancy's eye, we might have seen them lying in heaps upon heaps, like the enemies of the strong man in days of old. But let me bring back the gentleman's mind from this delightful scene of abolition death, to sober realities and solemn facts. I have now lying before me the names of thousands of living witnesses, that slavery has not entirely conquered liberty; that abolitionists (for so are all these petitioners called,) are not *all dead*. These are my first proofs to show the gentleman his ideas are all fancy. I have also, sir, since the commencement of this debate, received a newspaper, as if sent by Providence to suit the occasion, and by whom I know not. It is the Cincinnati Republican of the 2d instant, which contains an extract from the Louisville Advertiser, a paper printed in Kentucky, in Louisville, our sister city; and though about one hundred and fifty miles below us, it is but a few hours distant. That paper is the leading Administration journal too, as I am informed, in Kentucky. Hear what it says on the death of abolition :—

"ABOLITION—CINCINNATI—THE LOUISVILLE ADVERTISER.

"We copy the following notice of an article which we lately published, upon the subject of abolition movements in this quarter, from the Louisville Advertiser:—

'ABOLITION.—The reader is referred to an interesting article which we have copied from the Cincinnati Republican—a paper which lately supported the principles ot Democracy; a paper which has *turned*, but not quite far enough to act with the Adamses and Slades in Congress, or the Whig abolitionists of Ohio. It does not, however, give a correct view of the strength of the abolitionists in Cincinnati. There they are in the ascendant. They control the city elections, regulate what may be termed the morals of the city, give tone to public opinion, and "rule the roost," by virtue of their superior piety and intelligence. The Republican tells us, that they are not laboring Loco Focos—but "drones" and "consumers"—the "rich and well-born," of course; men who have leisure and means, and a disposition to employ the latter, to equalize whites and blacks in the slaveholding States. Even now, the absconding slave is perfectly safe in Cincinnati. We doubt whether an instance can be adduced of the recovery of a runaway in that place in the last four years. When negroes reach "the Queen city" they are protected by its intelligence, its piety, and its wealth. They receive the aid of the *elite* of the Buckeyes; and we have a strong faction in Kentucky, struggling zealously to make her one of the dependencies of Cincinnati! Let our mutual sons go on. The day of mutual retribution is at hand—much nearer than is now imagined. The Republican, which still looks with a friendly eye to the slaveholding States, warns us of the danger which exists, although its new-born zeal for Whiggery prompts it to insist, indirectly, on the right of petitioning Congress to abolish slavery. There are about two hundred and fifty abolition societies in Ohio at the present time, and, from the circular issued from head quarters, Cincinnati, it appears that agents are to be sent through every county to distribute books and pamphlets designed to inflame the public mind, and then organize additional societies — or, rather, form new clans, to aid in the war which has been commenced on the slaveholding States.' "

I do not, sir, underwrite for the truth of this statement as an entire whole; much of it I repel as an unjust charge on my fellow-citizens of Cincinnati; but, as it comes from a slaveholding State — from the State of the Senator who has so eloquently anathematized abolitionists that it is almost a pity they could not die under such sweet sounds — and as the South Carolina Senator pronounces them dead, I produce this from a slaveholding State, for the special benefit and consolation of the two Senators. It comes from a source to which, I am sure, both gentlemen ought to give credit. But suppose, sir, abolitionism is dead, is liberty dead also and slavery triumphant? Is liberty of speech, of the press, and the right of petition also dead? True, it has been strangled here; but gentlemen will find themselves in great error if they suppose it is also strangled in the country; and the very attempt in legslative bodies, to sustain a local and individual interest, to the destruction of our rights, proves that those rights are not dead, but a living principle, which slavery can not extinguish; and be my lot what it may, I shall, to the utmost of my abilities, under all circumstances, and at all times, contend for that freedom which is the common gift of the Creator to all men, and against the power of these two great interests — the slave power of the South, and banking power of the North — which are now uniting to rule this country. The cotton bale and the bank note have formed an alliance; the credit system with slave labor. These two congenial spirits have at last met and embraced each other, both looking at the same object — to live upon the unrequited labor of others, and have now erected for themselved a common platform, as was intimated during the last session, on which they can meet, and bid defiance, as they hope, to free principles and free labor.

With these introductory remarks, permit me, Sir, to say here, and let no one pretend to misunderstand or misrepresent me, that I charge gentlemen, when they use the word abolitionists, they mean petitioners here such as I now represent—men who love liberty and are opposed to slavery—that in behalf of these citizens I speak; and, by whatever name they may be called, it is those who are opposed to slavery whose cause I advocate. I make no war upon the rights of others. I do no act but what is moral, Constitutional and legal, against the peculiar institutions of any State; but acts only in defense of my own rights, of my fellow citizens, and, above all, of my State, I shall not cease while the current of life shall continue to flow.

I shall, Mr. President, in the further consideration of this subject, endeavor to prove, first, the right of the people to petition; second, why slavery is wrong, and why I am opposed to it; third, the power of slavery in this country, and its dangers; next, answer the question, so often asked, what have the free States to do with slavery? Then make some remarks by way of answer to the arguments of the Senator from Kentucky (Mr. Clay).

Mr. President—The duty I am requested to perform is one of the highest which a Representative can be called on to discharge. It is to make known to the legislative body the will and the wishes of his constituents and fellow-citizens; and, in the present case, I feel honored by the confidence reposed in me, and proceed to discharge the duty. The petitioners have not trusted to my fallible judgment alone, but have declared, in written documents, the most solemn expression of their will. It is true, these petitions have not been sent here by the whole people of the United States, but from a portion of them only; yet such is the justice of their claim, and the sure foundation upon which it rests, that no portion of the American people, until a day or two past, have thought it either safe or expedient to present counter petitions; and even now, when counter petitions have been presented, they dare not justify slavery, and the selling of men and women in this District, but content themselves with objecting to others enjoying the rights they practice, and praying Congress not to receive or hear petitions from the people of the States—a new device of the slave power this, never before thought of or practiced in any country. I would have been gratified if the inventors of this system, which denies to others what they practice themselves, had, in their petition, attempted to justify slavery and the slave-trade in the District, if they believe their practice just, that their names might have gone down to posterity. No, Sir; very few yet have the moral courage to record their names to such an avowal; and even some of these petitioners are so squeamish on this subject, as to say that they might, from conscientious principles, be prevented from holding slaves. Not so, Sir, with the petitioners which I have the honor to represent; they are anxious that their sentiments and their names should be made matter of record; they have no qualms of conscience on this subject; they have deep convictions and a firm belief that slavery is an existing evil, incompatible with the principles of political liberty, at war with our system of government, and extending a baleful and blasting influence over our country, withering and blighting its fairest prospects and brightest hopes. Who has said that these petitions are unjust in principle, and on that ground ought not to be granted? Who has said that slavery is not an evil? Who has said it does not tarnish the fair fame of our country? Who has said it does not bring dissipation and feebleness to one race, and poverty and wretchedness to another, in its train? Who has said, it is not unjust to the slave, and injurious to the happiness and best interest of the master? Who has said it does not break the bonds of human affection, by separating the wife from the husband, and children from their parents? In fine, who has said it is not a blot upon our country's honor, and a deep and foul stain upon her institutions? Few, very few, perhaps none but him who lives upon its labor, regardless of its misery; and even many whose local situations are within its jurisdiction, acknowledge its injustice, and deprecate its continuance; while millions of freemen deplore its existence, and look forward with strong hope to its final termination. SLAVERY! a word, like a secret idol, thought too obnoxious or sacred to be pronounced here but by those who worship at its shrine—and should one who is not such a worshiper happen to pronounce the word, the most disastrous consequences are immediately predicted, the Union is to be dissolved, and the South to take care of itself.

Do not suppose, Mr. President, that I feel as if engaged in a forbidden or improvident act. No such thing. I am contending with a local and "*peculiar*" interest, an interest which has already banded together with a force sufficient to seize upon every avenue by which a petition can enter this chamber, and exclude all without its leave. I am not now contending for the rights of the negro, rights which his Creator gave him and which his fellow-man has usurped or taken away. No, sir! I am contending for the rights of the white person in the free States, and am endeavoring to prevent them from being trodden down and destroyed, by that power which claims the black person as *property*. I am endeavoring to sound the alarm to my fellow-citizens that this power, tremendous as it is, is endeavoring to unite itself with the monied power of the country, in order to extend its dominion and perpetuate its existence. I am endeavoring to drive from the back of the *negro slave*, the politician who has seated himself there to ride into office for the purpose of carrying out the object of this unholy combination.

The chains of slavery are sufficiently strong, without being riveted anew by tinkering politicians of the free States. I feel myself compelled into this contest, in defense of the institutions of my own State, the persons and firesides of her citizens, from the insatiable grasp of the slaveholding power as being used and felt in the free States. To say that I am opposed to slavery in the abstract, are but cold and unmeaning words; if, however, capable of any meaning whatever, they may be fairly construed into a love for its existence; and such I sincerely believe to be the feeling of many in the free States who use the phrase. I, sir, am not only opposed to slavery in the abstract, but also in its whole volume, in its theory as well as its practice. This principle is deeply implanted within me; it has "grown with my growth and strengthened with my strength." In my infant years I learned to hate slavery. Your fathers taught me it was wrong in their Declaration of Independence: the doctrines which they promulgated to the world, and upon the truth of which they staked the issue of the contest that made us a nation. They proclaimed "that all men are created equal; that they are endowed by their Creator with certain inalienable rights; that among these are life, liberty and the pursuit of happiness." These truths are solemnly declared by them. I believed then, and believe now, they are self-evident. Who can acknowledge this, and not be opposed to slavery? It is, then, because I love the principles which brought your Government into existence, and which have become the corner-stone of the building supporting you, sir, in that chair, and giving to myself and other Senators seats in this body — it is because I love all this, that I hate slavery. Is it because I contend for the right of petition, and am opposed to slavery, that I have been denounced by many as an abolitionist? Yes; Virginia newspapers have so denounced me, and called upon the Legislature of my own State to dismiss me from public confidence. Who taught me to hate slavery and every other oppression? *Jefferson*, the great and good Jefferson! Yes, *Virginia Senators*, it was your own Jefferson, Virginia's favorite son, a man who did more for the natural liberty of man, and the civil liberty of his country, than any man that ever lived in our country; it was him who taught me to hate slavery; it was in his school I was brought up. That Mr. Jefferson was as much opposed to slavery as any man that ever lived in our country, there can be no doubt; his life and his writings abundantly prove the fact. I hold in my hand a copy, as he penned it, of the original draft of the Declaration of Independence, a part of which was stricken out, as he says, in compliance with the wishes of South Carolina and Georgia. I will read it. Speaking of the wrongs done us by the British Government, in introducing slaves among us, he says: "He (the British King) has waged cruel war against human nature itself, violating its most sacred right of life and liberty in the persons of a distant people, who never offended him, captivating and carrying them into SLAVERY in another hemisphere, or to incur miserable death in their transportation thither. This piratical warfare, the opprobrium of infidel Powers, is the warfare of the Christian King of Great Britain. Determined to keep open a market where MEN should be BOUGHT and SOLD, he has prostituted his prerogative for suppressing every legislative attempt to prohibit or restrain execrable commerce, and that this assemblage of horrors might want no fact of distinguished die, he is now exciting those very people to rise in arms against us, and purchase that liberty of which he has deprived them by murdering the people on whom he has also obtruded them, thus paying off former crimes committed against the liberties of one people, with crimes which he urges them to commit against the lives of another." Thus far this great statesman and philanthropist. Had his cotemporaries been ruled by his opinions, the country had now been at rest on this exciting topic. What abolitionist, sir, has used stronger language against slavery than Mr. Jefferson has done? "Cruel war against human nature," "violating its most sacred rights," "piratical warfare," "opprobrium of infidel Powers," "a market where men should be bought and sold," "execrable commerce," "assemblage of horrors," "crimes committed against the liberty of the people," are the brands which Mr. Jefferson has burned into the forehead of slavery and the slave trade.

When sir, have I, or any other person opposed to slavery, spoken in stronger and more opprobrious terms of slavery, than this? You have caused the bust of this great man to be placed in the center of your Capitol, in that conspicuous part where every visitor must see it, with its hand resting on the Declaration of Independence, engraved upon marble. Why have you done this? Is it not mockery? Or is it to remind us continually of the wickedness and danger of slavery? I never pass that statue without new and increased veneration for the man it represents, and increased repugnance and sorrow that he did not succeed in driving slavery entirely from the country. Sir, if I am an Abolitionist, Jefferson made me so; and I only regret that the disciple should be so far behind the master, both in doctrine and practice. But, sir, other reasons and other causes have combined to fix and establish my principles in this matter, never, I trust to be shaken. A free State was the place of my birth; a free Territory the theater of my juvenile actions. Ohio is my country, endeared to me by every fond recollection. She gave me political existence, and taught me in her political school;

and I should be worse than an unnatural son did I forget or disobey her precepts. In her Constitution it is declared, "That all men are born equally free and independent," and "that there shall be neither slavery nor involuntary servitude in the State, otherwise than for the punishment of crimes." Shall I stand up for slavery in any case, condemned as it is by such high authority as this? No, never! But this is not all, Indiana, our younger Western sister, endeared to us by every social and political tie, a State formed in the same country as Ohio, from whose territory slavery was forever excluded by the ordinance of July, 1787—she too, has declared her abhorrence of slavery in more strong and emphatic terms than we have done. In her Constitution, after prohibiting slavery, or involuntary servitude, being introduced into the State, she declares, "But as the holding any part of the human creation in slavery, or involuntary servitude, can originate only in *tyranny* and *usurpation*—no alteration of her Constitution should ever take place, so as to introduce slavery or involuntary servitude into the State, otherwise than for the punishment of crimes whereof the party had been duly convicted." Illinois and Michigan also formed their Constitutions on the same principles. After such a cloud of witnesses against slavery, and whose testimony is so clear and explicit, as a citizen of Ohio, I should be recreant to every principle of honor and of justice, to be found the apologist or advocate of Slavery in any State, or in any country whatever. No, I can not be so inconsistent as to say I am opposed to slavery in the *abstract*, in its separation from a human being, and still lend my aid to build it up, and make it perpetual in its operation and effects upon *man* in this or any other country. I also, in early life, saw a slave kneel before his master, and hold up his hands with as much apparent submission, humility, and adoration, as a man would have done before his Maker, while his master with outstretched rod stood over him. This, I thought, is slavery; one man subjected to the will and power of another, and the laws affording him no protection, and he has to beg pardon of man, because he has offended man, (not the laws,) as if his master were a superior all powerful being. Yes, this is slavery, boasted American Slavery, without which, it is contended even here, the union of these States would be dissolved in a day, yes, even in an hour! Humiliating thought, that we are bound together as States by the chains of slavery! It can not be—the blood and the tears of slavery form no part of the cement of our Union—and it is hoped that by falling on its bands they may never corrode nor eat them asunder. We who are opposed to and deplore the existence of slavery in our country, are frequently asked, both in public and private, what have you to do with slavery? It does not exist in your State; it does not disturb you! Ah, sir, would to God it were so—that we had nothing to do with slavery, nothing to fear from its power, or its action within our own borders—that its name and its miseries were unknown to us. But this is not our lot; we live upon its borders, and in hearing of its cries; yet we are unwilling to acknowledge, that if we enter its territories and violate its laws, that we should be punished at its pleasure. We do not complain of this, though it might well be considered just ground of complaint. It is our firesides, our rights, our privileges, the safety of our friends, as well as the sovereignty and independence of our State, that we are now called upon to protect and defend. The slave interest has at this moment the whole power of the country in its hands. It claims the President as a Northern man with Southern feelings, thus making the Chief Magistrate the head of an interest, or a party, and not of the country and the people at large. It has the cabinet of the President, three members of which are from the slave States, and one who wrote a book in favor of Southern slavery, but which fell dead from the press, a book which I have seen, in my own family, thrown musty upon the shelf. Here then is a decided majority in favor of the slave interest. It has five out of nine judges of the Supreme Court; here, also, is a majority from the slave States. It has, with the President of the Senate, and the Speaker of the House of Representatives, and the Clerks of both Houses, the army and the navy; and the bureaus, have, I am told, about the same proportion.

One would suppose that, with all this power operating in this Government, it would be content to *permit* — yes, I will use the word *permit* — it would be content to permit us, who live in the free States, to enjoy our firesides and our homes in quietness; but this is not the case. The slaveholders and slave laws claim that as property, which the free States know only as persons, a reasoning property, which, of its own will and mere motion, is frequently found in our States; and upon which THING we sometimes bestow food and raiment, if it appear hungry and perishing, believing it to be a human being; this perhaps is owing to our want of vision to discover the process by which a man is converted into a THING. For this act of ours, which is not prohibited by our laws, but prompted by every feeling, Christian and humane, the slaveholding power enters our territory, tramples under foot the sovereignty of our State, violates the sanctity of private residence, seizes our citizens, and disregarding the authority of our laws, transports them into its own jurisdiction, casts them into prison, confines them in fetters, and loads them with chains, for pretended offenses against their own laws, found by willing grand juries upon the oath, (to use the language of the late Governor of Ohio), of a perjured villain. Is this fancy, or is it fact, sober reality, solemn fact? Need I say all this, and much more, is now matter of history in the case of the Rev. John B. Mahan, of Brown county, Ohio? Yes, it is so;

but this is but the beginning — a case of equal outrage has lately occurred, if newspapers are to be relied on, in the seizure of a citizen of Ohio, without even the forms of law, and who was carried into Virginia and shamefully punished by tar and feathers, and other disgraceful means, and rode upon a rail, according to the order of Judge Lynch, and this, only because in Ohio he was an abolitionist. Would I could stop here — but I can not. This slave interest or power seizes upon persons of color in our States, carries them into States where men are property, and makes merchandize of them, sometimes under sanction of law, but more properly by its abuse, and sometimes by mere personal force, thus disturbing our quiet and harassing our citizens. A case of this kind has lately occurred, where a colored boy was seduced from Ohio into Indiana, taken from thence into Alabama, and sold as a slave; and to the honor of the slave States, and gentlemen who administer the laws there, be it said, that many who have thus been taken and sold by the connivance, if not downright corruption, of citizens in the free States, have been liberated and adjudged free in the States where they have been sold, as was the case of the boy mentioned who was sold in Alabama.

Slave power is seeking to establish itself in every State, in defiance of the Constitution and laws of the States within which it is prohibited. In order to secure its power beyond the reach of the States, it claims its parentage from the Constitution of the United States. It demands of us total silence as to its proceedings, denies to our citizens the liberty of speech and the press, and punishes them by mobs and violence for the exercise of these rights. It has sent its agents into the free States for the purpose of influencing their Legislatures to pass laws for the security of its power within such States, and for the enacting new offenses and new punishments for their own citizens, so as to give additional security to its interest. It demands to be heard in its own person in the hall of our Legislature, and mingle in debate there. Sir, in every stage of these oppressions and abuses, permit me to say, in the language of the Declaration of Independence — and no language could be more appropriate — we have petitioned for redress in the most humble terms, and our repeated petitions have been answered by repeated injury. A power, whose character is marked by every act which may define a tyrant, is unfit to rule over a free people. In our sufferings and our wrongs we have besought our fellow-citizens to aid us in the preservation of our Constitutional rights; but, influenced by the love of gain or arbitrary power, they have sometimes disregarded all the sacred rights of man, and answered in violence, burnings and murder. After all these transactions, which are now of public notoriety and matter of record, shall we of the free States tauntingly be asked what we have to do with slavery? We should rejoice, indeed, if the evils of slavery were removed far from us, that it could be said with truth, that we have nothing to do with slavery. Our citizens have not entered its territories for the purpose of obstructing its laws, nor do we wish to do so, nor would we justify any individual in such act; yet we have been branded and stigmatized by its friends and advocates, both in the free and slave States, as incendiaries, fanatics, disorganizers, enemies to our country, and as wishing to dissolve the Union. We have borne all this without complaint or resistance, and only ask to be secure in our persons, by our own firesides, and in the free exercise of our own thoughts and opinions in speaking, writing, printing and publishing on the subject of slavery, that which appears to us to be just and right; because we all know the power of truth, and that it will ultimately prevail, in despite of all opposition. But in the exercise of all these rights, we acknowledge subjection to the laws of the State in which we are, and our liability for their abuse.

We wish peace with all men; and that the most amicable relations and free intercourse may exist between the citizens of our State and our neighboring slaveholding States; we will not enter their States, either in our proper persons, or by commissioners, legislative resolutions, or otherwise, to interfere with their slave policy or slave laws; and we shall expect from them and their citizens a like return, that they do not enter our territories for the purpose of violating our laws in the punishment of our people for the exercise of their undoubted rights: the liberty of speech and of the press on the subject of slavery. We ask that no man shall be seized and transported beyond our State, in violation of our own laws, and that we shall not be carried into and imprisoned in another State for acts done in our own. We contend that the slaveholding power is properly chargeable with all the riots and disorders which take place on account of slavery. We can live in peace with all our sister States, if that power will be controlled by law, each can exercise and enjoy the full benefits secured by their own laws; and this is all we ask. If we hold up slavery to the view of an impartial public as it is, and if such view create astonishment and indignation, surely we are not to be charged as libelers. A State institution ought to be considered the pride, not the shame of the State; and if we falsify such institutions, the disgrace is ours, not theirs. If slavery, however, is a blemish, a blot, an eating cancer in the body politic, it is not our fault, if, by holding it up, others should see in the mirror of truth its deformity, and shrink back from the view.

We have not, and we intend not to use any weapons against slavery, but the moral power of truth and the force of public opinion. If we enter the slave States, and tamper with the slave contrary to law, punish us — we deserve it; and if a slaveholder is found in a free State, and is guilty of a breach of the law there, he also ought to be punished.

These petitioners as far as I understand them, disclaim all right to enter a slave State for the purpose of intercourse with the slave. It is the master whom they wish to address; and they ask and ought to receive protection from the laws, as they are willing to be judged by the laws. We invite the slaveholder into the arena of public discussion in our State; we are willing to hear his reasons and facts in favor of slavery, or against abolitionists; we do not fear his errors while we are ourselves free to combat them. The angry feelings which in some degree exist between the citizens of the free and slaveholding States, on account of slavery, are, in many cases, properly chargeable to those who support and defend slavery. Attempts are almost daily making to force the execution of slave laws in the free States; at least, their power and principles; and no term is too reproachful to be applied to those who resist such acts, and contend for the rights secured to every man under their own laws. We are often reminded that we ought to take color as evidence of property in a human being. We do not believe in such evidence, nor do we believe that a man can justly be made property by human laws. We acknowledge, however, that a *man*, not a *thing*, may be held to service or labor under the laws of a State, and, if he escapes into another State, he ought to be delivered up on claim of the party to whom such labor or service may be due; that this delivery ought to be in pursuance of the laws of the State where such person is found, and not by virtue of any act of Congress.

This brings me, Mr. President, to the consideration of the petition presented by the Senator from Kentucky, and to an examination of the views he has presented to the Senate on this highly important subject. Sir, I feel, I sensibly feel my inadequacy in entering into a controversy with that old and veteran Senator; but nothing high or low shall prevent me from an honest discharge of my duties here. If imperfectly done, it may be ascribed to the want of ability, not intention. If the power of my mind, and the strength of my body, were equal to the task, I would arouse every man, yes, every woman and child in the country, to the danger which besets them, if such doctrines and views as are presented by the Senator should ever be carried into effect. His denunciations are against abolitionists, and under that term are classed all those who petition Congress on the subject of slavery. Such I understand to be his argument, and as such I shall treat it. I, in the first place, put in a broad denial to all his general facts, charging this portion of my fellow citizens with improper motives or dangerous designs. That their acts are lawful he does not pretend to deny. I called for proof to sustain his charges. None such has been offered, and none such exist, or can be found. I repel them as calumnies doubly-distilled in the alembic of slavery. I deny them, also, in the particulars and inferences; and let us see upon what ground they rest, or by what process of reasoning they are sustained.

The very first view of these petitioners against our right of petition, strikes the mind that more is intended than at first meets the eye. Why was the Committee on the District overlooked in this case, and the Senator from Kentucky made the organ of communication? Is it understood that anti-abolitionism is a passport to popular favor, and that the action of this District shall present for that favor to the public a gentleman upon this hobby? Is this petition presented as a subject of fair legislation? Was it solicited by members of Congress, from citizens here, for political effect? Let the country judge.

The petitioners state that no persons but themselves

are authorized to interfere with slavery in the District; that Congress are their own Legislature; and the question of slavery in the District is only between them and their constituted legislators; and they protest against all interference of others. But, sir, as if ashamed of this open position in favor of slavery, they, in a very coy manner, say that some of them are not slaveholders, and might be forbidden by conscience to hold slaves. There is more dictation, more political heresy, more dangerous doctrine in this petition, than I have ever before seen couched together in so many words. We! Congress their OWN Legislature in all that concerns this District! Let those who may put on the city livery, and legislate for them and not for their constituents, do so; for myself, I came here with a different view, and for different purposes. I came a free man, to represent the people of Ohio; and I intend to leave this as such representative, without wearing any other livery. Why talk about executive usurpation and influence over the members of Congress? I have always viewed this District influence as far more dangerous than that of any other power. It has been able to extort, yes, extort from Congress, millions to pay District debts, make District improvements, and in support of the civil and criminal jurisprudence of the District. Pray, sir, what right has Congress to pay the corporate debts of the cities in the District more than the debts of the corporate cities in your State and mine? None, sir. Yet this has been done to a vast amount; and the next step is, that we, who pay all this, shall not be permitted to petition Congress on the subject of their institutions, for, if we can be prevented in one case, we can in all possible cases. Mark, sir, how plain a tale will silence these petitioners. If slavery in the District concerns only the inhabitants and Congress, so do all municipal regulations. Should they extend to granting lottery, gaming-houses, tippling-houses, and other places calculated to promote and encourage vice — should a representative in Congress be instructed by his constituents to use his influence, and vote against such establishments, and the people of the District should instruct him to vote for them, which should he obey? To state the question is to answer it; otherwise the boasted right of instruction by the constituent body is "mere sound," signifying nothing. Sir, the inhabitants of this District are subject to State legislation and State policy; they can not complain of this, for their condition is voluntary; and as this city is the focus of power, of influence, and considered also that of fashion, if not of folly; and as the streams which flow from here irradiate the whole country, it is proper, that it should be subject to State policy and State power, and not used as a leaven to ferment and corrupt the whole body politic.

The honorable Senator has said the petition, though from a city, is the fair expression of the opinion of the District. As such I treated it, am willing to acknowledge the respectability of the petitioners and their rights, and I claim for the people of my own State equal respectability and equal rights to those the people of the District are entitled to: any peculiar rights and advantages I can not admit.

I agree with the Senator, that the proceedings on abolition petitions, heretofore, have not been the most wise and prudent course. They ought to have been referred and acted on. Such was my object, a day or two since, when I laid on your table a resolution to refer them to a committee for inquiry. You did not suffer it, sir, to be printed. The country and posterity will judge between the people whom I represent, and those who caused to be printed the petition from the city. It can not be possible that justice can have been done in both cases. The exclusive legislation of Congress over the District is as much the act of the constituent body, as the general legislation of Congress over the States, and to the operation of this act have the people within the District submitted themselves. I can not, however, join the Senator in supposing that the majority, in refusing to receive and refer petitions, did not intend to destroy or impair the right in this particular. They certainly have done so.

The Senator admits the abolitionists are now formidable; that something must be done to produce harmony. Yes, sir, do justice, and harmony will be restored. Act impartially, that justice may be done: hear petitions on both sides, if they are offered, and give righteous judgments, and your people will be satisfied. You can not compromise them out of their rights, nor lull them to sleep with fallacies in the shape of reports. You can not conquer them by rebuke, nor deceive them by sophistry. Remember you can not now turn public opinion, nor can you overthrow it. You must, and you will, abandon the high ground you have taken, and receive petitions. The reason of the case, the argument and judgment of the people, are all against you. One in this cause can "chase a thousand," and the voice of justice will be heard whenever you agitate the subject. In Indiana, the right to petition has been most nobly advocated in a protest, by a member, against some puny resolutions of the Legislature of that State to whitewash slavery. Permit me to read a paragraph worthy an American freeman:

"But who would have thought until lately, that any would have doubted the right to petition in a respectful manner to Congress? Who would have believed, that Congress had any authority to refuse to consider the petitions of the people? Such a step would overthrow the Autocrat of Russia, or cost the Grand Seignior of Constantinople his head. Can it be possible, therefore, that it has been reserved for a Republican Government, in a land boasting of its free institutions, to set the first precedent of this kind? Our city councils, our courts of justice, every department of Government are approached by petition, however unanswerable, or absurd, so that its terms are respectful. None go away unread, or unheard. The life of every individual is a perfect illustration of the subject of petitioning. Petition is the language of want, of pain, of sorrow, of man in all his sad variety of woes, imploring relief, at the hand of some power superior to himself. Petitioning is the foundation of all government, and of all the administrations of law. Yet it has been reserved for our Congress, seconded indirectly by the vote of this Legislature, to question this right, hitherto supposed to be so old, so heaven-deeded, so undoubted, that our fathers did not think it necessary to place a guaranty of it in the first draft of the Federal Constitution. Yet this sacred right has been, at one blow, driven, destroyed, and trodden under the feet of slavery. The old bulwarks of our Federal and State Constitutions seem utterly to have been forgotten, which declare—'that the freedom of speech and the press shall not be abridged, nor the right of the people peaceably to assemble and *petition* for the redress of their grievances.'"

These, Sir, are the sentiments which make Abolitionists formidable, and set at nought all your councils for their overthrow. The honorable Senator not only admits that Abolitionists are formidable, but that they consist of three classes. The friends of humanity and justice, or those actuated by those principles, compose one class. These form a very numerous class, and the acknowledgment of the Senator proves the immutable principles upon which opposition to slavery rests. Men are opposed to it on principles of humanity and justice — men are Abolitionists, he admits, on that account. We thank the Senator for teaching us that word; we intend to improve it. The next class of Abolitionists, the Senator says, are so, apparently, for the purpose of advocating the right of petition. What are we to understand from this? That the right of petition needs advocacy. Who has denied this right, or who has attempted to abridge it? The slaveholding power; that power which avoids open discussion, and the free exercise of opinion; it is that power alone which renders the advocacy of the right of petition necessary, having seized upon all the powers of the Government. It is fast uniting together those opposed to its iron rule, no matter to what political party they have heretofore belonged; they are uniting with the first class, and act from principles of humanity and justice; and if the mists and shades of slavery were not the atmosphere in which gentlemen were enveloped, they would see constant and increasing numbers of our most worthy and intelligent citizens attaching themselves to the two classes mentioned, and rallying under the banners of Abolitionism. They are compelled to go there, if the gentleman will have it so, in order to defend and perpetuate the liberties of the country. The hopes of the oppressed spring up afresh from this discussion of the gentleman.

The third class, the Senator says, are those who, to accomplish their ends, act without regard to consequences. To them, all the rights of property, of the States, of the Union, the Senator says, are nothing. He says they aim at other objects than those they profess—emancipation in the District of Columbia. No, says the Senator, their object is *universal emancipation*, not only in the District, but in the Territories and in the States. Their object is to set free three millions of negro slaves. Who made the Senator, in his place here, the censor of his fellow-citizens? Who authorized him to charge them with other objects than those they profess? How long is it since the Senator himself, on this floor, denounced slavery as an evil? What other inducements or object had he then in view? Suppose universal emancipation to be the object of these petitioners; is it not a noble and praiseworthy object, worthy of the Christian, the philanthropist, the statesman, and the citizen? But the Senator says, they (the petitioners) aim to excite one portion of the country against another. I deny, Sir, this charge, and call for the proof; it is gratuitous, uncalled for, and unjust toward my fellow citizens. This is the language of a stricken conscience, seeking for the palliation of its own acts by charging guilt upon others. It is the language of those who, failing in argument, endeavor to cast suspicion upon the character of their opponents, in order to draw public attention from themselves. It is the language of disguise and concealment, and not that of fair and honorable investigation, the object of which is truth. I again put in a broad denial to this charge, that any portion of these petitioners, whom I represent, seek to excite one portion of the country against another; and without proof I can not admit that the assertion of the honorable Senator establishes the fact. It is but opinion, and naked assertion only. The Senator complains that the means and views of the Abolitionists are not confined to securing the right of petition only; no, they resort to other means, he affirms, to the BALLOT BOX; and if that fail, says the Senator, their next appeal will be to the bayonet.

Sir, no man, who is an American in feeling and in heart, but ought to repel this charge instantly, and without any reservation whatever, that if they fail at the ballot box they will resort to the bayonet. If such a fratricidal course should ever be thought of in our country, it will not be by those who seek redress of wrongs, by exercising the right of petition, but by those only who deny that right to others, and seek to usurp the whole power of the Government. If the ballot box fail them, the bayonet may be their resort, as mobs and violence now are. Does the Senator believe that any portion of the honest yeomanry of the country entertain such thoughts? I hope he does not. If thoughts of this kind exist, they are to be found in the hearts of aspirants to office, and their adherents, and none others. Who, sir, is making this question a political affair? Not the petitioners. It was the slaveholding power which first made this move. I have noticed for some time past that many of the public prints in this city, as well as elswhere, have been filled with essays against Abolitionists for exercising the rights of freemen.

Both political parties, however, have courted them in private and denounced them in public, and both have equally deceived them. And who shall dare say that an Abolitionist has no right to carry his principles to the *ballot box? Who fears the ballot box?* The honest in heart, the lover of our country and its institutions? No, sir! It is feared by the tyrant; he who usurps power, and seizes upon the liberty of others; he, for one, fears the ballot box. Where is the slave to party in this country who is so lost to his own dignity, or so corrupted by interest or power, that he does not, or will not, carry his principles and his judgment into the ballot box? Such an one ought to have the mark of Cain in his forehead, and be sent to labor among the negro slaves of the South. The honorable Senator seems anxious to take under his care the ballot box, as he has the slave system of the country, and direct who shall or who shall not use it for the redress of what they deem a political grievance. Suppose the power of the Executive Chair should take under its care the right of voting, who should proscribe any portion of our citizens who should carry with them to the polls of election their own opinions, creeds, and doctrines. This would at once be a death-blow to our liberties, and the remedy could only be found in revolution. There can be no excuse or pretext for revolution while the ballot box is free. Our Government is not one of force, but of principle; its foundation rests on public opinion, and its hope is in the morality of the nation. The moral power of that of the ballot box is sufficient to correct all abuses. Let me, then, proclaim here, from this high arena, to the citizens not only of my own State, but to the country, to all sects and parties who are entitled to the right of suffrage, To THE BALLOT BOX! carry with you honestly your own sentiments respecting the welfare of your country, and make them operate as effectually as you can, through that medium, upon its policy and for its prosperity. Fear not the frowns of power. It trembles while it denounces you. The Senator complains that the Abolitionists have associated with the politics of the country. So far as I am capable of judging, this charge is not well founded; many politicians of the country have used Abolitionists as stepping stones to mount into power; and, when there, have turned about and traduced them. He admits that political parties are willing to unite with them any class of men, in order to carry their purposes. Are Abolitionists, then, to blame if they pursue the same course? It seems the Senator is willing that his party should make use of even Abolitionists; but he is not willing that Abolitionists should use the same party for their purpose. This seems not to be in accordance with that equality of rights about which we heard so much at the last session. Abolitionists have nothing to fear. If public opinion should be for them, politicians will be around and among them as the locusts of Egypt. The Senator seems to admit that, if the Abolitionists are joined to either party, there is danger — danger of what? That humanity and justice will prevail? that the right of petition will be secured to ALL EQUALLY? and that the long-lost and trodden African race will be restored to their natural rights? Would the Senator regret to see this accomplished by argument, persuasion, and the force of an enlightened public opinion? I hope not; and these petitioners ask the use of no other weapons in this warfare.

These ultra-abolitionists, says the Senator, invoke the power of this Government to their aid. And pray, sir, what power should they invoke? Have they not the same right to approach this Government as other men? Is the Senator or this body authorized to deny them any privileges secured to other citizens? If so, let him show me the charter of his power and I will be silent. Until he can do this, I shall uphold, justify, and sustain them, as I do other citizens. The exercise of power by Congress in behalf of the slaves within this District, the Senator seems to think, no one without the District has the least claim to ask for. It is because I reside without the District, and am called within it by the Constitution, that I object to the existence of slavery here. I deny the gentleman's position, then, on this point. On this, then, we are equal.

The Senator, however, is at war with himself. He contends the object of the cession by the States of Virginia and Maryland, was to establish a Seat of Government *only*, and to give Congress whatever power was necessary to render the District a valuable and comfortable situation for that purpose, and that Congress have full power to do whatever is necessary for this District; and if to abolish slavery be necessary, to attain that object, Congress have power to abolish slavery in the District. I am sure I quote the gentleman substantially; and I thank him for this precious confession in his argument; it is what I believe, and I know it is all I feel disposed to ask. If we can, then, prove that this District is not as comfortable and convenient a place for the deliberations of Congress, and the comfort of our citizens who may visit it, while slavery exists here, as it would be without slavery, then slavery ought to be abolished; and I trust we shall have the distinguished Senator from Kentucky to aid us in this great national reformation. I take the Senator at his word. I agree with him that this ought to be such a place as he has described; but I deny that it is so. And upon what facts do I rest my denial? We are a Christian nation, a moral and religious people. I speak for the free States, at least for my own State; and what a contrast do the very streets of your capital daily present to the Christianity and morality of the nation? A race of slaves, or at least colored persons, of every hue from the jet-black African, in regular gradation, up to the almost pure Anglo-Saxon color. During the short time official duty has called me here, I have seen the really red haired, the freckled, and the almost white negro; and I have been astonished at the number of the mixed race, when compared with those of full color, and I have deeply deplored this stain upon our national morals; and the words of Dr. Channing have, thousands of times, been impressed on my mind, that "a slave country reeks with licentiousness." How comes this amalgamation of the races? It comes from slavery. It is a disagreeable annoyance to those who come from the free States, especially to their Christian and moral feelings. It is a great hindrance to the proper discharge of their duties while here. Remove slavery from this District, and this evil will disappear. We argue this circumstance alone as sufficient cause to produce this effect. But slavery presents within the District other and still more appalling scenes; scenes well calculated to awaken the deepest feelings of the human heart. The slave-trade exists here in all its HORRORS, and unwhipt of all its crimes. In view of the very chair which you now occupy, Mr. President, if the massy walls of this building did not prevent it, you could see the prison, the *pen*, the HELL, where human beings, when purchased for sale, are kept until a cargo can be procured for transportation to a Southern or foreign market; for I have little doubt slaves are carried to Texas for sale, though I do not know the fact.

Sir, since Congress have been in session, a mournful group of these unhappy beings, some thirty or forty, were marched, as if in derision of members of Congress, in view of your Capitol, chained and manacled together, in open day-light, yes, in the very face of Heaven itself, to be shipped at Baltimore for a foreign market. I did not witness this cruel transaction, but speak from what I have heard and believe. Is this District, then, a fit place for our deliberations, whose feelings are outraged with impunity with transactions like this? Suppose, Sir, that mournful and degrading spectacle was at this moment exhibited under the windows of our Chamber, do you think the Senate could deliberate, could continue with that composure and attention which I see around me? No, Sir; all your powers could not preserve order for a a moment. The feelings of humanity would overcome those of regard for the peculiar institutions of the States; and though we would be politically and legally bound not to interfere, we are not morally bound to withhold our sympathy and our execration, in witnessing such inhuman traffic. This traffic alone, in this District, renders it an uncomfortable and unfit place for your Seat of Government. Sir, it is but one or two years since I saw standing at the railroad depot, as I passed from my boarding house to this Chamber, some large wagons and teams, as if waiting for freight; the cars had not then arrived. I was inquired of, when I returned to my lodgings, by my landlady, if I knew the object of those wagons which I saw in the morning? I replied, I did not; I suppose they came and were waiting for loading. "Yes, for slaves," said she; "and one of those wagons was filled with little boys and little girls, who had been bought up through the country, and were to be taken to a Southern market. Ah, Sir!" continued she, "it made my very heart ache to see them." The very recital unnerved and unfitted me for thought or reflection on any other subject for some time. It is scenes like this, of which ladies of my country and my State complained in their petitions, some time since, as rendering this District unpleasant, should they visit the capital of the nation as wives, sisters, daughters or friends of members of Congress. Yet, Sir, those respectable females were treated with contemptuous sneers; they were compared, on this floor, to the fish-women of Paris, who dipped their fingers in the blood of revolutionary France. Sir, if the transaction in slaves here, which I have mentioned, could make such an impression on the heart of a lady, a resident of the District, one who had been used to slaves, and was probably an owner, what would be the feelings of ladies from the free States on beholding a like transaction? I will leave every gentleman and every lady to answer for themselves. I am unable to describe it. Shall the capital of your country longer exhibit scenes so revolting to humanity, that the ladies of your country can not visit it without disgust? No; wipe off the foul stain, and let it become a suitable and comfortable place for the Seat of Government.

The Senator, as if conscious that his argument on this point had proved too much, and of course had proven the converse of what he wished to establish, concluded this part by saying, that if slavery is abolished, the act ought to be confined to the city alone. We thank him for this small sprinkling of correct opinion upon this arid waste of public feeling. Liberty may yet vegetate and grow even here.

The Senator insists that the States of Virginia and Maryland would never have ceded this District if they had thought slavery would have been abolished in it. This is an old story twice told. It was never, however, thought of, until the slave power imagined it, for its own security. Let the States ask a retrocession of the District, and I am sure the free States will rejoice to make the grant.

The Senator condemns the Abolitionists for desiring that slavery should not exist in the Territories, even in Florida. He insists that, by the treaty, the inhabitants of that country have the right to remove their EFFECTS when they please; and that, by this condition, they have the right to retain their slaves as effects, independently of the power of Congress. I am no diplomatist, sir, but I venture to deny the conclusion of the Senator's argument. In all our intercourse with foreign nations, in all our treaties in which the words "goods, effects," etc., are used, slaves have never been considered as included. In all cases in which slaves are the subject matter of controversy, they are specially named by the word "slaves;" and, if I remember rightly, it has been decided in Congress, that slaves are not property for which a compensation shall be made when taken for public use, (or rather, slaves can not be considered as taken for public use,) or as property by the enemy, when they are in the service of the United States. If I am correct, as I believe I am, in the position I have assumed, the gentleman can say nothing, by this part of his argument, against Abolitionists, for asking that slavery shall not exist in Florida.

The gentleman contends that the power to remove slaves from one State to another, for sale, is found in that part of the Constitution which gives Congress the power to regulate commerce within the State, etc. This argument is a *non sequitur*, unless the honorable Senator can first prove that slaves are proper articles for commerce. We say that Congress have power over slaves only as persons. The United States can protect persons, *but can not make them property*, and they have full power in regulating commerce, and can, in such regulations, prohibit from its operations every thing but property; property made so by the laws of nature, and not by any municipal regulations. The dominion of men over things, as property, was settled by his Creator when man was first placed upon the earth. He was to subdue the earth, and have dominion over the fish of the sea, and fowls of the air, and over every living thing that moveth upon the earth; every herb bearing seed, and the fruit of the tree yielding seed, was given for his use. This is the foundation of all right in property of every description. It is for the use of man the grant is made, and of course man can not be included in the grant. Every municipal regulation, then, of any State, or any of its peculiar institutions, which makes man property, is a violation of this great law of nature, and is founded in usurpation and tyranny, and is accomplished by force, fraud, or an abuse of power. It is a violation of the principles of truth and justice, in subjecting the weaker to the stronger man. In a Christian nation such property can form no just ground for commercial regulations, but ought to be strictly prohibited. I therefore believe it is the duty of Congress, by virtue of this power to regulate commerce, to prohibit, at once, slaves being used as articles of trade.

The gentleman says, the Constitution left the subject of slavery entirely to the States. To this position I assent; and, as the States can not regulate their own commerce, but the same being the right of Congress, that body can not make slaves an article of commerce, because slavery is left entirely to the States in which it exists; and slaves within these States, according to the gentleman, are excluded from the power of Congress. Can Congress, in regulating commerce among the several States, authorize the transportation of articles from one State, and their sale in another, which they have not power so to authorize in any State? I can not believe in such doctrine; and now solemnly protest against the power of Congress to authorize the transportation to, and the sale in, Ohio, of any negro slave whatever, or for any possible purpose under the sun. Who is there in Ohio, or elsewhere, that will dare deny this position? If Ohio contains such a recreant to her Constitution and policy, I hope he may have the boldness to stand forth and avow it. If the States in which slavery exists love it as a household god, let them keep it there, and not call upon us in the free States to offer incense to their idol. We do not seek to touch it with unhallowed hands, but with pure hands, upraised in the cause of truth and suffering humanity.

The gentleman admits that, at the formation of our Government, it was feared that slavery might eventually divide or distract our country; and, as the BALLOT BOX seems continually to haunt his imagination, he says there is real danger of dissolution of the Union if Abolitionists, as is evident they do, will carry their principles into the BALLOT BOX. If not disunion in fact, at least in feeling, in the country, which is always the precursor to the clash of arms. And the gentleman further says we are taught by holy writ, "that the race is not to the swift, nor the battle to the strong." The moral of the gentleman's argument is, that truth and righteousness will prevail, though opposed by power and influence; that Abolitionists, though few in number, are greatly to be feared; one, as I have said, may chase a thousand, and two put ten thousand to flight; and, as their weapons of warfare are not "carnal, but mighty to the pulling down of strong holds," even slavery itself; and as the ballot box is the great moral lever in political action, the gentleman would exclude Abolitionists entirely from its use, and for opinion's sake, deny them this high privilege of every American citizen. Permit me, sir, to remind the gentleman of another text of holy writ. "The wicked flee when no man pursueth, but the righteous are bold as a lion." The Senator says that those who have slaves, are sometimes supposed to be under too much alarm. Does this prove the application of the text I have just quoted? "Conscience sometimes makes cowards of us all." The Senator appeals to Abolitionists, and beseeches them to cease their efforts on the subject of slavery, if they wish, says he, "to exercise their benevolence." What! Abolitionists benevolent! He hopes they will select some object not so terrible. Oh, sir, he is willing they should pay tithes of "mint and rue," but the weightier matters of the law, judgment and mercy, he would have them entirely overlook. I ought to thank the Senator for introducing holy writ into this debate, and inform him his arguments are not the sentiments of Him, who, when on earth, went about doing good.

The Senator further entreats the clergy to desist from their efforts in behalf of Abolitionism. Who authorized the Senator, as a politician, to use his influence to point out to the clergy what they should pray? Would the Senator dare exert his power here to bind the consciences of men? By what rule of ethics, then, does he undertake to use his influence, from this high place of power, in order to gain the same object, I am at a loss to determine. Sir, this movement of the Senator is far more censurable and dangerous, as an attempt to unite Church and State, than were the petitions against Sunday mails, the report in opposition to which gained for you, Mr. President, so much applause in the country. I, Sir, also appeal to the clergy to maintain their rights of conscience; and if they believe slavery to be a sin, we ought to honor and respect them for their open denunciation of it, rather than call on them to desist, for between their conscience and their God, we have no power to interfere; we do not wish to make them political agents for any purpose.

But the Senator is not content to entreat the clergy alone to desist; he calls on his country-women to warn them, also, to cease their efforts, and reminds them that the ink shed from the pen held in their fair fingers when writing their names to abolition petitions, may be the cause of shedding much human blood! Sir, the language toward to this class of petitioners is very much changed of late; they formerly were pronounced idlers, fanatics, old women, and school misses, unworthy of respect from intelligent and respectable men. I warned gentlemen then that they would change their language; the blows they aimed fell harmless at the feet of those whom they were intended to injure. In this movement of my country-women I thought was plainly to be discovered the operations of Providence, and a sure sign of the final triumph of *universal emancipation.* All history, both sacred and profane, both ancient and modern, bears testimony to the efficacy of female influence and power in the cause of human liberty. From the time of the preservation, by the hands of women, of the great Jewish law-giver, in his infantile hours, and who was preserved for the purpose of freeing his countrymen from Egyptian bondage, has woman been made a powerful agent in breaking to pieces the rod of the oppressor. With a pure and uncontaminated mind, her actions spring from the deepest recesses of the human heart. Denounce her as you will, you can not deter her from her duty. Pain, sickness, want, poverty, and even death itself form no obstacles in her onward march. Even the tender virgin would dress, as a martyr for the stake, as for her bridal hour, rather than make sacrifice of her purity and duty. The eloquence of the Senate, and clash of arms, are alike powerful when brought in opposition to the influence of pure and virtuous woman. The liberty of the slave seems now to be committed to her charge, and who can doubt her final triumph? I do not. You can not fight against her and hope for success; and well does the Senator know this; hence this appeal to her feelings to terrify her from that which she believes to be her duty. It is a vain attempt.

The Senator says that it was the principles of the Constitution which carried us through the Revolution. Surely it was; and to use the language of another Senator from a slave State, on a former occasion, these are the very principles on which the Abolitionists plant themselves. It was the principle that all men are born FREE AND EQUAL, that nerved the arm of our fathers in their contest for independence. It was for the natural and inherent rights of *man* they contended. It is a libel upon the Constitution to say that its object was not liberty, but slavery, for millions of the human race.

The Senator, well fearing that all his eloquence and his arguments thus far are but chaff, when weighed in the balance against truth and justice, seems to find consolation in the idea, and says that which opposes the ulterior object of Abolitionists, is that the General Government has no power to act on the subject of slavery, and that the Constitution or the Union would not last an hour if the power claimed was exercised by Congress. It is slavery then, and not liberty, that makes us one people. To dissolve slavery, is to dissolve the Union. Why require of us to support the Constitution by oath, if the Constitution itself is subject to the power of slavery, and not the moral power of the country? Change the form of the oath which you administer to Senators on taking seats here, swear them to support slavery, and according to the logic of the gentleman, the Constitution and the Union will both be safe. We hear almost daily threats of dissolving the Union; and from whence do they come? From citizens of the free States? No! From the slave States only. Why wish to dissolve it? The reason is plain — that a new government may be formed, by which we, as a nation, may be made a slaveholding people. No impartial observer of passing events can, in my humble judgment, doubt the truth of this. The Senator thinks the Abolitionists in error, if they wish the slaveholder to free his slave. He asks, why denounce him? I can not admit the truth of the question; but I might well ask the gentleman, and the slaveholders generally, "why are you angry at me, because I tell you the truth?" It is the light of truth which the slaveholder can not endure; a plain, unvarnished tale of what slavery is, he considers a libel upon himself. The fact is, the slaveholder feels the leprosy of slavery upon him. He is anxious to hide the odious disease from the public eye; and the ballot box, and the right of petition, when used against him, he feels as sharp reproof; and being unwilling to renounce his errors, he tries to escape from their consequences, by making the world believe that HE is the persecuted, and not the persecutor. Slaveholders have said here, during this very session—"the fact is, slavery will not bear examination." It is the Senator who denounces Abolitionists for the exercise of their most unquestionable rights; while Abolitionists condemn that only which the Senator himself will acknowledge to be wrong at all times, and under all circumstances. Because he admits that if it was an original question whether slaves should be introduced among us, but few citizens could be found to agree to it, and none more opposed to it than himself. The argument is, that the evil of slavery is incurable; that the attempt to eradicate it would commence a struggle which would exterminate one race or the other. What a lamentable picture of our Government, so often pronounced the best upon earth! The seeds of disease, which were interwoven into its first existence, have now become so incorporated into its frame, that they can not be extracted without dissolving the whole fabric; that we must endure the evil without hope and without complaint. Our very natures must be changed before we can be brought tamely to submit to this doctrine. The evil will be remedied: and to use the language of Jefferson again, "this people will yet be free." The Senator finds consolation, however, in the midst of this existing evil, in color and caste. The black race (says he) is the strong ground of slavery in our country. Yes, it is *color*, not right and justice, that is to continue forever slavery in our country. It is prejudice against color, which is the strong ground of the slaveholder's hope. Is that prejudice founded in nature, or is it the effect of base and sordid interest? Let the mixed race which we see here, from black to almost perfect white, springing from white fathers, answer the question. Slavery has no just foundation in color; it rests exclusively upon usurpation, tyranny, oppressive fraud, and force. These were its parents in every age and country of the world.

The Senator says, the next or greatest difficulty to emancipation is, the amount of property it would take from the owners. All ideas of right and wrong are confounded in these words: emancipate property. Emancipate a horse, or an ox, would not only be an unmeaning, but a ludicrous expression. To emancipate, is to set free from slavery. To emancipate, is to set free a man, not property. The Senator estimates the number of slaves—*men* now held in bondage—at three millions, in the United States. Is this statement made here by the same voice which was heard in this Capitol in favor of the liberties of Greece, and for the emancipation of our South American brethren from political thraldom? It is; and has all its fervor in favor of liberty been exhausted upon foreign countries, so as not to leave a single whisper in favor of three millions of men in our own country, now groaning under the most galling oppression the world ever saw? No, Sir. Sordid interest rules the hour. Men are made property, and paper is made money; and the Senator, no doubt, sees in these two peculiar institutions a power which, if united, will be able to accomplish all his wishes. He informs us that some have computed the slaves to be worth the average amount of five hundred dollars each. He will estimate within bounds, at four hundred dollars each; making the amount twelve hundred millions worth of slave property. I heard this statement, Mr. President, with emotions of the deepest feeling.

By what rule of political or commercial arithmetic does the Senator calculate the amount of property in human beings? Can it be fancy or fact, that I hear such calculation, that the people of the United States own twelve hundred millions' (double the amount of all the specie in the world) worth of human flesh! And this property is owned, the gentleman informs us, by all classes of society, forming part of all our contracts within our own country and in Europe. I should have been glad, Sir, to have been spared the hearing of a declaration of this kind, especially from the high source and the place from which it emanated. But the assertion has gone forth that we have twelve hundred millions of slave property at the South; and can any man so close his understanding here, as not plainly to perceive that the power of this vast amount of property at the South, is now uniting itself to the banking power of the North, in order to govern the destinies of this country? Six hundred millions of banking capital is to be brought into this coalition, and the slave power and the bank power are thus to unite in order to break down the present administration. There can be no mistake, as I believe, in this matter. The aristocracy of the North, who, by the power of a corrupt banking system, and the aristocracy of the South, by the power of the slave system, both fattening upon the labor of others, are now about to unite in order to make the reign of each perpetual. Is there an independent Amercan to be found, who will become the recreant slave to such an unholy combination? Is this another compromise to barter the liberties of the country for personal aggrandiezment? "Resistance to tyrants is obedience to God."

The Senator further insists, "that what the law makes property is property." This is the predicate of the gentleman; he has neither facts nor reason to prove it; yet upon this alone does he rest the whole case that negroes are property. I deny the predicate and the argument. Suppose the Legislature of the Senator's own State should pass a law declaring his wife, his children, his friends, indeed, any white citizen of Kentucky, *property*, and should they be sold and transferred as such, would the gentleman fold his arms and say, "Yes, they are property, for the law has made them such?" No, sir; he would denounce such law with more vehemence than he now denounces Abolitionists, and would deny the authority of human Legislation to accomplish an object so clearly beyond its power.

Human laws, I contend, can not make human beings property, if human force can do it. If it is competent for our legislatures to make a black man *property*, it is competent for them to make a white man the same; and the same objection exists to the power of the people in an organic law for their own government; they can not make property of each other; and, in the language of the Constitution of Indiana, such an act "can only originate in usurpation and tyranny." Dreadful, indeed, would be the condition of this country, if these principles should not only be carried into the ballot box, but into the Presidential chair. The idea that the Abolitionists ought to pay for the slaves if they are set free, and that they ought to think of this, is addressed to their fears, and not their judgment. There is no principle of morality or justice that should require them or our citizens generally to do so. To free a slave is to take from usurpation that which it has made property and given to another, and bestow it upon the rightful owner. It is not taking property from its true owner for public use. Men can do with their own as they please, to distroy their peace if they wish, but can not be compelled to do so.

The gentleman repeats the assertion that has been repeated a thousand and one times: that Abolitionists are retarding the emancipation of the slave, and have thrown it back fifty or a hundred years; that they have increased the rigors of slavery, and caused the master to treat his slave with more severity. Slavery, then, is to cease at some period; and because the Abolitionists have said to the slaveholder, "Now is the accepted time," and because he thinks this an improper interference — not having the Abolitionists in his power, he inflicts his vengeance on his unoffending slave! The moral of this story is, the slaveholder will exercise more cruelty because he is desired to show mercy. I do not envy the Senator the full benefit of his argument. It is no doubt a true picture of the feelings and principles which slavery engenders in the breast of the master. It is in perfect keeping with the threat we almost daily hear; that if petitioners do not cease their efforts in the exercise of their Constitutional rights, others will dissolve the Union. These, however, ought to be esteemed idle assertions and idle threats.

The Senator tells us that the consequences arising from the freedom of slaves, would be to reduce the wages of the white laborer. He has furnished us with neither data nor fact upon which this opinion can rest. He, however, would draw a line, on one side of which he would place the slave labor, and on the other side free white labor; and looking over the whole, as a general system, both would appear on a perfect equality. I have observed, for some years past, that the Southern slaveholder has insisted that his laborers are, in point of integrity, morality, usefulness, and comfort, equal to the laboring population of the North. Thus endeavoring to raise the slave in public estimation, to an equality with the free white laborer of the North; while, on the other hand, the Northern aristocrat has, viz: by comparison, endeavored to reduce his laborers to the moral and political condition of the slaves of the South. It is for the free white American citizens to determine whether they will permit such degrading comparisons longer to exist.

Already has this spirit broken forth in denunciation of the right of universal suffrage. Will free white laboring citizens take warning before it is too late?

The last, the great, the crying sin of Abolitionists, in the eyes of the Senator, is that they are opposed to colonization, and in favor of amalgamation. It is not necessary now to enter into any of the benefits and advantages of colonization; the Senator has pronounced it the noblest scheme ever devised by man; he says it is powerful but harmless. I have no knowledge of any resulting benefits from the scheme to either race. I have not a doubt as to the real object intended by its founders; it did not arise from principles of humanity and benevolence toward the colored race, but a desire to remove the free of that race beyond the United States, in order to perpetuate and make slavery more secure.

The Senator further makes the broad charge that Abolitionists wish to *enforce* the unnatural system of amalgamation. We deny the fact, and call on the Senator for proof. The citizens of the free States, the petitioners against slavery, the Abolitionists of the free States, in favor of amalgamation! No Sir! If you want evidence of the fact, and reasoning in support of amalgamation, you must look into the slave States; it is there it spreads and flourishes from slave mothers, and presents all possible colors and complexions, from the jet black African to the scarcely to be distinguished white person. Does any one need proof of this fact? let him take but a few turns through the streets of your capital, and observe those whom he shall meet, and he will be perfectly satisfied. Amalgamation, indeed! The charge is made with a very bad grace on the present occasion. No, sir; it is not the negro *woman*, it is the *slave* and the contaminating influence of slavery that is the mother of amalgamation. Does the gentleman want facts on this subject? let him look at the colored race in the free States; it is a rare occurrence there. A colony of blacks, some three or four hundred, were settled, some fifteen or twenty years since, in the county of Brown, a few miles distant from my former residence in Ohio, and I was told by a person living near them, a country merchant with whom they dealt, when conversing with him on this very subject, that he knew of but one instance of a mulatto child being born among them for the last fifteen years; and I venture the assertion, had this same colony been settled in a slave State, the cases of a like kind would have been far more numerous. I repeat again, in the words of Dr. Channing, it is a slave country that reeks with licentiousness of this kind, and for proof I refer to the opinions of Judge Harper, of North Carolina, in his defense of southern slavery.

The Senator, as if fearing that he had made his charge too broad, and might fail in proof to sustain it, seems to stop short, and make the inquiry, where is the process of amalgamation to begin? He had heard of no instance of the kind against Abolitionists; they (Abolitionists) would begin it with the laboring class; and if I understand the Senator correctly, that Abolitionism, by throwing together the white and the black laborers, would naturally produce this result. Sir, I regret, I deplore, that such a charge should be made against the laboring class—that class which tills the ground; and in obedience to the decree of their Maker, eat their bread in the sweat of their face—that class, of whom Mr. Jefferson says, if God has a chosen people on earth, they are those who thus labor. This charge is calculated for effect, to induce the laboring class to believe, that if emancipation takes place, they will be, in the free States, reduced to the same condition as the colored laborer. The reverse of that is the truth of the case. It is the slaveholder NOW, he who looks upon labor as only fit for a servile race, it is him and his kindred spirits who live upon the labor of others, endeavoring to reduce the white laborer to the condition of the slave. They do not yet claim him as property, but they would exclude him from all participation in the public affairs of the country. It is further said, that if the negroes were free, the black would rival the white laborer in the free States. I can not believe it while so many facts exist to to prove the contrary. Negroes, like the white race, but with stronger feelings, are attached to the place of their birth, and the home of their youth; and the climate of the South is congenial to their natures, more than that of the North. If emancipation should take place at the South and the negroes be freed from the fear of being made merchandize, they would remove from the free States of the North and West, and immediately return to that country, because it is the home of their friends and fathers. Already in Ohio, as far as my knowledge extends, has free white labor, (emigrants,) from foreign countries, engrossed almost entirely all situations in which male or female labor is found. But, Sir, this plea of necessity and convenience is the plea of tyrants. Has not the free black person the same right tothe use of his hands as the white person; the same right to contract and labor for what price he pleases? Would the gentleman extend the power of the government to the regulation of the productive industry of the country? This was his former theory, but put down effectually by the public voice. Taking advantage of the prejudice against labor, the attempt is now being made to begin this same system, by first operating on the poor black laborer. For shame! let us cease from attempts of this kind.

The Senator informs us that the question was asked fifty years ago that is now asked, can the negro be continued forever in bondage? Yes; and it will continue to be asked, in still louder and louder tones. But, says the Senator, we are yet a prosperous and happy nation. Pray, Sir, in what part of your country do you find this prosperity and happiness? In the slave States? No! no! There all is weakness, gloom, and despair; while in the free States, all is light, business, and activity. What has created the astonishing difference between the gentleman's State and mine—between Kentucky and Ohio? Slavery, the withering curse of slavery, is upon Kentucky, while Ohio is free. Kentucky—the garden of the West, almost the land of promise, possessing all the natural advantages, and more than is possessed by Ohio—is vastly behind in population and wealth. Sir, I can see from the windows of my upper chamber, in the city of Cincinnati, lands in Kentucky, which, I am told, can be purchased from ten to fifty dollars per acre; while lands of the same quality, under the same improvements, and the same distance from me in Ohio, would probably sell from one to five hundred dollars per acre. I was told by a friend, a few days before I left home, who had formerly resided in the county of Bourbon, Kentucky—a most excellent county of lands adjoining, I believe, the county in which the Senator resides—that the white population of that county was more than four hundred less than it was five years since. Will the Senator contend, after a knowledge of these facts, that slavery in this country has been the cause of our prosperity and happiness? No, he can not. It is because slavery has been excluded and driven from a large proportion of our country, that we are a prosperous and happy people. But its late attempts to force its influence and power into the free States, and deprive our citizens of their unquestionable rights, has been the moving cause of all the riots, burnings, and murders that have taken place on account of Abolitionism; and it has, in some degree, even in the free States, caused mourning, lamentation and woe. Remove slavery, and the country, the whole country, will recover its natural vigor, and our peace and future prosperity will be placed on a more extensive, safe, and sure foundation. It is a waste of time to answer the allegations that the emancipation of the negro race would induce them to make war on the white race. Every fact in the history of emancipation proves the reverse: and he that will not believe those facts, has darkened his own understanding, that the light of reason can make no impression; he appeals to interest, not to truth, for information on this subject. We do not fear his errors, while we are left free to combat them. The Senator implores us to cease all commotion on this subject. Are we to surrender all our rights and privileges, all the official stations of the country into the hands of the slaveholding power, without a single struggle? Are we to cease all exertions for our own safety, and submit in quiet to the rule of this power? Is the calm of despotism to reign over this land, and the voice of freedom to be no more heard? This sacrifice is required of us, in order to sustain slavery. *Freemen*, will you make it? Will you shut your ears and your sympathies, and withhold from the poor, famished slave, a morsel of bread? Can you thus act, and expect the blessings of Heaven upon your country? I beseech you to consider for yourselves.

Mr. President—I have been compelled to enter into this discussion from the course pursued by the Senate on the resolutions I submitted a few days since. The cry of Abolitionist has been raised against me. If those resolutions are Abolitionism, then I am an Abolitionist from the sole of my foot to the crown of my head. If to maintain the rights of the States, the security of the citizen from violence and outrage; if to preserve the supremacy of the laws; if insisting on the right of petition, a medium through which *every person* subject to the laws has an undoubted right to approach the Constitutional authorities of the country—be the doctrines of Abolitionists, it finds a response in every beating pulse of my veins. Neither power, nor favor, nor want, nor misery, shall deter me from its support while the vital current continues to flow.

Condemned at home for my opposition to slavery, alone and single handed here, well may I feel tremor and emotion in bearding this lion of slavery in his very *den* and upon his own ground. I should shrink, Sir, at once, from this fearful and unequal contest, was I not thoroughly convinced that I am sustained by the power of truth and the best interests of the country.

I listened to the Senator of Kentucky with undivided attention. I was disappointed, sadly disappointed. I had heard of the Senator's tact in making compromises and agreements on this floor, and though opposed in principle to all such proceedings, yet I hoped to hear something upon which we could hang a hope that peace would be restored to the borders of our own States, and all future aggression upon our citizens from the free States be prevented. Now, Sir, he offers us nothing but unconditional submission to political death; and not political alone, but absolute *death.* We have counted the cost in this matter, and are determined to live or die free.

Let the slaveholder hug his system to his bosom in his own State, we will not go there to disturb him; but, Sir, within our own borders we claim to enjoy the same privileges. Even, Sir, here in this District, this ten miles square of common property and common right, the slave power has the assurance to come into this very Hall, and request that we—yes, Mr. President, that my constituents — be denied the right of petition on the subject of slavery in this District. This most extraordinary petition against the right of others to petition on the same subject as theirs, is graciously received and ordered to be printed, pæans sung to it by the slave power; while the petitions I offer, from as honorable, free, high-minded and patriotic American citizens as any in this District, are spit upon, and turned out of doors as an *unclean thing!* Genius of liberty! how long will you sleep under this iron power of oppression? Not content with ruling over their own slaves, they claim the power to instruct Congress on the question of receiving petitions; and yet we are tauntingly and sneeringly told that we have nothing to do with the existence of slavery in the country, a suggestion as absurd as it is ridiculous. We are called upon to make laws in favor of slavery in the District, but it is denied that we can make laws against it; and at last the right of petition on the subject, by the people of the free States, is complained of as an improper interference. I leave it to the Senator to reconcile all these difficulties, absurdities, claims and requests of the people of this District, to the country at large; and I venture the opinion that he will find as much difficulty in producing the belief that he is correct now, as he has found, in obtaining the same belief, that he was before correct, in his views and political course on the subject of banks, internal improvements, protective tariff, etc., and the regulation, by acts of Congress, of the productive industry of the country, together with all compromises and coalitions he has entered into for the attainment of those objects. I rejoice, however, that the Senator has made the display he has on this occasion. It is a powerful shake to awaken the sleeping energies of liberty, and his voice, like a trumpet, will call from their slumbers, millions of freemen, to defend their rights; and the overthrow of his theory now, is as sure and certain, by the force of public opinion, as was the overthrow of all his former schemes, by the same mighty power.

I feel, Mr. President, as if I had wearied your patience, while I am sure my own bodily powers admonish me to close; but I can not do so, without again reminding my constituents of the greetings that have taken place on the consummation and ratification of the treaty, offensive and defensive, between the slaveholding and bank powers, in order to carry on a war against the liberties of our country, and to put down the present administration. Yes, there is no voice heard from New England now. Boston and Faneuil Hall are silent as death. The free day-laborer is, in prospect, reduced to the political, if not moral, condition of the slave; an ideal line is to divide them in their labor; yes! the same principle is to govern on both sides. Even the farmer, too, will soon be brought into the same fold. It will be again said, with regard to the government of the country, "The farmer with his huge paws upon the statute book, what can he do?" I have endeavored to warn my fellow-citizens of the present and approaching danger, but the dark cloud of slavery is before their eyes, and prevents many of them from seeing the condition of things as they are. That cloud, like the cloud of summer, will soon pass away, and its thunders cease to be heard. Slavery will come to an end, and the sunshine of prosperity warm, invigorate and bless our whole country.

I do not know, Mr. President, that my voice will ever again be heard on this floor. I now willingly, yes, gladly return to my constituents, to the people of my own State. I have spent my life among them, and the greater portion of it in their service, and they have bestowed upon me their confidence in numerous instances. I feel perfectly conscious that, in the discharge of every trust which they have committed to me, I have, to the best of my abilities, acted solely with a view to the general good, not suffering myself to be influenced by any particular or private interest whatever; and I now challenge those who think I have done otherwise, to lay their finger upon any public act of mine, and prove to the country its injustice or anti-republican tendency. That I have often erred in the selection of means to accomplish important ends, I have no doubt; but my belief in the truth of the doctrines of the Declaration of Independence, the political creed of President Jefferson, remains unshaken and unsubdued. My greatest regret is that I have not been more zealous, and done more for the cause of individual and political liberty than I have done. I hope, on returning to my home and my friends, to join them again in rekindling the beacon-fires of liberty upon every hill in our State, until their broad glare shall enlighten every valley, and the song of triumph will soon be heard; for the hearts of our people are in the hands of a just and holy Being, (who can not look upon oppression but with abhorrence), and he can turn them whithersoever he will, as the rivers of water are turned. Though our national sins are many and grievous, yet repentance, like that of ancient Nineveh, may divert from us that impending danger which seems to hang over our heads as by a single hair. That all may be safe, I conclude that THE NEGRO WILL YET BE SET FREE.

This noble Speech startled the Senate, and produced a marked sensation throughout the country. A Southern Senator arose, and said, Mr. Morris deserved expulsion from the Senate, that his presence there was contamination; and he soiled the very carpet on which he stood. The Legislature of Virginia, suggested that Ohio's Senator be expelled.

The friends of freedom, however, hailed the speech with delight. Numerous Conventions passed resolutions, commending his Roman integrity and firmness. He received numerous letters, saying: "Your very able and timely speech, in reply to Mr. Clay, will be remembered with gratitude by millions till the end of time." "You are regarded as the chief defender of the liberty of speech, of the right of petition, and freedom of debate, among all the Senators who compose that august Body."

"We beg the reader," said a paper, "will not throw

down this splendid speech unread, because it is a long one. Read it attentively, and then say what paragraph might have been omitted. We have read it three times, with profit and pleasure. It embraces, as will be seen, a recapitulation of all the arguments in Mr. Clay's celebrated speech in favor of slavery, and is a capital expose of the whole budget of fine-spun fallacies brought forward by the Kentucky slaveholder. Mr. Morris could not have chosen a better topic for a valedictory speech on the eve of his retirement from the Senate. We have for years held this man in high regard. His profession of Democracy amounts to something more than enrollment. He has no need to advertise the public of his political creed, so far, at least, as concerns the great question of human rights. The old painters, in the imperfection of their art, were wont to underwrite upon their canvass, "*this* is a *horse*" — "*that* is a *lion*." Morris needs no label. He stands confessed the lion of the day."

"When Mr. Morris began his speech, the audience was small, as Mr. Webster had attracted the great and fashionable to hear his argument before the Supreme Court in another wing of the Capitol; but before Morris had proceeded far, the tide set the other way, and soon *he* had the Senate-chamber crowded to listen to his noble speech!"

Almost all the Senators who participated in that memorable debate are dead. Calhoun lies in his own graveyard, in the State which he loved so passionately, and to whose interests, his logical and masterly intellect and energies were devoted. The imperial Webster, whose massive mind, and rich intellectual resources are the glory of his country, rests in his home farm, in Marshfield, Massachusetts. His name has lost the prestige of its former power and glory, because, on several occasions, he declined to defend, by his eminent abilities, the cause of freedom. Clay, the idol of his party, and ever potential in the politics and civil councils of his country, was borne in a funeral pageant, from the Capital of the Nation, where he died, to the shades of Ashland, Kentucky, where he sleeps in death. A son of Kentucky, himself an ardent admirer of Mr. Clay, says: "Strong considerations would restrain me from undervaluing his work, but some of the measures he originated and pursued with ceaseless toil, are cast aside as obselete ideas, his party is disbanded, the talismanic charm of his name is powerless, and it will remain for future ages to decide how great and enduring his influence shall be."

Morris also is dead. He rests in the free soil of Ohio, (buried in a spot of ground consecrated to freedom by a special Act,) a State, of which it was a passion of his nature to love, and to whose welfare he devoted the energies of a long life; closing his last official efforts for Ohio and his country, by this speech in the Senate of the United States; but the great principles enunciated, and so fearlessly maintained in it, still live and will live forever.

"Truth crushed to earth, will rise again,
The eternal years of God are hers
While error writhing in her pains,
Shall die amid her worshipers."

CHAPTER XIV.

Various Resolutions offered on Slavery—Refused Printing—Opinion of a Southern Senator—A Northern Senator—Social and Civil Proscriptions of Anti-Slavery Senators.

The vigilant watchfulness of Mr. Morris, in reference to the spirit and aggression of the slave power, was developed in his efforts, to test the view of the Senate of the United States, on its growing pretensions and power. It demanded not only security and protection from the Government, within its own limits, but also, complete exemption from discussion in and out of Congress; nor would it permit any examination of the system of slavery. The pro-slavery sentiment, so entirely triumphant in Congress, was subjected to a new development in the Senate, through the vigilant efforts of Mr. Morris. On the 5th of February, 1839, he offered for the consideration of the Senate, the following resolutions :

Whereas, the right and privilege of petition is an existing principle, established by the laws of nature, and is designed to be exercised not for opposition or resistance but to obtain relief or favor; and this right, when the people peaceably exercise it, is placed by the Constitution of the United States above the power of legislative bodies, who can not rightfully control the time, or the manner, or the matter, in or for which, the people shall petition. And, whereas, recent events in Congress, on this important subject, render it doubtful, how far that body consider the people justifiable, in the exercise of this right, especially on the subject of slavery, the slave trade, and the abolition of slavery; and since, upon all subjects, on which legislative bodies may Constitutionally act, it seems clear that every intelligent being, who is subject to this action, ought to enjoy the right of petition to the fullest extent.

Resolved, therefore, That as the people of the United States, or certain portions of them, claim to have an undeniable right to petition Congress to abolish slavery in the District of Columbia, to suppress the slave trade therein, and between the different States and Territories of the United States; or between any of the States and the Republic of Texas; and against the admission of any new State into the Union whose Constitution permits or tolerates slavery; in as full, free and ample manner, as they can exercise this right on any other subject; it is therefore expedient, that all petitions, on the aforesaid subjects, or any of them, be referred to the Committee on the Judiciary, which committee is instructed to inquire into and report to the Senate, their opinion on the following points:

First, Whether the people of the United States, or any portion of them, have an indisputable right to petition Congress on the subjects, or any of them, mentioned in the foregoing resolution.

Second, Whether Congress, possess the power to abolish slavery in the District of Columbia.

Third, Whether Congress possess the power to prohibit slavery in the Territories of the United States.

Fourth, Whether Congress have power to create, introduce, or establish slavery, in any territory acquired by the United States, in which slavery did not exist at the time the United States became possessed thereof.

Fifth, Whether Congress have the power and ought to restrain or abridge any Constitutional right of the citizens, because the exercise of such right may tend, by calling in question the justice and policy of slavery, to weaken or abolish that system in any of the States.

Sixth, Whether Congress in any case can, either directly or indirectly, Constitutionally restrain or abridge the freedom of the press, or of speech, or the right of petition.

Seventh, Whether Congress have power to provide for the safety and protection of persons and property of the citizens of one State, from violence and injury being done such citizens or their property, in another State; and also to protect the citizens of any State, who think proper, within their own State, to speak, write, print, and publish their opinions against the political, moral, or religious institutions of another State, from trial and punishment in the State whose institutions such speaking, writing, printing and publishing were designed to affect.

Eighth, Whether Congress have power to declare what shall or shall not be, made property in any of the States.

Ninth, Whether Congress have power to authorize the sale of slaves as property, to discharge a judgment in favor of the United States.

Tenth, Whether a removal of the Seat of Government into a State in which slavery does not exist, would not be expedient, consistent with sound policy, and promote the quiet, safety, and interest of the country.

Resolved, further, That as Congress has no power over the persons of slaves as property, in any State, or the subject of slavery therein, a retrocession of the District of Columbia to the States of Virginia and Maryland ought to be made, to prevent, or take away, the exercise of such power in the District.

Resolved, further, That it belongs exclusively to the States in this Union, to provide that a person who may be held to service or labor in one State, under the laws thereof, and who shall escape into another State, shall be delivered up by such State to the party to whom such service or labor may be due; and that the States, as parties to the compact of Union, are in good faith bound to make such provision.

Resolved, That Congress have not the power to authorize or permit a person to take into, or to hold, as property, in any State, that which the Constitution and laws of such State declare shall not be held as property therein; but the citizens of each State ought to be protected in the several States, in the enjoyment of all privileges and immunities that citizens of the State are entitled to, and none other.

Resolved, That it would be expedient and proper for Congress to ascertain the number of slaves in the District of Columbia, the extent of the slave trade carried on therein, and from the District; whether such slaves are purchased in the District, or bought within the same from the States, for exportation, and how many have been taken from the District within the last two years, for sale, and to what market they were taken, whether within or without the United States.

A year previous to the introduction of the foregoing resolutions, on the 19th of February, 1838, Mr. Morris offered the following:

Resolved, That the Committee on the Judiciary be instructed to inquire, whether the present laws of the United States, on the subject of the slave trade, will prohibit that trade being carried on between the citizens of the United States and the citizens of the Republic of Texas, whether by land or sea; and whether it would be lawful in vessels owned by citizens of that Republic, and not lawful in vessels owned by citizens of this, or lawful in both, and by citizens of both countries; and also, whether a slave carried from the United States, into a foreign country, and brought back or returning into the United States, is considered a free person, or is liable to be sent back, if demanded, as a slave into that country from which he or she in the past came; and also, whether any additional legislation by Congress is necessary on any of these subjects.

When read, a Southern Senator (Mr. Foster) expressed his surprise, that the Senate had not the power, by an instantaneous vote, to refuse even to receive such resolutions.

A Senator from New Hampshire, Mr. Hubbard, said, "it was a matter of policy to let the whole subject alone. These resolutions have been fully discussed through the public press; and notwithstanding their author has received the most unmerited abuse from public journals, yet he was free to say, that he most sincerely concurred with his friend, Mr. Morris, in every sentiment expressed by him, in these resolutions; and he might add that a large majority of the constituents of his friend, (he had reason to believe,) were prepared fully to sustain him in the course he had pursued on this subject."

Mr. Buchanan said, "He should vote against the proposition to lay upon the table. From his whole course on the subject of these Abolition petitions, he supposed no person would suspect him of being friendly to them, or to their objects. But fair play is a jewel; and he thought the Senator from Ohio, (Mr. Morris,) had a right to be heard, and to reply to the remarks that were made in the Senate on this subject yesterday."

Mr. Hubbard said: "That there was no want of "fair play!" The Senator from Ohio, by this motion, is not precluded from offering his views on the subject of slavery. This right he has, this privilege he now enjoys, if he chooses to exercise it. No rule of the Senate could prevent him from going fully into the subject of slavery at any time.

Mr. Morris said: "He felt very much obliged to the Senator from New Hampshire for the information, that *he had the same right as any other Senator to express his opinions* on subjects brought before the Senate. He supposed he ought to tender his profound thanks for *this gracious privilege.*"

The resolutions were refused to be entertained or printed.

Mr. Morris, by his fearless defense of freedom, and bold denunciations of Slavery, did not lose political or social caste among his co-Senators. At each session of Congress he served on important Committees, such as the Judiciary and Agricultural, and was Chairman of the Committee on Pensions. Southern Senators, treated him with the urbanity of gentlemen, and admitted his honesty and admired his fearlessness. A Senator from Georgia, remarked to him, that if it was known who he was, he might travel with safety through his State, though holding and proclaiming the sentiments he then did on the subject of slavery.

A change has come over the spirit and action of the slave Power. Now, its imperious authority, disregarding the rules of Parliamentary right and justice, declares certain Senators, eminent for talents and patriotism, "to belong to an unhealthy political organization," and forbids them a place on Senatorial Committees. Seward from New York; Chase and Wade, from Ohio; Sumner and Wilson, from Massachusetts; Hale, from New Hampshire; Collamer, from Vermont; Trumbell, from Illinois; Durkee, from Wisconsin, and others; statesmen of eminent abilities, and of exalted patriotism and purity in public and private character and life, have been proscribed by a pro-slavery Senate from their Constitutional privileges, and from the social urbanities of pro-slavery Senators. Persecution, for righteousness, and for freedom's sake, is no novelty in the history of the world. The days of the martyrs are not ended. Let the freemen of the nation embalm these, and other champions of freedom in grateful and perpetual remembrance.

"In Freedom's field advancing their firm feet
They plant them on the line that Justice draws,
And will prevail or perish in her cause!"

CHAPTER XV.

Alliance of Democracy with the Slave Power—Degeneracy in a great party a great calamity—Resolutions of the Democracy of Cincinnati, on the 8th of January, 1839—Mr. Morris's Answer—Letter from A. A. Guthrie, 3d of January, 1839—Mr. Morris's Reply—Vermont Resolutions refused to be Printed—Predictions fulfilled.

Ardent, and consistent, in his devotion to the principles of true Democracy, it was a source of profound sorrow to Mr. Morris, to see the party, with which he had so long acted, yielding the purity and power of their noble principles, to the corrupting and contagious influences of slavery. Harmonizing, as he believed they did, with all that is true in political science, and civil government, and adapted, in their beneficent action and progress, to give freedom and elevation to men and nations — degeneracy or apostacy, from these noble landmarks of freedom, by a great and dominant party, is always a great national calamity. "A nation can suffer no greater calamity than the loss of its principles. Lofty and pure sentiment is the life and hope of a people." Decay or defection from the vital principles of freedom, right, religion, and humanity, betokens the approach of national ruin. As the sturdy oak when girdled must die, so the nations that denounce the principles of Christian rectitude, and of true Democracy, must tend to degeneracy and destruction. "If the foundations be destroyed" what hope is there that the stately temple of freedom can stand.

A great party, then, who represent the *beau ideal* of Democracy, whose doctrines have a natural charm for the popular ear and popular heart, and which controls the masses, and so forms the resistless current of political public sentiment, and directs political policy and action, should guard with watchful vigilance, the integrity and purity of its principles. Every interest and motive, that clusters around patriotism and national honor, and safety, and the hope of the final freedom of the world, from bondage — demands of a great party, whose creed is truly Democratic, to be firm and loyal in their unfaltering fidelity to its fundamental principles.

It was the development of unhealthy symptoms, in regard to the disposition of the Democratic party of the country, to yield to the usurpations and dictations of the slave power, that went like iron, to the free heart of Thomas Morris. With great grief he heard the leaders of the party declare, that "Democracy was the natural ally of the South, and of slavery;" and that the surest, reliable strength of the institution of slavery, was found in the Democratic party of the free States. Both of the two great parties of the country, Democratic and Whig, had succumbed, in humble subserviency to the aggressions of slavery; but to the Democratic party, with all its noble principles and professions, belongs the humiliation of yielding most to the demands of the slave power, and opening new and wide fields for the tread of the oppressor.

This policy had a development during the Senatorial term of Mr. Morris. He, as a true Democrat, could not, and did not, yield to its influence. Though it cost him the loss of power, and banishment from his party, yet he stood firm in resisting oppression, and in defense of the true doctrines of Democracy. The following letter was written, in the midst of his earnest conflicts with slavery, in the Senate; and addressed to a Democratic citizen of Cincinnati, who had forwarded to him, the proceedings of a meeting of some of the Democracy, who approved his course as a Senator of Ohio.

WASHINGTON, January 15, 1839.

DEAR SIR—I received your favor, enclosing the proceedings and resolutions, passed by a meeting of our Democratic friends on the 8th inst., at the Lafayette Hall, in the city of Cincinnati. For the favorable notice the meeting was pleased to take of my course here, as Senator, and my efforts in the support of the Democratic cause, the object of which is, equal rights and impartial justice, the gentlemen who composed the meeting, as well as yourself, for the kind manner in which you transmitted me the proceedings, will be pleased to accept my grateful acknowledgments and my sincere thanks.

The approbation of my Democratic fellow citizens, with whom I have personally acted, and to whom I am individually known, is an honor which I more highly prize, than that which wealth and power can bestow. It is my highest ambition, next to a faithful and honest discharge of duty, to preserve the favorable opinion of my friends in the State, by a constant, unwavering adherence to Democratic principles; *believing there, where they* are found, liberty is; where liberty disappears, or is trodden down, they are lost.

The time, the place, the circumstances under which I received the proceedings you enclosed, were calculated to make a deep impression on my mind. Condemned by the Legislature of my own State, as an unfit or unsafe Representative of her Democratic principles in Congress, on account (as I have been informed) of my opposition to slavery, and my defense of the right of petition, the freedom of speech and of the press, and the free use of the Post-Office to Abolitionists, as well as to other men; it was consolatory to learn, that those great principles are still sustained and cherished, in her primary assemblies, not to be abandoned for any local or private interest whatever.

Past experience has taught us that, when liberty and the Constitutional rights of our citizens, or of any portion of them, have been stricken down, in Legislative Assemblies, they have found support in the country, and are resuscitated and sustained by the people, as common rights and common blessings, which all ought to enjoy. This reflection ought to fill the heart of every friend to his country, and of the human race, with the most lively hope and unshaken confidence, that our Government rests upon the most safe foundation which human wisdom can devise; and that the privileges and rights, which it has left free and unrestrained by the power of law, will remain perpetual with the people. The *people*, and not politicians, *must be the guardians of freedom.*

Though contemned, I am not convinced, that, on the now agitated question of slavery, I am in error. Though trodden down, I am not discouraged; because I am well satisfied that the American people will never consent that the records of the Declaration of Independence, and the provisions of their Constitutions, which declare that the natural rights of man are inalienable, shall be thrown aside, as mere waste parchment, and the words therein contained considered as mere rhetorical flourishes. No! this will never be done, to sustain slavery, or any other interest, which is at war with the "general welfare." The system of slavery is not only at war with such welfare, but with the most sacred rights of human nature.

I deeply deplore, that that spirit of proscription for opinion's sake, which is sometimes exercised by power, for its own selfish purposes, is now *stalking openly through our country*, with too little rebuke; that it should find its way into the *Halls of Legislation is still more alarming.* The moral power of the country, the expression of public sentiment, is the only weapon which can rightfully be used against these opinions. The power of the Government can justly punish for ACTS done, but not for opinions entertained; and "error of opinion may be safely tolerated, while reason is left free to combat it." The countenance given by men in places of power, and indeed their assertions made, that opinions adverse to slavery ought not to be expressed or promulgated, have stirred men, of the baser sort, to engage in mobs, and to use violence against their fellow citizens, for *no other cause than an honest* expression of opinion. Such transactions are not only a libel on our Government, a fatal stab aimed at the vital principles of our institutions, and a reproach to our people; but they have caused the land to mourn, and weakened the confidence of our citizens, in those guarantees of person and property, which the Government affects to throw around them.

To strike down an individual by the hand of another—a politician by the hands of politicians—is, comparatively, nothing; the waves of time soon close over the wrong, and it is forgotten, and retributive justice may overtake the wrong-doer. But when Legislative Assemblies, the Rulers of the country, strike at principles on which rest all our invaluable rights and privileges, the blow vibrates through the whole nation; every person feels its full force, as much as if aimed at himself singly. It rends the political fabric, forming a chasm which time seldom closes.

These reflections will be excused, when you remember that my *opinions* have been so arraigned and condemned, that they seem to be *unpardonable political sins.*

The decree of condemnation was first pronounced against me in the newspapers of the slave States. The power which can put a gag into the mouths of members of Congress; can prevent petitions being received in one branch, and can lay them on the table without further action thereon in the other, if on the subject of slavery, is a power not to be overlooked or disregarded in its operation on the free States. If it assumes to dictate, who shall represent the States in Congress? and if such dictation is submitted to, the so-called free States, instead of being independent and governing themselves, will be governed by the slaves of the other States, acting through the medium of their masters!

Do not suppose I speak from any personal feeling on this subject. No! I speak my sober judgment upon facts, which almost daily transpire before the face of the whole country. What are these facts?

The President, (Mr. Van Buren,) is claimed, by many, as a Northern man with Southern principles and feelings. The Cabinet is composed of six members, three from slave States, and one who wrote a book in favor of Southern slavery. Two-thirds, then, of this branch of the Government, are in favor of slavery. The Supreme Court of the United States, is composed of nine Judges, five of whom are from slave States. The President of the Senate, (Vice President of the United States,) and Speaker of the House of Representatives, are also from slave States; the Secretary of the Senate is from this District, a slave country; and the Clerk of the House from a slave State.

We might reasonably suppose, that, with all this power and patronage of the General Government in their hands, the slave-holders ought to feel satisfied, without making any further demands, for security for their *peculiar institution*, on the free States. But this is not so. They ask to abridge our Constitutional and undeniable rights,—the liberty of speech and the press, and the right of petition on the subject of slavery,—and so far as the General Government has acted, they have obtained this also. Still they are not satisfied. *Their march is onward.*

They enter the territories of the free States, seize upon the white as well as the black man, and convey him into their own States; sometimes under pretence of law, at others by mere personal force. They confine our citizens, who have not violated their laws, in their jails, load them with irons and fasten them with chains. But they do not stop here.

The General Assemblies in the slave States pass resolutions, and send them to the Legislatures of the free States, requiring such laws to be passed, as *they think*, are necessary for the security and protection of their *slave property*. Still, like the grave, this slave power can not be satisfied. Enough has not been done. Their Newspapers assume the prerogative of dictating, who shall, and who shall not be elected to Congress in the free States.

Are we disposed to bow to any power on earth, in obedience to these demands? If made by a foreign power, a universal burst of indignation, from the American people, would answer, NO! NEVER! Shall we not then resist them, when made by sister States, with a view to *compel* us to uphold their "*peculiar institution*"? *Resist them*, NOT BY A DISSOLUTION OF THE UNION; not by Legislative resolves sent into the slave States; not by the physical power of the free States. No! not by any of these means. But by the moral power of TRUTH and the force of public opinion; by the BALLOT BOX, THAT HOPE AND ROCK OF SALVATION FOR THE FREEDOM OF OUR COUNTRY. Resist the aggressions of slavery by these means.

Against the further extension of this slave power, which I have but faintly described, I, as a Senator here, coming from a free State, have constantly opposed, by my best exertions. I have claimed for the free States an equality of official station and influence, in conducting the affairs of the General Government; and I am clearly of the opinion, that they ought to possess the ascendency, because they contain a majority of the people. I claim for my own State absolute sovereignty, over persons and things within her jurisdiction; that neither shall be abducted or carried away, without our consent, and in pursuance of our laws. I claim, for my fellow citizens, the full enjoyment of their Constitutional rights, liberty of speech and of the press, and the right of petition, without the fear of mobs or personal violence. I claim for them the peaceable enjoyment of their fire-sides and their bed chambers, secure from the rude assaults of slave-hunters or slave-dealers.

Who will stand by me in support of these claims, and bear the reproach of being an ABOLITIONIST? — A name now made unpopular by interest, misrepresentation, and the love of despotic power; but one WHICH CHRISTIANITY APPROVES, PHILOSOPHY RESPECTS, AND POSTERITY WILL HONOR. A name, however, which has brought into notice a class of politicians, who, taking advantage of existing prejudices against the negro race, have made many believe, that Abolitionism is destructive to the best interests of the country, and that an Abolitionist "to be hated needs but to be seen!" It is by this class I have been charged with being an Abolitionist, the High Priest of Abolitionism in Ohio. They have thus denied and rejected all the doctrines and opinions, I have advanced on this subject, and without meeting me by argument, have been able, by the aid of the slaveholding power, to strike me down in your presence.

I have been with you in opposition to the power of concentrated wealth; to Banks and systems that band together men in sustaining any particular or private object, by which they can operate on, and control the Legislation and government of the county. I have said to you, that immediately after the settlement of the Money question, there was one of far more importance which the people must decide — the question of equal rights and civil liberty, in opposition to which would be arrayed the whole force of the slaveholding power: An interest, which private, local, and arrogant in its nature, has *united together* more persons for selfish purposes, and is more powerful and dangerous to the peace and prosperity of the country, than Banks or any other interest, that has ever existed among us.

Is it for the *welfare* and *perpetuity* of the Democratic party in the United States, to be *governed by* and to sustain their power? Can they drive from their ranks all, who have contended against it, and who oppose slavery, and still out-number their opponents at the polls? In short, will the Democracy of Ohio support the system of slavery, and disown all who use their moral influence and power for its extinction? These are grave considerations, which, I am sure, you will give a candid examination before you join in such a crusade. Count first the probable results of such a course; and, if your way is clearly seen, and can promise safety, still it would not be safe to act. The power of our political opponents is not to be despised. Their forces are still unbroken and ready to act. Take care then, that you do not, for the love of any "*peculiar institution,*" weaken the Democratic party.

I shall soon, I hope be with you, freed from the high responsibility under which I have been acting. I shall then breath more freely and deeply in the support and maintenance of principles, which I believe are essentially connected with the peace, prosperity and best interests of our country. I feel under everlasting obligations to my Democratic fellow citizens of Cincinnati, for the kindness they have shown me, during the short time I have been a resident of the city. I shall return with augmented resolution to aid them in sustaining their individual and political rights. But still on *all occasions,* must insist, on the *full, free use of all my moral powers to overthrow slavery in our country;* or confine it strictly to its present limits; and wrest from it, if I can, some portion of the political power of the county. *Unless this be done, I fear that the citizens of the free States will neither enjoy peace, nor safety from the arrogance of its pretensions, nor be permitted to hold any office under this Government, but by its leave.*

I am yours, with respect,

THOMAS MORRIS.

The following letter to A. A. Guthrie, of Putnam, Ohio, will explain itself. On the presenting the resolutions of the State of Vermont, Southern Senators were roused to the highest state of indignation and alarm.

Mr. Calhoun regarded them, "as striking at the very foundation of the Union, and tending to the overthrow of the best hopes of mankind. The strongest minds of the country were carried away by the Abolition excitement. He was amazed to see the Senator from Vermont pursuing the course he did." "The progress of Abolitionism must be arrested at home, or the South will take care of itself."

Mr. Lumpkin, of Georgia, declared "that he felt no disposition to countenance or respect attempts to agitate the question of slavery, the more because it was brought before the Senate by the proceedings of a sovereign State. Every lover of this Union, should cease to agitate this question. These proceedings are rapidly alienating the affections of one portion of the Union from another. We should not print these resolutions, nor circulate anything from this Senate, calculated to increase the excitement and prejudice."

WASHINGTON, January 9, 1839.

DEAR SIR—I received your letter of the 3d inst., to-day in the Senate, under circumstances calculated to make a deep and lasting impression on my mind. A vote had just been taken in the Senate, which, I am sure, once understood by the free citizens of the United States, would suffuse their face with shame, for the degradation of the free States, and their prostration at the footstool of slavery, and arouse their indignation to defend their rights as citizens, as well as the honor of their States.

One of the Senators from Vermont (Mr. Prentiss), introduced the following resolutions, passed by the Legislature of his State:

Resolved, by the Senate and House of Representatives, That our Senators in Congress be instructed, and our Representatives be requested, to use their utmost efforts to prevent the annexation of Texas to the United States, and to procure the abolition of slavery, and the slave trade between the several States and Territories of the Union.

Resolved, That the adoption by the House of Representatives of the United States, on the 21st of December last, of the resolution by which "all petitions, memorials, and papers, touching the abolition of slavery, or the buying, selling, or transferring of slaves in any State, District, or Territory of the United States, were laid on the table, without being debated, printed, read, or referred, was a daring infringement of the right of the people to petition, and a flagrant violation of the Constitution of the United States; and we do, in the name of the people of Vermont, protest against the passage of the same, or any similar resolution, by the present or any future Congress of the United States.

Resolved, That our Senators in Congress be instructed, and our Representatives be requested, to present the foregoing resolutions to their respective Houses, and use their influence to carry the same into effect.

Resolved, That the Governor be requested to transmit a copy of the foregoing resolutions to the President of the United States, and to each of our Senators and Representatives in Congress.

STATE OF VERMONT, SECRETARY OF STATE'S OFFICE,
Montpelier, *November* 30, 1838.

I certify the foregoing to be true copies of resolutions passed by the Legislature of this State, on the 5th day of November, A.D. 1838.

CHAUNCEY L. KNAPP,
Secretary of State.

The introduction of these resolutions created instant excitement among the slaveholders in the Senate, and objections were made to their reception; but to refuse to receive resolutions solemnly passed by one of the sovereign States of this Confederacy, was a measure of so high and extravagant a character, that even the slaveholding power, haughty as it is, shrunk back from its exercise; one of them observing, that if this was a petition from a poor, miserable, individual fanatic, he would not receive it. He thought, as it was from a sovereign State, it should be received and laid on the table. Mr. Prentiss then moved it be laid on the table and printed. Arogance always, when checked in its violence, descends to meanness. A division of the question was called for; the motion to lay on the table agreed to; and the whole slaveholding and slave-loving power of the Senate exploded its indignation by refusing to PRINT.

Yes! the slaveholding power of the country commanded that the Senate of the United States should not print the resolutions of a sovereign State, instructing their own delegation in Congress; and the Senate obeyed. When that vote was taken, my colleague (Hon. William Allen), whose name was called first, voted against the printing. Ah! thought I, and *you, too, Ohio!* you, who owe all your wealth and your prosperity to your free institutions! the land which slavery, as yet, has never polluted! the country within which neither slavery nor involuntary servitude can exist, except as a punishment for crime, and whose Constitution declares all men are born equally free and independent! Yes, Ohio! in the councils of the nation, subjecting her own principles and her own Constitution to be trodden down as "worthless parchment," under the foot of slavery. It was a degradation which I could not have anticipated, and one which I would gladly have been spared the mortification of witnessing.

I retired to my room, after this attempt at foul murder of State rights, and that, too, by men who profess to hold them inviolate. I took the Declaration of Independence, to examine, once more, the wrongs done the Colonies, and see if any therein enumerated, exceeded that of the contempt offered by the Senate of the United States to the sovereignty of a State; or if the slaveholding power was not inflicting greater injuries upon the free States, than the British King had inflicted on the Colonies. Let any one, who will remove the blackness of a negro's skin from before his eyes, examine the wrongs complained of in that Document, and see if they are not such as the wrongs done by the slaveholder to the free States.

"Our citizens have been subjected to a judicial trial foreign to our Constitution and unacknowledged by our laws"—[Recollect the case of Rev. J. B. Mehan]; "Protecting, by a mock trial, from punishment for murder"—[even in the borders of a free State—case of Rev. E. P. Lovejoy]; "Depriving our citizens, in many cases, of the trial by jury"—[Mr. Morris seems here, as if by prophecy, to refer to the Fugitive Slave Law, passed in 1850, by which any man, white or colored, may be carried off without a jury trial]. "In every stage of these oppressions (and those I have mentioned are but small), the people have petitioned for redress, in the most humble terms, and their repeated petitions have been answered only by repeated rejections." "A power," in this country, "whose character is thus marked by every act which may define a tyrant," is unfit to exist among a free people.

In the midst of these reflections, how cheering was your letter! It was indeed, "Good news from a far country." It was evidence, that not *all* Ohioans were willing to sell their birthrights for the products of the unrequited labor of the slave! No! my dear Sir, you have not said too much. Who is a greater tyrant than he, who seizes upon his fellow man, and not only wrests from him the profits of his labor, his wife and his children, but makes use of his very flesh, his sinews, and his bones, as articles of merchandize in a foreign market.

Shall we hesitate, in this matter? No! Whoever is on the side of freedom, of safety, of Union, of the Constitution, of humanity, of justice; in fact, whoever loves his country more than he loves negro slavery, let him come over to us. Resistance to slavery is our duty. It is both a political and religious duty; and the only question is, how shall we best discharge that duty? We must do it with much forbearance and suffering. *The moral power of truth will bring us off more than conquerors;*—if we are faithful to our Maker, our country, and ourselves; if we carry with us our opposition to slavery into all the *social circles of life; talk of it there as it is;* protect ourselves against its blighting influences in the discharge of our political duties; *remember it at the polls;* bestow our suffrages on no man, no matter what he is in other respects, who will treat with contempt the sovereignty of the States, to feed the monster slavery, which, like the grave, is never satisfied.

I have written to you as a man and a brother. I know not to what political party you belong, nor do I care. THAT PARTY IS MY PARTY, which *sustains* those inalienable rights upon which the very foundations of this Government are laid. I have endeavored to maintain those rights, through life, in every situation in which it has been the pleasure of my fellow citizens to place me. I shall not desert them now, for age has confirmed my belief in their truth. And I have consolation in this thought, more than in any other connected with my political life, that *my name*, humble as it is, *will be found among* those who have stood FAITHFUL in defense of the Constitutional liberty and equal rights of the free citizen; and in opposition to that cruel bondage under which the slave is now groaning.

Use no other weapons, then, in this holy warfare, but such as are spiritual, moral, and political, and which are in strict obedience to the laws of the country under which we live. I have written in terms which may be considered harsh: but I have not written with the least disrespect to men, as individuals, or legislators.

The great principles for which we are contending require from us energy, firmness and decision.

I am, with respect,

Yours, etc.,

THOMAS MORRIS.

A. H. Guthrie, Esq.

How patriotic, and, alas! how prophetic are the utterances of these letters. The successful aggressions of the slave power, since his voice rang for freedom in the Senate and through the hills of Ohio, are mournful fulfillments of his political predictions. The slave power still rules the Government. "*Judah still stoops down; he couches as a lion, and as an old lion: Who, or what, shall rouse him up?*"

CHAPTER XVI.

Creed of Parties—Their Tendencies and Results—Warning of Washington—Mr. Morris a Democrat from Principle—Catechised by the Democratic Legislature—His Answer—Rejected for a Second Term—Benjamin Tappan his Successor—Letter to the Ohio Statesman—Charles Hammond Read out of the Party—A Poem written after his Rejection and dedicated to Mr. Morris.

The rigid creed of political parties, allows no liberal latitude in the expression of opinion. If a public man does not hold the doctrines of the party, with a dovetail exactness, he is, in the technical language of the party, read out; is a rotten member, unworthy of party confidence. His private judgment and conscience are subsidized to the inflexible tactics of party machinery; so that he is not free to act, or to follow where conscience and duty would lead. The political creed, formed often by selfish, ambitious politicians, is *fixed*, and no man can be a loyal member of the party, unless he adopts and carries out, in every particular, its doctrines. If he does not, he forfeits his party standing, and suffers disfranchisement from all political favors. Under this anti-democratic rule, politicians, and public men in office, have, against the convictions of their conscience and deliberate judgment, voted for public measures, because they were the measures of the party.

The dangers and evils of this political despotism are manifold. It is subversive of true manhood and independence. It substitutes a partisan spirit for national patriotism. It is a political inquisition, that tortures men to affect to believe what they can not. It enthrones the power of party, above conscience, truth, and patriotism, and thus tends to the demoralization of the national heart. It disintegrates politics and political creeds from moral principles; and so subverts the strongest pillars of national prosperity and safety. It encourages corruption in public men, and creates a class of politicians, who live for party purposes, and labor only to reap the spoils of office. It is a virtual interdiction of freedom of thought, allowing no generous expansion of views, no act, except it is in exact conformity with party.

It was in view of such results of parties, that Washington, in his Farewell Address to his countrymen, declared:

"The common and continual mischiefs of the spirit of party, are sufficient to make it the duty and interest of a wise people to discourage and restrain it. Their being constant danger of *excess*, the effort ought to be, by force of public opinion, to mitigate and assuage it. A fire not to be quenched, it demands a uniform vigilance to prevent its bursting into a flame, lest instead of warming it should consume."

It is a hopeful and healthy indication, now in its incipient stage of development, among the people of the United States, that political Platforms made by politicians, have lost the confidence of the American people. A new political and moral Millenium, will be inaugurated under such a dispensation.

Senator Morris was a Democrat, not because it was the synonym and watchward of a party, but because it was the representative of doctrines, that were free, universal, beneficent, and equal in their operations on all men; and if carried out, in their true intent, would enfranchise the world, and bestow on every man, the boon of personal liberty and all civil and natural rights. Hence, he was constitutionally incapable of working in the traces of a modern party. Indeed he thought party organizations frequently detrimental to the success of principles. "I follow party," said he, "where the *Constitution* and *prin-*

ciples lead." And it was his unfaltering fidelity to true Democratic principles, that secured his banishment from the Democratic party.

The year subsequent to his retirement from the Senate of the United States, he was a delegate from Hamilton County to the Democratic Convention, which assembled at Columbus, Ohio, on the 8th of January, 1840. That Convention passed strong resolutions against any political movement or agitation, connected with slavery, and declared that no sound Democrat would have part or lot with it."

Mr. Morris, faithful to the great principles of Democracy, attempted to speak, in defense of the repudiated principles. He was *permitted*, as an act of grace, to go on a short time, and then coughed down, and silenced by a Democratic Convention, which, in their address to the people of the State, reckoned it one of the chief glories of Jefferson's administration that "the freedom of speech and of the press were restored to the people."

After Mr. Morris had been silenced, a member rose (Mr. Sawyer) and declared—"That the Democratic party had no affinity with Abolitionists; and that he considered the gentleman from Hamilton (Mr. Morris) *as a rotten branch that should be lopped off*." This was received with loud shouts of—"Agreed!" "Agreed!" "Let him go!" "Turn him out of the party, and all other Abolitionists with him!"

Previous to the defeat of Mr. Morris, for a second term, to the Senate of the United States, the Democratic Committee of the Legislature of Ohio, sent him the Democratic Creed, for his approval.

To that communication he sent the following answer:

WASHINGTON, December 11th, 1838.

GENTLEMEN—I received yours of the 7th instant, this morning, and I reply thereto as soon as possible. You inform me that, having been selected by the Democratic members of the Legislature of Ohio, as a committee to interrogate the several persons named for United States Senator, you request my answer to the following interrogatories:

1. Are you in favor of an Independent Treasury Bill?

My answer is, that I view the independence of the Treasury as essentially necessary to the independence of the country itself. I am, therefore, in favor of an Independent Treasury, free from all local and private influence.

2. Are you a supporter of the leading measures of the present Administration?

I answer—I shall give my support to the Administration, in whatever situation I may be placed, in its opposition to a Bank of the United States; in its views with regard to the safe-keeping of the public money, and the disbursment thereof; the rights of the States, and the limitations of the powers of Congress. I say, further, that I know of no recommendation made by the present incumbent of the Presidential chair, of a general character, in which I do not concur. I am, therefore, in favor of the leading measures of the present Administration.

3. Are you for or against modern Abolitionism?

I am opposed to slavery in all its forms; and against its further extension in our country; believing it to be wrong in itself, and injurious to the best interests of the people, I view it as a creature of State law only, and that Congress have no power over it, as it exists in the States; neither have Congress the power to create a system of slavery where it does not exist, or to give it new and additional security. I believe that, if the citizens of a free State, when within the jurisdiction of a slave State, violate the slave laws of such a State, they are as justly punishable for such acts as they would be for the violation of the laws of such State in any other particular. I hold that the citizens in each and every State, have an indisputable right *to speak, write, or print, on the subject of slavery, as on any other subject;* always liable to the laws of the State where the act is done, for the abuse of that liberty. The right of petition to the Legislature for a redress of grievances, I hold to be inviolate on all subjects, and above the power of law.

I believe also, however much we feel opposed to slavery, and however wicked and unjust we may believe the system, we are still, under our Government, bound to protect the slaveholder in his slave property, by aiding in the suppression of servile insurrection, or war. I believe it to be the *duty of the States as well as their interest, to abolish slavery where it exists*, but that no other State would be justifiable in interfering for that purpose.

I also believe the African race, born in our country, or brought into it against their will, ought to be protected in, and enjoy their natural rights; but I do not believe it would be good policy, or promote the safety of the country, the happiness of ourselves, or the Negro race, to admit them to the enjoyment of equal political or social privileges. I believe that the moral power of truth and reason, ought alone to be employed on behalf of the slaves; and that every citizen has the right to exercise this power, which, if rightfully used, will be sufficient for the downfall of slavery; and that, in all our intercourse with the colored race, we ought, constantly, to give them to understand, that we will not aid, but suppress, any attempt that may be made for their liberation in any other way.

I have thought it best to answer your third interrogatory, as I have done, because a direct answer might be liable to misconception or misunderstanding. As to what modern Abolitionism is; as it is *represented by many*, I believe it entirely wrong, but whether the representation be correct or not, I do not pretend to say. My opinions on this question have been often, both in public and private, heretofore expressed; but I have answered you, briefly, as it seemed to me I ought, in the same manner as if the subject was altogether a new one. I trust you will be able fully to comprehend my views, from what I have said.

"4. Are you willing to submit to the selection made by your political friends?"

I am always willing to sustain my political friends in their selection of men for the purpose of sustaining public measures. Without this unity, every measure, however valuable, would be liable to fail.

I have thus, Gentlemen, answered you briefly, and in much haste; and whatever course you may pursue, I hope it may prove satisfactory to our friends, and tend to promote the best interests of the country.

I am, with respect,
Your obedient Servant
THOMAS MORRIS.

MESSRS. T. J. BUCHANAN, JOHN BROUGH,
AND DAVID TOD, *Committee, etc.*

Mr. Morris was succeeded as Senator, by Hon. Benjamin Tappan, with whom he had acted as a politician, and a legislator, in the early history of Ohio. They were personal and political friends. Both were prominent members of the Democratic party, and active in the Legislation of Ohio. Mr. Tappan was elected for his *avowed* discountenance and opposition to anti-slavery doctrines; and Mr. Morris rejected for favoring and advocating them. During a series of years, which had ripened into mutual friendship, their sentiments, not only on the general principles of politics, but *especially* on the subject of American slavery, were in harmony. Mr. Tappan belonged to a distinguished anti-slavery family, who were among the pioneers of the anti-slavery enterprise; and who suffered persecution for the cause. *Arthur Tappan*, who was mobbed in New York, in 1832, and for whose head the

South offered a reward of ten thousand dollars; and Lewis Tappan, who has been connected officially with the anti-slavery cause from the beginning almost, were brothers of Benjamin Tappan.

Charles Hammond, the veteran editor of the Cincinnati Gazette, said of Mr. Tappan, when elected Senator: "I have known him nearly forty years. Not Arthur Tappan, nor Lewis Tappan have either ever evinced a more settled scorn for the slaveholder's pretensions, *on the whole subject of slavery*, than Benjamin Tappan has manifested in his whole life and conduct, until a surrender of opinion has been made a party test. If he has surrendered, it is but another instance of the debasing power of party drill. But Benjamin Tappan is anti-slavery, and his whole soul is as strong as that of John Quincy Adams against the assumptions of the slaveholder. He distinguished himself in his profession, in Jefferson County, for a succession of years, in maintaining the rights of the Negro."

Mr. Tappan signalized his first effort in Congress, by refusing to present to the Senate, petitions, on the subject of slavery, from his own constituents.

He said, that "slavery and the slave trade, in the District of Columbia, were no grievances to the people of Ohio, and that for myself, I can not recognize the right of my fair country-women to meddle in public affairs."

On the 21st of December, 1838, Mr. Tappan was elected Senator from Ohio. When the result of the election reached Mr. Morris, he wrote to the Editors of the Ohio *Statesman*, then and now, the organ of the Democratic party, at the capitol of the State, the following letter:

WASHINGTON, December 26, 1838.

Messrs. Medary, and Brothers—I received your paper of the 21st, in the afternoon of the 24th, in which is stated the result of the election of Senator in Congress, by the Legislature of the State. There is also in the same paper, some remarks of yours, which, I believe, require from me a justification of my official conduct here. I would have immediately written to you, but it was the Eve of Christmas, and the time and place, seemed rather unfavorable.

There was not a man among all the contending candidates, whom I would prefer before Judge Tappan; and I should rejoice at his election, did I not understand from your remarks, and from other information, derived from a source in which I have full confidence, that this election is to be considered a rebuke, for the course I have, as Senator, taken here; and the opinions, I have, as a private citizen, expressed on the subject of Abolition. I hope this may not be the case, but as facts now stand before the country, I should feel myself recreant to the Constitution, to the people, and to myself, did I not, on this occasion, re-assert the principles on which I have constantly acted.

I have known my worthy successor for many years. We, I think, have constantly and uniformly agreed on political subjects; and on the subject of slavery, my memory is, that he was a more strenuous opposer of that system than myself. I am fortified in this position, because I well remember that his opposition to slavery, was an objection urged against him when he was a candidate for District Judge of our State. What his opinions now are on this subject, I am unable to say, but would be much pleased to learn.

You say: "That a great number of Democratic visitors, with the members of the Legislature, met Judge Tappan in the large Hall of the American Hotel; that the Judge, in reply to the complimentary toast, to the Senator elect, replied in a neat and most satisfactory manner. He dwelt with effect upon the slanders that had been put into circulation in regard to his being an Abolitionist, and was responded to with the most thrilling acclamations, and (as I understood you) his views on this subject, as well as upon others, correspond entirely with the present Administration, and the present majority in Congress."

It has, perhaps, been my misfortune to love and respect the Constitution of my country, and the rights of the people under it, more than an *Administration* or a *majority*. Placed in this situation, and under the ban of a MAJORITY, I respectfully ask the Legislature to recall me, if I have, in any act or vote here, done that which they deem injurious to the best interests of the country. The shortness of the remaining time of my service, I consider no objection or excuse for the Legislature; as in a case like the present, the man and the time are nothing, the example everything. I would follow the example set me by members of the House of Representatives from our own State, if I had satisfactory evidence, clear to my mind, that the Constitutional Body, the Legislature of State, disavowed my principles and doctrines.

In order that I may stand correctly before the country, I will state, as succinctly as I can, my actions and opinions as a Senator in Congress, and even some of the private opinions I entertain as a citizen; and hope the General Assembly if they think them incorrect, will promptly disavow them, and instruct me to act otherwise, even during the present session. The question is considered by all as one of vast importance. It is one on which the country requires their action; though an individual might very properly complain of injustice if stricken down without a hearing. I will briefly state some votes I have given here, on the different propositions connected with the slavery question, for the consideration of the Legislature and the people of the State, in order to give a full understanding of the subject.

President Jackson, in his Message to the first session of the 24th Congress, invited the attention of Congress "to the painful excitement produced in the South, by attempts to circulate, through the mail, inflammatory appeals addressed to the slaves." After speaking in strong terms against such proceeding, he seems to remind the State authorities that to them properly belongs this part of the subject. He further says: "I would, therefore, call the attention of Congress to the subject, and especially suggest the propriety of passing such a law as will prohibit, under severe penalties, the circulation, in the Southern States, of incendiary publications, intended to instigate the slave to insurrection."

To this recommendation of the President I strongly objected at the time; a Bill, however, was brought in, in pursuance of the recommendation. It progressed as it is usual, until Mr. Calhoun proposed certain amendments, which were rejected by an even vote. When the question was taken on the engrossment, and the vote stood 18 to 18, the Vice President, (Mr. Van Buren,) voted for the engrossment; both the Senators from New York were on the same side. On the third reading of the Bill the vote stood 19 for the Bill, 25 against it. In every stage of this anti-Abolition Bill, I opposed it. To preserve the correspondence of individuals from inspection, and the right of the people to use the Post Office Department, and the system from being broken down under the slaveholding power, was my most ardent wish. We succeeded after a long struggle; the slaveholding interest not then being organized and banded together, as it afterward was and now is. This I think ought to be considered my first Abolition sin. I *ask no forgiveness*, but hope the Legislature will disavow the act, if they think I erred.

The next prominent question on this subject, was, the presentation of petitions praying for the abolition of slavery in the District of Columbia. I presented these petitions, and advocated their reference to a committee, to consider the subject. I am willing to admit, that they were the petitions of actual Abolitionists. Petitions of this kind I have now in my possession, and I feel it my duty to present them, and move for the action of the Senate on the same. I respectfully ask the Legislature to instruct me on this point, as I do not wish to misrepresent the State a single moment. If the Legislature are of the opinion that the petitions of Abolitionists, praying for the abolition of slavery in the District of Columbia, ought not to be presented to Congress; or when presented, that the right of petition is not abridged, by a member objecting to their reception, and laying the motion on the table, without deciding whether the petition shall be received or not, is a correct and Constitutional proceeding—it is a very easy matter so to inform me. My course of duty will then be plain.

Mr. Calhoun's resolutions were the next great Anti-Abolition movements. They speak for themselves. I voted against them all, as I think, without an examination of the vote, as it may appear on the Journal. The resolutions can be approved, and my course censured, if it be necessary as a peace-offering to sustain slavery. The counter-resolutions I offered are before the public. I, soon after their introduction, abandoned the idea of asking for them a separate vote, as those offered by Mr. Calhoun brought the whole subject into debate. There is one specific proposition, however, which I submitted, which is in the following words, and to which I would ask particular attention. It is:

"And the privilege of the people to speak, write, print, and publish their opinions, on any subject whatever, whether the same concern the political, moral, or religious institutions of any State, or on the nature and condition of man, as born equally free and independent, is indisputable; and those exercising that privilege are responsible for the abuse of this liberty to the State alone, in which such writing, speaking, printing, or publishing actually takes place." In favor of this proposition there were 9 votes against 32.

I pronounce this solemn denial of the truth of this proposition I submitted, one of the most extraordinary votes ever given in Congress. (You will pardon me for speaking against *majorities.*) *Thirty-two* members of the Senate have, by this vote, asserted that the converse of the propostion is true, that the people have no such rights as are there enumerated, and that the people may be individually responsible for acts done in one State to the laws of another State. The practical effect of this vote, Mr. Mahan, of Brown county, has felt; but even the court of a slaveholding State could not be made to swallow this monstrous doctrine. My colleague, Mr. Allen, voted against this proposition, and on this question he and I differed widely.

You seem to think that no State in the Union will HAVE abler and warmer supporters of the President and his measures (not of the Constitution and rights of the people, but of the PRESIDENT and his MEASURES), in both branches of the NEXT Congress, than the Buckeye State. Do the Democratic members of the Legislature deny the truths of the propositions I submitted? It seems to me they *do;* for I have been condemned as the friend of Abolitionism, without one redeeming quality. In perfect respect to the Body, may I hope they will instruct or reprove me on this point also.

I could enlarge on the subject, but I fear I have already been tedious. I have not set down one word in bitterness, but with the most entire respect to the Legislature of my State, who have thought my opinions, as expressed on the subject of slavery, of sufficient importance to ostracise me. This is in exact accordance with the demands of the slaveholder—"You *shall not* express an opinion against our slavery institutions; if you do, we will revenge our injuries," say the slaveholders. Do the Democracy of Ohio respond to this sentiment, and say—"We want no one to belong to our ranks who speaks against slavery; that will make Southern gentlemen very wrathy?" I drop the subject. I grow sick at the reflection; I hope it all may be fancy, but I fear its reality.

I have never, to my recollection, brought forward or urged a single proposition, in favor of the down-trodden and suffering slave. My only apology, before God, and my country, is, that I have as yet discovered no ray of hope for him, until public opinion shall become more united and vigorous in his behalf. In order to keep his fetters secure, the freedom of speech and debate on his behalf is stricken down, and now lies dead in the Halls of Congress. But I rejoice to know, that, when individual rights have been broken down, and trodden upon in Congress, they have found support in the State Legislatures; and when liberty has been strangled there, she has been resuscitated by the people, and bestowed upon all as a common birthright.

To preserve the Constitutional rights of man has been my constant object. There is, perhaps, no instance to be found, in which the first advocates of liberty in any country, were not few in number, and a persecuted class by those, who in power, were gaining by the oppression of others. *They have been branded with every odious epithet*, and charged with seeking to destroy the peace, and happiness of the country. The promulgation of their opinions has been prohibited, because power, unrighteously exercised, always seeks to carry on its operations secretly, darkly, and without examination by others.

Do not suppose I regret the loss of power; I would not wish to exercise it against the opinions of my State; nor would I wish its possession for a moment, if I should feel constrained to use it to depress or destroy human liberty. I *feel devoutly thankful to my Maker, and deeply grateful to my State, for the situation I occupy, where my humble name, appears upon the highest records of my country, in opposition to slavery, and among the friends of the poor, trodden down, and broken-hearted slave. I have no wish to occupy any situation, in which all the powers of my mind, may not be fully exercised in this high, and permit me to say, holy duty, always subject to the laws of the country in which I may be.*

And when the hand of time shall point to the last hour of my existence; I trust that my fervent prayer may be, that the Almighty, in his good time, will deliver the Negro race, from that cruel slavery under which they are now groaning; and that the liberties and happiness of my country may be perpetual. That this will be accomplished in good time there can be but little doubt; and that an overruling Providence, will so order the affairs of our land, that this event may take place without disturbing the peace of our people, I trust is the ardent desire of every citizen, who is attached to the true principles upon which our Government rests.

I am, with respect, yours, etc.,

THOMAS MORRIS.

N. B. When I commenced this letter, I intended it for your private inspection only, but my mind changed as I progressed, and I leave it to you to publish, if you think proper.

Every rising sun confirms me in the truth of the opinions I entertain on this subject. The power of slavery here is *tremendous — its march is onward.* It avows the bold determination, that by the Constitution of the United States, MEN ARE PROPERTY; and that every citizen has the right to use his property in each and every State in the Union; therefore, slavery, at the will of the slaveholder, may exist in all the States. Constitutions and laws of States are mere cobwebs, when they come in contact with this claim to make men property. Even this cant phrase, Negro property, is used by many of our own citizens in Ohio. There can be no doubt but, he who seems to dwell with pleasure on this idea, would feel much pleasure also, in aiding to establish slavery among us, with all its withering influences. I ask the vigilant and solemn attention of our citizens to this point.

"This letter," said Dr. Bailey, "must exalt the character of Thomas Morris, in the estimation of every one, whose opinions are of any value. It is his praise, rare praise for a politician, that he loves his country and the Constitution, better than his party or its measures. Few except those, whose generous feelings have been destroyed by pro-slavery rancor or party bigotry, will deny to Thomas Morris the credit of being an able, honest, independent, a consistent and high-minded patriot." After his defeat, it was proclaimed through the country, that Thomas Morris was a martyr to his principles. He is laid on the altar of Slavery as a peace offering to the South. Slaveholders commanded, and the party obeyed. He will rejoice in being counted worthy to suffer for the *truth*.

After his defeat, the following Poem was published and dedicated—

"To the Hon. Thomas Morris.

The heart and lip are dumb!
And the Southern taunt is tamely met
Our kneeling day is come!
Freedom's bright Star hath set!
The recreant West hath kneeled
To the footstool of the South;
And the voice of her own free son is sealed,
The gag is in *her* mouth.

And what hast *thou* done, that they
  Should frown upon thee now;
And what is the crime they thus repay,
  With a dark and clouded brow?
While our country's banner's wave,
  In pride and pomp, on high,
Thou hast lent an ear to the dying slave,
  In his bitter agony.

Thou hadst eyes, and could not be blind
  To his hot and bitter tears;
Nor deaf to the shrieks that load the wind
  Nor cold to the mother's fears.
Thy lip *could not* be dumb
  To plead for the down-trodden poor,
Though the stern rebuke should harshly come
  From the sons of the high and the pure.

Thou art one of the few who art better
  Than those they represent;
Who rise to break the bondman's fetter,
  Ere Mercy's day be spent;
Who cherish the golden words
  That are from oblivion won,
Undying gems that flash from the lips
  Of the glorious Jefferson.

There are some whose nerves are strong,
  Who can see the slave all gory,
And scarred with the mark of the driver's thong,
  Yet talk of their country's glory!
Who can smite on the bowed with years
  As he perisheth in the sun;
And coldly look on the orphan's tears
  As she prays her life were done.

Thank God *there are* hearts that feel
  For the out-cast bleeding poor;
Thank God, there are *men* who will not kneel
  And laud the evil-doer.
And *thou* art one of those,
  Who as they feel dare speak;
Who can not spurn the bondman's woes,
  Or spurn the poor and weak.

And thou the wise and good,
  We oft will pray for thee;
Thou hast done as thy country's freemen should,
  While battling for her free.
Thou hast our warmest love—
  Thou hast our freshest tears;
And shalt have, while the bright stars shine
  Down to our latest years!

Farewell! farewell!! Unknown
  Though the minstrel is to thee,
He hath tuned his harp to an humble tone
  For the Champion of the free.
And in its dying cadence-moans—
  "May sorrow find thee never;
And love and truth, with their kindest tones,
  Be with thee, now and ever."

CHAPTER XVII.

Erection of Pennsylvania Hall in Philadelphia — Distinguished Politicians and Divines invited to its Dedication — Its destruction by a mob — The Continental State House — Its Bell — Its Bible Motto — Mr. Morris invited to the Dedication — His Answer — Its just and noble sentiments.

On the 18th of May, 1838, the friends of free discussion, in Philadelphia, completed a large and beautiful hall, and with imposing ceremonies, dedicated it to Truth and Freedom, and Free discussion. It was stipulated by those who erected it that "it is not to be used for Anti-slavery purposes alone, but for any purpose not of an immoral character." It was a Temple open for free discussion on all subjects relating to the progress of society, and the elevation and freedom of all men.

It bore the title of "Pennsylvania Hall." Ionic columns graced its interior, and on these rested a beautiful arch, on which was engraven, the motto of the Commonwealth of Pennsylvania,

Virtue, Liberty, and Independence.

Distinguished men from all parties in politics, and from various sects in religion, were invited to be present at its dedication. A host of the sons of freedom were present, and very many, wrote letters of congratulation and sympathy.

John Quincy Adams, in response to a letter of invitation, wrote from his seat in Congress: "The right of discussion upon slavery and an indefinite extent of topics connected with it, banished from one half of the States of this Union. It is *suspended* in both Houses of Congress,—opened and closed at the pleasure of the slave representation; opened for the promulgation of nullification sophistry; closed against the question, WHAT IS SLAVERY? at the sound of which the walls of the Capitol staggered like a drunken man."

"For this suppression of the freedom of speech, of the freedom of the press, and of the right of petition, the people of the FREE States of this Union, (by which I mean the people of the non-slaveholding States,) are responsible, and the people of Pennsylvania most of all." "I rejoice that in the city of Philadelphia, the friends of free discussion, have erected a Hall for its unrestrained exercise. My fervent wishes are, that Pennsylvania Hall may fulfill its destination, by demonstrative proof, that freedom of speech in the city of Penn shall no longer be an abstraction."

Distinguished Ministers, also, rejoiced in so auspicious an event. Rev. Nathan S. Beman, D. D., of Troy, New York, a man of great pulpit talents and celebrity, in the New-School, Presbyterian Church, wrote to the committee on this wise: "I felt honored in your choice, and my feelings were deeply enlisted. My own heart is with you. We can not forbear to express our abhorrence of *chains* and stripes; and should we do it, *the very stones would cry out.* I rejoice that there is a spirit still in existence, that will not bow to the altar of *slavery*, nor tamely submit to the dictation of those, who declare in high places, that it is a wise and holy institution, and that it shall be perpetual. What a contest is this to be waged in a land of Republicanism, and a land of Christianity! But if the charter of these two systems—the Declaration of Independence and the Bible, are permitted to speak, now, certain is it that *the rights of man will be triumphant.*"

David Paul Brown, a distinguished lawyer of Philadelphia; and Alvan Steuart, a noble hearted philanthropist of New York; and other distinguished and patriotic men, were present, and made eloquent orations at its dedication.

The day of its dedication was but a speedy prelude to its destruction. The festive and the funeral song almost mingled in union. Three days a Temple dedicated to freedom was permitted to stand, in a city founded by William Penn, and in a country whose civil Constitutions proclaim freedom of speech as one of the cardinal doctrines of the Government, one of the inalienable rights of man. On the 17th of May, 1838, a mob countenanced by men of intelligence and by the municipal authorities of Philadelphia, put the torch to the noble temple, and in a few hours it stood a sacrificial monument to incendiarism and slavery.

"That Temple now in ruin lies;
The fire-stain's on its shattered wall,
And open to the changing skies
Its black and roofless hall.
It stands before a nation's sight,
A grave-stone over buried right!

"But from that ruin, as of old,
The fire-scorched stones themselves are crying,
And from their ashes, white and cold,
Its timbers are replying!
A voice which slavery can not kill,
Speaks from the crumbling arches still!"
WHITTIER.

The old State-House, redolent with Revolutionary inspirations, and forever sacred to freedom — where the the patriots and statesmen of 1776 counseled and prayed, and pledged their "lives, their fortunes, and their sacred honor," to the cause of freedom and of human rights — stood, and yet stands, in the city of Philadelphia. On that old State-House hangs a Bell, imported from England in

Colonial times; and on it, is engraven this inspired and prophetic motto of Freedom:

"Proclaim Liberty throughout the land unto all the inhabitants thereof."

When the torch of the incendiary was put to that Temple of Freedom, that old Bell which had, in the dark days of the Revolution called patriots together, should have sent forth its peals of warning to those enemies of freedom and their country.

Thomas Morris, defending the true principles of the Government and of liberty in the Senate of the United States, being invited to aid in the Dedication, wrote from his seat the following letters:

WASHINGTON, January 30, 1838.

FRIENDS—I received on yesterday, your esteemed favor of the 26th instant; and I congratulate you and the country, that in your city a Hall has been erected sacred to liberty and free discussion. Born in Pennsylvania, but at a very early age removed into the Western Country, I was a citizen of Ohio, at the adoption of her Constitution, and during the greater part of the last thirty years, have borne an humble part in the Legislative Assembly of my own State, where by my best efforts, I have constantly endeavored to maintain and establish those great principles, in support of which your society is now engaged. I feel unable to express my heartfelt emotions, on receiving your invitation to be present at the opening of the Hall in the emporium of my native State, a city renowned for its philanthropy and benevolence, and now affording new evidence of those inestimable virtues, by the erection of a hall, in which liberty and equality of civil rights can be FREELY discussed, and the evils of slavery fearlessly portrayed. While the spirit of slavery is grasping at the power of our country, threatening a disunion of the States unless free discussion concerning it be destroyed, and even in the free States marking its progress in scenes of blood; it is a cause for joy and congratulation that Pennsylvania — that PHILADELPHIA is about to consecrate one spot, at least, where its evils may be fearlessly portrayed. Slavery is a spirit which hates the light, because its deeds are evil, and to banish it entirely from our country, free discussion alone is amply sufficient. I rejoice in the awakening energies of the country, and in receiving almost daily assurance that my fellow citizens are determined to maintain those inalienable rights, without which they would be in a situation little in advance of the African slave himself.

I will, if life and health permit, endeavor to be present at the opening of your Hall, but I would gladly dispense with the delivery of an address on that occasion, could I do so consistent with your wishes, as I can not suppose myself capable of adding any information to that mass which is already before the public, on this interesting topic; but whatever feeble service I can render to the great and good cause in which you are engaged, will be cheerfully offered.

You will, for yourselves, and those whom you represent, accept the assurance of my highest regard.

THOMAS MORRIS.

MESSRS. SAMUEL WEBB, J. M. TRUMAN,
AND WM. M'KEE, *Committee.*

The following letter from Thomas Morris was also received by the Committee:

WASHINGTON, May 11, 1838.

GENTLEMEN: — I have seen in the *Pennsylvania Freeman* of the 3d inst., with sensations of the deepest gratitude, the favorable notice you have been pleased to take of my name, in your general invitation to the public to attend the opening of the Pennsylvania Hall on the 14th of the present month, which Hall, I understand, is dedicated to free discussion.

It would afford me the highest pleasure to be present and join you in this work of universal charity and love, could I feel that my public duties as well as my health would justify it — domestic concerns having lately called me to Ohio; I have but just resumed my seat here; it seems proper, therefore, that I should not willingly, at this time, absent myself from the Senate.

Your Hall, as I have said, is to be dedicated to free discussion. What a train of solemn reflections does the very thought create in the mind. Is it possible, that in the free State of Pennsylvania, in the quiet and orderly city of Philadelphia, (a city not inaptly called the city of "brotherly love,") that in all places, and all times, *free* discussion on all questions connected with the religion, morality, the welfare of the country, or the rights of man, can not be had with safety to the citizen, and the peace and quiet of the community? I presume this *can not* be the case in your city, and was not the great moving cause that induced your humane, philanthropic, and patriotic citizens to erect the Hall which they are about to open.

If, however, Pennsylvania is safe, if Philadelphia is secure from all attempts to put down the right of free discussion, the liberty of speech, and the press, your fellow citizens have seen and felt that all parts of our beloved country is not thus highly favored. It is gratifying, indeed, that while the enemy of human rights and Constitutional liberty, is, in our country, making rapid advances to power, endeavoring as far as in him lies, not to silence discussion, but even to muzzle the press itself, knowing that his principles can not stand the test of examination, Philadelphia has the honor to erect a barrier which he can not pass, and a battery which he can not silence, but which will effectually destroy his whole power, by the consecration of a spot where all his pretensions may be fully and fairly discussed.

This act of your citizens I regard not as a local act merely. It is not for Philadelphia alone to receive its benefits, but the whole country — the whole world. Its objects are universal and impartial justice to all men in every condition, to establish each in his own inherent, individual, and inalienable rights, to give warning of approaching danger, and stay the rod of the oppressor; and as such, we claim for the day of consecration a bright page in the history of our country.

Every philanthropist, every moralist must mourn and deplore the riots, burnings, and murders, that of late have taken place in our country. Your own recollections will be sufficient to place before your mind scenes of the most outrageous atrocity. How often has tidings of the destruction of the press, because it has spoken fearlessly in defense of human rights, tingled in your ears! Have you not heard that free born AMERICAN CITIZENS have been, by a lawless mob, subjected to the infamous torture of the WHIP? Has not the weapon of the assassin laid its victim bleeding at his feet, for no crime, for no act but that which you intend to practice in the Hall you have erected — the exercise of the right of FREE DISCUSSION? While I rejoice that your citizens are embodying themselves to march forward to the rescue, I mourn for my country that this same fell spirit which has urged mobs, not only of the "baser sort," but of citizens who claim to be respectable, to deeds of violence and blood, has found its way in some degree into the councils and the official stations of the country, into the bosom of society, and I much fear into the very PULPIT itself, thus rendering insecure all that is dear and sacred to man.

I would willingly draw a veil over the proceedings of that body, of which I have the honor to be a member, in regard to the important right of *free discussion*, if the deep sense of the obligations of duty which I feel to you and the country, would permit me to do so. This same spirit, which you are about so nobly to rebuke, has been able, in the very halls of Congress, to silence debate at its pleasure. It has been able to strike its deadly fangs into the most vital part of American liberty. It has denied the right of petition, in all its essential qualities, to a large portion of our fellow citizens, on a subject they deemed worthy of their highest consideration, and materially affecting the honor and interest of our country. If it were possible, I would that I could persuade myself not to believe this; but while the records of our country bear witness to the fact, it can not be. I fervently pray that the tear of some recording angel may yet be dropped upon the words of shame and dishonor, and blot them out forever.

If the supreme Legislature of the country can rightfully, in any one possible instance, refuse to receive, hear, and act upon petitions sent by *any portion of the human race* who are subject to our laws, or owe allegiance to our Government, I can see no safe guaranty for this high privilege in any case whatever, when it shall come in contact with power, interest, or influence. For if an individual right which was deemed of a character too sacred to be regulated or controlled by the people themselves, by their highest fundamental law, (the Constitution,) and placed by that instrument above the power of Congress to ABRIDGE—can be withheld or restrained by that body, it is hard to discover what political or natural right you, or I, or any other citizen, can calculate upon as secure. If the right of petition fail us, will it not prove that the whole fabric of the Constitution is rotten and not worth our care; its preservation in such case for any valuable purpose might well be considered doubtful.

It is not only the right of petition that has been abridged. *The freedom of debate has been stricken down, and lies dead in the halls of Congress.* We are compelled to submit not only to a rule which imposes silence on a question to lay a motion or proposition on the table, and which a majority can always use to put an end to discussion disagreeable to them, however important it may be to others; but the country now mourns the loss of one of her most talented sons, whose life, it is believed, was sacrificed for the exercise of the right of free discussion in the very hall of Congress itself. It would be some consolation if, in the midst of this war upon individual rights, this want of personal security, this waste of political privileges in the chambers of legislation, the judiciary of the country remained firm and uncontaminated. But here we have also to deplore, that the incendiary with the torch in his hand, scarcely extinguished, with which he had attempted to fire his neighbor's dwelling, because of that neighbor's exercise of his unquestionable right in the free expression of his opinion; and the mobocrat who has attempted to silence the press by its destruction, together with the assassin whose red hands are yet dripping with the blood of his innocent victim, find not only protection but favor; and this new code of morals which would impose restraint upon the expression of our thoughts, because the truth may affect some pecuniary interest, or expose some wicked practice, teaches the doctrine that a printing press may be broken up, a man's house may be burnt, and the owner slain by violence, and yet no one be GUILTY! It has been said, and I think truly, that the verdicts of juries give the character of the country. What, then, will be the character of our country before an impartial world, if juries shall continue to lend themselves to this same spirit of misrule, and violence, and blood?

But if we withdraw our view from the constituted authorities of the land, from men in official stations, and extend it over the country at large, what do we behold? The Bowie-knife and the pistol substituted for reason and argument, usurping the power of the laws, or setting them at defiance,—the actors professing to draw the example from high places of power, and justifying themselves by the actions of men who claim to be among our most respectable citizens. It is against the freedom of speech, the right of free discussion, that these ruffians in society wage their fiercest war.

I am aware that it may be thought that I have written hard things against my fellow citizens; but do not the facts that exist justify me? And should I not be faithless, indeed, and recreant to all my principles, if, when writing to you on the important event which you are about to celebrate, I should either fail or fear to express my thoughts fully and freely? If I did not do so, I might well be considered a mocker of the institutions I profess to honor. The picture I have presented, I know is one not calculated to flatter our vanity; but it is no fancy sketch—it has all the painful vividness of reality.

We should ponder on the signs of the times with serious deliberation. We have been and are still a prosperous and favored people; but I fear that in the eyes of Him in whose hands are our destinies, and who can search the heart, we are viewed as a proud and sinful nation. And if his chastisements have not already commenced, our wickedness, without repentance, must call them down at last.

To understand our errors, and know the evil that besets us, is the first step toward reformation. To examine into, and ascertain the causes which have produced those evils, is necessary to their radical cure. This examination I shall now attempt. There is implanted in our very nature a love of power and dominion, no doubt for wise and beneficial purposes; but dominion, in the creation of man, was only given him over "the fish of the sea, the fowl of the air, the cattle, and every creeping thing that creepeth upon the face of the earth." It was never intended by the Creator that man should have dominion over his fellow-man, but by his full and free consent. Had this been intended, it would have been given when the boundaries of man's dominion were fixed and established. The exercise, then, of all power which subjects man to involuntary servitude, and to a dominion to which he has not given his full and free consent, is a violation of the laws of heaven, and contrary to the very nature of man, who, though formed for dominion and imbued with its love, yet has authority from his Maker to exercise it only over inanimate matter, and over creatures not made in the bright image of God!

But when man became wicked and corrupt, he began to usurp dominion over his fellow-man, reducing the weaker and less guarded portions of the race to the condition of the cattle of the field. This, however, could not totally destroy the principle of reason within the immortal creature thus degraded; he knew still that he was entitled to the same rights as his fellow-man, and that his condition was the effect of gross injustice and grinding oppression. This produced the constant strife between the oppressed and oppressor, the fruitful source of violence and crime through all time, and created the desire and stimulated the action of those in power to prevent, as far as possible, all examination into the rights of man as established by his Creator.

The exercise of dominion begat the love of ease and opulence. This could more readily be obtained by appropriating to his own use the labor of others without any just compensation therefor. Thus the love of money, the root of all evil, grew and expanded. In our own time and day, those principles which our father's intended to subdue and eradicate, if possible, in the formation of a Constitution founded upon the natural and inalienable rights of man, have sprouted afresh, with a luxuriance which is calculated to fill the mind of the just and good with deep and solemn reflection.

I have heard it stated by a sagacious statesman of our own country, that it was one of the unchanged and unchangeable laws of Providence, that one man should live upon the labor of another, that this always had and always would be the case, and *that American slavery, as it existed in the Southern States, was the best human modification of that unalterable decree.* This was the language of a Southern gentleman, from a slaveholding State. The practical operation of this despotic system, of man as an individual usurping dominion over man, and endeavoring to live upon the labor of others, began in our country with the slaveholders, and its ramifications are now seen and felt in all parts of our country. The desire to live upon the unrequited labor of others, is acquiring a dreadful universality. It is the slaveholding power,—this Goliath of all monopolies,—that now brandishes his spear and threatens the overthrow of our most essential rights, and the most sacred of all our privileges. It defies even the Constitution itself, to engage in single combat. It claims to be before and superior to that instrument, which it contends has acknowledged its superiority, and has guaranteed its existence and perpetual duration. It imperiously asserts that it has converted men into property; and, as a matter of course, any person, when he becomes a CITIZEN of the United States, has a right to the enjoyment and use of this species of property, in each and every State in the Union. It is upon this false position, that a person can be converted by law into a thing, that slavery rests its whole claim — a position at war with the Constitution of the United States, and which ought not to be sustained in our courts of justice. It is provided in the fourth article of the amendments to the Constitution, that the right of the PEOPLE to be secure in their PERSONS against unwarrantable seizure shall not be violated; and that warrants when issued, shall particularly describe the PERSONS OR THINGS to be seized. I suggest, then, as the settled conviction of my own mind, that our courts of justice can not rightfully adjudge that a Negro slave is property, BECAUSE HE IS NOT A THING, and property consists in things ONLY. That he may be claimed as owing labor or service to another, does not shake, but confirms the argument.

If the free States intend to continue free, as it respects negro slavery, and all its concomitant evils, they must not permit that system to take one single step beyond its Constitutional, legal, and present geographical boundaries. If it can break one bar of its enclosure, it will be like the unchained lion escaping from his cage — it will make war upon and destroy every obstacle that opposes its onward march. It will be insatiate until all Constitutional barriers which may impede its progress shall be broken down and destroyed; we shall be unable to stay its fury, or appease its rage, or again reduce it to Constitutional limits; and the consequences will be that our entire liberties will be annihilated. The evils and propensities of the slaveholding system, which I have but faintly attempted to describe, are not the workings of imagination. I draw on sober realities and solemn facts. Who in our country justified slavery during the war of the Revolution? No one, who was willing to defend his country from the grasp of the oppressor, or shed his blood in defense of her liberties. Who justified the practice, or contended for its perpetual duration, at the close of that memorable contest? Not a single hero or patriot of that day. Did any one attempt to make its chains more strong, or bind its victims more securely, or enlarge its borders by any Constitutional provision? No, not one. Slavery at that day was deemed so dissonant to the principles of American liberty, that none were found to render it so much respect as to insert its name, or even the word "slave," in the Constitution.

All then looked for and desired the speedy downfall of the entire system; and Congress proceeded to fix limits to its power, and rebuke its practice upon every possible occasion, as in the ordinance in the year 1787, for the government of the North-Western Territory, and in subsequent acts passed after the adoption of the Constitution.

But slavery flattered the pride of man, because it enabled him to extend his legitimate dominion beyond its just and rightful landmarks. It gratified his cupidity by increasing the means of enjoyment. It was adhered to, not as a political, but as an individual claim, and was left subject to the power of the laws; and in that day, like all other subjects, it was freely discussed at all times and in all places without fear or restraint. But what is the condition of the country now? Slaves have increased vastly in number, and the power of the slaveholder in equal degree. The acquisition of Louisiana gave new impulse to this power; but it was never practically demonstrated until the application by Missouri to be admitted into the Union. It was on this occasion that the first triumph was obtained on the floor of Congress, by the slaveholding power, over the Constitution of the United States, as well as of that of Missouri.

The people of Missouri formed for themselves a Constitution, in which they had given their Legislature full authority to prohibit the introduction of any slave into that State, for the purpose of speculation, or as an article of trade or merchandise. When she presented herself for admission into the Union, the slaveholding power in Congress objected to the exercise of this authority remaining with her Legislators; and the final compromise was not to compel Missouri to change her Constitution, but that her Legislature, by a solemn public act, to be made in pursuance of a resolution of Congress, should provide and declare that the before-mentioned provision in her Constitution should never be construed to authorize the passage of any law, and that no law should be passed in conformity thereto, by which any citizen of either of the States of this Union should be excluded from the enjoyment of any of the privileges and immunities to which such citizens were entitled, under the Constitution of the United States. This compromise, which I consider one of the darkest pages in the history of Congress, though submitted to by the people of Missouri, was severely rebuked by them at that time. This was the first open step to place slavery under the provisions of that Constitution which was formed for the safety and security of liberty. It assumes the principle, though covertly, that man may be made property, and that a citizen of either State has a right to make merchandize of him if a slave, to use him in trade as a chattel, to sell him in any State in which slavery exists for the purpose of speculation, and that such State has no power to prohibit the sale. This to my mind is a monstrous principle, and at open variance with every provision of a Constitution, immolated, in this compromise, on the altar of slavery.

The slaveholding power having thus obtained a foothold on the ramparts of the Constitution, by a violation of its spirit and its letter, now claims that violation as evidence of the right itself, and boldly asserts that the Constitution recognises slavery as one of the institutions of the country, and that the right of the slaveholder to his slave is derived from that instrument. It is here the question must be met, and decided. The arrogance of the slaveholding power, in trampling down the right of petition, and denying the freedom of debate, are only consequences resulting from this assumption of power, and is a foretaste of what we may expect, when it shall have completely established itself (should it be permitted to do so), within the provisions of the Constitution. That instrument will then be no longer what it now is, the home of Liberty. It will be made its grave. This is the first great and combined interest in this country which strikes at equal rights; but all other special and local interests have the same tendency, when they claim peculiar or exclusive privileges.

The monied interest is next to be feared, and whenever that or any other shall have acquired sufficient strength, to induce or influence Congress to legislate for its special benefit, there will be an end to that equality of rights which the Constitution designed to establish for the benefit of all.

That our liberties are assailed, and individual as well as political rights disregarded by men in high places of power, none I think, will presume to deny; but that the Union or the Constitution are yet so far endangered as to create despondency, I can by no means admit. The unnatural matter which slavery is attempting to engraft upon the Constitution, will soon be blown off by the breath of popular opinion. The remedy for all evils in the system or administration of our Government is in the hands of the people, and FREE DISCUSSION—discussion without fear of the pistol of the duellist, the knife of the assassin, the faggot of the incendiary, or the still more dangerous fury of the unbridled mob—that free discussion which the people *must* and *will* have, soon will work out an effectual cure. It is not in the nature of man, to remain forever deprived of his rights in a country like our own.

But free discussion must be practised to produce its salutary effects. You and your fellow-citizens of Philadelphia have set a noble example. Though the sectarian and bigot may exclude you from his sanctuary, and the cringing sycophant to power may shut you out from the Halls erected at your expense, and consecrated to justice, yet you are not discouraged but have again erected your own

Hall for a noble purpose—for the purpose of that free discussion, without which religion would languish, and liberty and justice would die. I congratulate the friends of equal rights everywhere, on this praiseworthy effort. I trust its influence will be productive of much good to the human race. I hope that it may cross the mountains, and descend the valley of the Mississippi, until free discussion shall have restored the purity of the Constitution, and the reign of righteous law. It will be then, and not till then, that the value and merit of your proceeding in this matter will be duly appreciated, and Pennsylvania will be considered as having furnished new evidence that she is, in reality, the Keystone of our political arch, **THE ARK OF OUR POLITICAL SAFETY.**

With great respect, I am, gentlemen,

Your obedient servant,

THOMAS MORRIS.

JOSEPH M. TRUMAN, WM. H. SCOTT, WM. MCKEE, SAMUEL WEBB—*Committee.*

CHAPTER XVIII.

RETIREMENT from the Senate—Return to Ohio—Addresses a large meeting in Cincinnati—Applauded by the Democracy—Activity in the cause—An address to the Liberty Party—Nominated for Vice-President—Letter on that subject—Attends the State Liberty Convention—His Address.

THE 4th of March, 1839, closed his official responsibilities as Senator of the United States; but he went forth into a wider field of action and usefulness. Returning to Ohio, and his home, with the armor of Liberty on, he re-entered the contest, and until the day of his death fought as a veteran in the army of freedom.

"His sword was in his hand,
Still warm with recent fight,
Ready, that moment, at command
Through rock and steel to smite!"

The 7th of May, 1839, finds him in the city of Cincinnati, before a large meeting of his fellow-citizens, the unconquered friend of freedom, the inveterate enemy of slavery. That meeting is described by Dr. Bailey, the present accomplished editor of the National Era, then editor of the Cincinnati Herald, as follows:

"Ex-Senator Morris holds a court-house meeting, in which he exposes the fearful inroads of the slave power on the liberties of the nation, vindicates Abolitionists, defends his own course, as a Senator, on slavery, and insists on the duty of every citizen in the free States, solemnly to engage in lawful efforts for the abolition of slavery.

"The court-house was well filled—the speaker occupied the evening till some time past 10 o'clock. We should like to report the whole speech; particularly those parts of it which were most applauded. But we can not. A majority of the Abolitionists of the city knew nothing of the meeting till it was over. Of course, the larger portion of those present, was composed of the speaker's political friends.

"The speech was listened to with intense interest, and many tokens of sympathetic feelings. There was no vituperation in any part of it—nothing sordid. Mr. Morris has a peculiarly happy way of presenting a point with force and clearness, so that the mind immediately appreciates and firmly retains it. The secret of his influence over his party is to be found, no less in his self-reliance, and inimitable boldness, than his strong intellect. Perfectly calm, and deliberate almost to a fault, there is yet so much strength in the views he presents, and such a tone of deep sincerity in every word he utters, that he never loses the attention of his audience.

"It is a fact, worthy of particular notice, that the boldest passages in Mr. Morris's speech, those containing sentiments which Abolitionists themselves, as a body, have not generally insisted on, were precisely the parts most cordially applauded.

"While commenting on the passage of the Servile Bill, and the base subserviency of the Legislature to the dictation of Kentucky, his condemnation of its conduct was promptly echoed by his audience. He then alluded to the fact, that he had, perhaps, occupied a seat in the Legislature, for a longer period than any citizen in the State, and remarked, that had such an embassy, as was commissioned by Kentucky last winter, been sent to Columbus at any time when he was a member of the legislative body, he could have secured members enough, and would have done it, to have committed those gentlemen to prison!

On which the people, wrought up to a pitch of high indignation at foreign dictation, made the house ring with applause.

"On the subject of the recovery of fugitive slaves, he begged leave to throw out a suggestion. It might startle them; but he must express his opinion frankly—others had a right to think for themselves. And he would be happy to discuss the point with any Constitutional lawyer in Cincinnati, the suggestion "THAT OHIO, UNDER THE FEDERAL CONSTITUTION, WAS NOT BOUND TO DELIVER UP RUNAWAY SLAVES." Loud cheering followed this remark; and, be it remembered, Abolitionists were but a small portion of the meeting. The applause came chiefly from citizens uncommitted to Abolition—most of them Democrats.

"Another remark much applauded, was, that so far from passing laws to enable a slaveholder to re-capture men and women, whom he called his slaves, in Ohio, he would be in favor of the passage of a law, punishing severely, every person, who, for a pitiful reward, would in any way aid in the capture of a slave.

"If we mistake not, slaveholders will yet have cause to repent that they ousted Thomas Morris from office, and thus furnished him leisure for advocating more extensively and effectively Anti-slavery doctrines and measures. Mr. Morris has energy and influence enough to work a great change in his party."

He became identified with the Liberty party, and labored for its efficient organization and success. In the summer of 1843, he issued to the friends of Constitutional liberty, in Hamilton county, the following address:

FELLOW-CITIZENS:—At a late meeting of the friends of Liberty, in Cincinnati, the undersigned was appointed a Committee to address you, and urge the necessity of more prompt and efficient action on your part, in the cause in which you are engaged; for without such action, the friends of slavery here and elsewhere, will say in derision (and probably with too much truth), that all your professions of love for liberty, are but hollow pretensions.

It is necessary *now*, that every one of you, every friend of liberty, should faithfully and fearlessly put his hand to the work, and do all in his power to abolish the wicked, the deplorable, and ruinous system of slavery in our country. There is but one way by which this can lawfully be done; and that is the ballot box.

The principal disorders in our country are engendered in, and flow from the bitter and corrupting fountain of slavery; and the reason is, the slave power has become omnipotent. It governs the suffrages of the people, and thus it keeps millions of the human race, in our professedly free land, in the most abject and servile bondage—making one portion of our people the chattels of the other. No person can enjoy that liberty promised, and intended to be secured, by the Constitution, while another is held in slavery. It is a perfect solecism to say, that slavery is the corner stone of our republican edifice.

No! it is more like a pile of unstable sand, a heap of putrid, rotten dust, blown by its own effervescence into the eyes of our fellow-citizens, perverting their vision. It is an eating cancer, gnawing at the very vitals of our republican institutions. That spirit of liberty which breathes through our Constitution, must soon crush and destroy it, or slavery will soon stifle and destroy that spirit. Then, indeed, will our republican institutions become rotten and corrupt as slavery.

There is no mistaking the signs of the times. The slave power, itself, is in possession of all the important stations of the country. It directs all our councils and State affairs; the ballot box, itself, is controlled by it; the press and the pulpit are trampled upon by it; while every principle of *justice* and *morality, is its scoff and scorn.* It has eaten out our substance, and brought upon us pecuniary embarrassment and public disgrace. Can such a system continue forever. If it can, then indeed are our declarations, that Justice, Liberty and Union, are established among us, idle words, vain and illusory; calculated only to deceive and destroy.

No! this can not be. There is yet vitality enough in the country to restore the Government to healthy action; and this too, in spite of the contending political parties, in our State, who are sacrificing all their professed principles on the altar of slavery, and striving with each other, who shall be its most humble apologists. It is admitted that Liberty men now hold the balance of power between them, and are constantly on the increase. We say to them in a political view, "Ye are the salt of the earth. Ye are the light of the world." You *now* stand conspicuous before the nation and the world; and a high and important duty is required of you. *Redeem the ballot box from the power of slavery.* This you most assuredly will do if you vote right. Sink not your individuality into clanship. Believe not the man who tells you, he is opposed to slavery as much as you, and yet votes for a slave-dealer, or the advocate of slavery, to fill the official stations in our country. Remember, "you can not serve two masters;" you can not be the friend of slavery and the friend of freedom. Whence come the oppression and depression of your country and its affairs? The hard times and the want of credit and confidence. Does all this come by too much liberty, or too much slavery? Answer this to your judgment, your conscience, and your country.

Recollect, we beseech you, that a Liberty Convention is to be held at Mount Pleasant, in this county, on Tuesday, the first day of August next; a day and a month made memorable in the annals of time, by the emancipation of hundreds of thousands, if not millions of the human family from the thraldom of slavery, in the West India

Islands. We implore, then, one and all, to be present at that Convention; and we earnestly invite all who differ from us in this matter to come, hear and judge us; and if they believe we are wrong, arraign us at the bar of public opinion. We fear not the strictest scrutiny into all we say, and all we do.

We are always ready to make known our doctrines, and test our principles in every proper place, and under all circumstances. The object of our opponents is to silence us and extinguish the *lights we are kindling*. They have no other hope of ultimate triumph over us, but by covering us with darkness. Come then, to the Convention, and trim your fires anew! Come and convince gainsayers that you intend to live up to the political faith you profess — Justice and Liberty to ALL! Come and form a ticket for yourselves to be voted the ensuing election; composed of men who have not the brand of slavery on their foreheads, or upon their flesh, nor love of slavery in their hearts; and whose souls are not withered and almost dried up by the blasting influence and poisonous breath of that system. Come, and swear on the altar of your country's liberty, that you will uniformly and constantly hereafter attend the polls of your elections, and vote to sustain liberty. THOMAS MORRIS.

This earnest address, brought a large Convention, and the name of Thomas Morris was placed on the Liberty ticket as State Senator. He who had for twenty-five years been elected by triumphant majorities, to the Legislature by the Democratic party, in Clermont county, now entered the political field for freedom.

On the 31st of July, 1839, a large National Anti-Slavery Convention was held in the city of Albany, New York, the object of which, was "the thorough discussion of those great principles, which lie at the foundation of the Abolition enterprise throughout the civilized world; and of the measures which are suited to its accomplishment in the United States, and especially those which relate to the right of suffrage by the citizens of the free States." Mr. Morris having been but a few months from his seat in the Senate, was invited to attend. He sent the following answer to the Convention.

CINCINNATI, July 22, 1839.

It was my intention to have been with you at the National Anti-Slavery Convention, at Albany on the 31st inst., and I had made preparations to leave here, for that purpose on this morning; but the state of my health and domestic affairs have prevented me.

I rejoice, however, that the abolition of slavery throughout the civilized world, is no longer problematical. It seems to be almost universally conceded, that this stupendous fraud upon a portion of the human race, is fast issuing to a close; and the great question truly with us is, what measures are best to accomplish this desired result in the United States. In our otherwise free and favored country, slavery seems to have erected its strongest hold, and is not only striving to govern the councils of the country, the press, and the pulpit, but even mind itself, is attempted to be made.

It is true, they are yet in the minority; but, if I am not mistaken, in every age and country of the world, in which men have been compelled, by oppression, to strike for freedom, they have been at first but few in number and a persecuted race. But where they have been sincere, making truth and justice their guide, success has been, universally, the final result of their efforts.

With us the slave has no power of action; nor can we consent that his freedom shall be purchased by his own arm. A merciful Providence, in order to prevent such a dreadful catastrophe has brought to his rescue, and united for his deliverance, the warmest hearts and soundest heads of the nation ; and they present to the world the new and cheering phenomenon, of men enjoying all the blessings of liberty themselves, yet willing to devote their time, their means, their all, to procure for the oppressed and down-trodden slave, those natural rights to which he is entitled, and which, in our charters of freedom, we promise to all men. The moral power of such men is sufficient for this work, but that moral power must operate by means to make it effectual. *Political action is necessary to produce moral Reformation in a nation ; and that action, with us, can only be effectually exercised through the Ballot Box. And surely the Ballot Box can never be used for a more noble purpose, than to restore and secure to any man, his inalienable rights.* It seems to me almost impossible, that a man can be in favor of perpetuating American slavery, and yet be a friend to the principles of our Government. If the Ballot Box, then, is honestly and independently used, it alone will soon produce the extinguishment of slavery in our country.

I am able to say to you, and to those who are endeavoring to restore the slave to his long lost rights, that, in the West, the cause of freedom is onward. Men speak, as well as think, on the subject. Mind is meeting mind, and mutual confidence and mutual support will be the result.

I sincerely regret I was denied the pleasure of meeting the friends of liberty in Convention at Albany; but there is much to do here, and I find it not in my power, to comply with the numerous invitations to attend meetings in different parts of my own State. Though the friends of the slave are scattered throughout our vast country, yet they seem to be actuated by the same impulse. This I trust, will afford motives to perseverance and give encouragement to *all.*

I am, with respect,

Your obedient servant,

THOMAS MORRIS.

The 28th of December, 1842, found him in the Capital of Ohio, a member of the State Liberty Convention. Through Mr. Morris, the Convention requested the use of the Hall of the Legislature then in session, for its sittings. The request was virtually denied by its being postponed to the second Tuesday of October. He whose voice had rung in that same Hall, for twenty-four years, as a Democratic Representative, was refused the privilege of holding a Convention in it, to favor the true doctrines of Democracy, and to resist the aggressions of slavery! The Convention met in the Second Presbyterian church.

In that Convention, Mr. Morris was prominent. A brief sketch is preserved of his address. He quoted the remark of Coleridge—"It is a profound question to answer, why it is that, since the sixteenth century, the Reformation has not advanced one step in Europe." He showed the reason to be, that Luther contended for truth and principles, and not for a mere sect, and that his followers had labored for sect more than for principle.

In reference to the subserviency of the two great parties of the country to slavery, he said—"Both parties are very subservient." "The Democrats," said he, "*hold the truth in unrighteousness.*" Petitions are received as a matter of courtesy, in the Legislative Halls of Ohio; the *right* of petition is not acknowledged at all. He said that, in the Democratic proscriptive Convention of 1840 (the one in which he was cut off as a rotten branch), it was stated that no Democrat could be an Abolitionist. He would reverse the proposition, and say—"Every Democrat must be an Abolitionist."

At another point in the deliberations of the Convention, he made some very extended remarks, of which a brief sketch is subjoined.

Mr. Morris said, the American people were responsible for slaveholding under National legislation. He did not believe there was any warrant for such legislation in the

Constitution; he was *sure there was none in the moral code, which was at the foundation of all valid law.* He could not assent to the monstrous proposition that, "What the law makes property is property." He did not believe a slave could breathe in Ohio. A person held to service in another State, escaping into this, might be reclaimed as an escaping servant—not as an article of property—not as a slave. Such a person, in Ohio, has every right that any other person has, subject only to liability to reclamation. He said, no slave ought to be content with his condition. He would go farther than the Poet, who said—

> "The day
> That makes a man a slave, takes half his worth away."

It takes all his worth away. He could not, he said, blame the slave for desiring to escape, nor could he blame those who aided their escape. To charge such persons as criminals, was to offend common sense and common justice. If slavery is right, it is right to aid in sending back the fugitive—not otherwise. He would, he said, make Ohio a free State in reality. He would enforce the great principles of liberty proclaimed in the Constitution. He would have no State officer or State magistrate desecrating his office, by prostituting it to the purposes of the slaveholder. He commented on the wavering and unstable conduct of the other parties; on the repeal of the Fugitive Bill of Ohio; on the fact of the existence of one of the greatest slave-marts in the world, at the Seat of Government; on the slave representation of twenty-five members in Congress; on the compact and concentrated energy of the slave power; on the negotiations set on foot and carried on, for the purpose of extending the market for slave labor products; the total neglect of all effort to extend the markets for free labor; on the sinking of three or four hundred millions of the earnings of free labor in the gulf of slaveholding bankruptcy. He said, that slavery had literally eaten up the Banks, and, like Pharaoh's lean cattle, had devoured the prosperity of others, without promoting their own.

During the meeting of this Convention, Mr. Morris rose and said, that he had been honored, by a Convention which met in New York, in May, 1841, with a nomination for the Vice-Presidency. He felt it to be a very high honor. He prized that mark of confidence beyond any office which either of the other parties could bestow But when the nomination was made, the Liberty-Party was imperfectly organized, and much smaller than at present. He had, therefore, delayed the acceptance of the nomination; and now, in view of the rapid progress of the Party, and of future unanimity of action, he had come to the conclusion to decline it, in order that another Convention, representing the greater numbers which now compose and are continually joining the Liberty Party, might have an opportunity to act upon it.

Mr. Morris retired; and the Convention unanimously declared by a resolution, that we "do cordially approve the course pursued by that veteran and consistent friend of liberty; and invite the Liberty Men of the United States to meet in Convention at Buffalo, on the 28th day of June, 1843."

CHAPTER XIX.

Recapture of Fugitive Slaves — Compromises of the Constitution; Readjustment of Compromise Measures in 1850 — Fugitive Slave Bill; Opposition to it—President Pierce's opinion of it — Approved by President Fillmore — His former Anti-slavery Sentiments —Commissioners sent from the Legislature of Kentucky to Ohio, in 1839—Ask Ohio to aid in Recapturing their Slaves — How received by the Legislature of Ohio; Black Laws of Ohio — Mr. Morris's labors for their overthrow — His views on the duties of States in the rendition of Slaves — Report of Judge Smith in the Senate of Ohio in 1837 —Mr. Morris's elaborate reply to it.

The Recapture of fugitive slaves, has given to the system of American slavery a profound interest and agitation both North and South. Slaves are human beings, and have longings for liberty. This living spark, not extinguished, even in the soul of the bondman of the South, has led thousands of slaves, to seek deliverance from slavery, and the blessing of personal freedom. Some of the most romantic and heroic achievements in history, are those that record the daring efforts and adventures of slaves to escape from bondage. Their heroism, in ancient days, would have secured them monuments, and immortalized their names.

In the organization of the Government, a provision was inserted in the Constitution, that "No person held to service or labor in one State, under the laws thereof, escaping into another State, shall, in consequence of any law or regulation therein, be discharged from such service and labor; but shall be delivered up on claim of the party to whom such service or labor may be due."

This was a compromise between the North and the

South, in order that the Union might be formed, and the Government go into harmonious operation. This Constitutional provision was a temporary sacrifice of rights, for the purpose of adjusting the interests of all sections of country. The North and South expected, and desired, the speedy extinction of slavery, and its extension into new territory, was not contemplated by the framers of the Constitution. Hence it was agreed, that the South would not attempt to carry slavery into new Territories, and the North would extend a certain degree of protection to the interests of the South, by allowing the recovery of fugitive slaves in the Free States.

This provision, however, in the course of time, was found inadequate for the slave interests of the South. The growing sentiments of the country against the evils of slavery, and the growing sentiments of freedom among a large number of slaves, who, by increasing numbers escaped, made the property of human chattels, more and more insecure. A new surrender must be made on the part of the North.

In a new adjustment of political affairs, in 1850, when California was admitted into the Union, a Fugitive Slave Bill was passed by Congress, far more stringent and oppressive than any previous legislation. This Bill, in the North, produced general dissatisfaction.

It made every man a " slave catcher." "*All good citizens are hereby commanded*, to aid and assist in the prompt and efficient execution of this law, whenever their services may be required," and any attempt to aid a slave, directly or indirectly to escape, subjected the offender to a fine of $1000, and six months imprisonment. It also destroyed the right of trial by jury, by allowing the claimant of a slave to file his certificate before a Commissioner, and on that certificate the slave must be surrendered, in the face of " a process issued by any Court or Judge, Magistrate or other person whomsoever." This feature of the

Bill, conflicts with the Constitution of the United States, where it declares that "The privilege by the writ of Habeas Corpus, shall not be suspended unless when in cases of rebellion or invasion the public safety may demand it." It made humanity a crime, and is in direct conflict with the "higher law" of God, that declared, "*Thou shalt not deliver unto his master, the servant which is escaped from his master unto thee,*" and against that Christian law, "That whatsoever ye would that men should do unto you, do ye also unto them."

This bill passed Congress and became the law of the nation. Northern statesmen gave it their votes and influence, and on the 18th of September, 1850, it received the approval of President Fillmore, who, as a Representative in Congress, and through most of his political life, had been distinguished for his opposition to slavery.

In October, 1838, the Anti-Slavery Society of Erie county, New York, asked Mr. Fillmore's views on the subject of slavery. He returned the following answer:

BUFFALO, Oct. 17, 1838.

SIR—You solicit my answer to the following interrogatories:

1st, Do you believe that petitions to Congress, on the subject of slavery and the slave-trade, ought to be received, read, and respectfully considered by the representatives of the people?

2nd, Are you opposed to the annexation of Texas to this Union, so long as slaves are held therein?

3d, Are you in favor of Congress exercising all the Constitutional powers it possesses, to abolish the internal slave trade between the States?

4th, Are you in favor of immediate legislation for the abolition of slavery in the District of Columbia?

I answer all your interrogatories in the affirmative.

MILLARD FILLMORE.

The present President of the United States, Mr. Pierce, on the 2d of January, 1852, expressed his opinions and feelings on the Fugitive Slave Bill as follows: "I have been asked if I like this Fugitive Slave Bill. I answer, No. I *loathe* it. I have a most revolting feeling at giving up a slave. The law is opposed to moral right and humanity. Slavery is contrary to the Constitution, in some respects."

Not only the National Legislature, but many of the free States, legislated for the recapture of fugitive slaves, giving legal facilities to slave hunters, to arrest the fugitive in his pursuit of freedom.

In this work Ohio, in her legislative capacity, was prominent. Kentucky was losing her human chattels, from their strong love of liberty. A large number of slaves, from year to year, made their escape, and passed through Ohio to Canada, their only safe city of refuge on the American Continent.

To remedy this, the Legislature of Kentucky appointed a special embassy to the Legislature of Ohio. The embassadors, in the persons of Charles T. Morehead and John Speed Smith, entered upon the immediate execution of their mission, and arrived in Columbus, the capital of Ohio, on the 26th of January, 1839. They were received by the Legislature of Ohio with distinguished consideration, and by the citizens with princely attention and courtesy.

In an address to the Legislature of Ohio, they entreated that body, by their love of the Union, and of the Constitution, and by every motive of patriotism, "to provide all needful enactments, to prevent evil disposed persons, who may shelter themselves within the jurisdiction or limits of Ohio, from enticing away the slaves of the citizens of Kentucky, or aiding, or assisting, or concealing them after they shall have reached the borders of that State; and also, to pass an act, to provide more efficient and certain means for recapturing and bringing away absconding slaves, by their masters, or their legally authorized agents." "The confidence of Kentucky is full in the justice, good feeling, and comity of Ohio."

The commissioners were entirely successful. In less than thirty days, the Legislature passed "An Act relating to Fugitives from Labor, or Service from other States," which passed on the 24th of February, 1839, and which declared that "If any person, or persons, in this State, shall counsel, advise, or entice any other person or persons, who by the laws of another State shall owe labor or service to any other person or persons, to leave, abandon, abscond, or escape, or shall furnish money, or conveyance, or any other facility for enabling such persons owing labor, or service, to escape from, or elude the claimant, every person so offending shall be fined in any sum not exceeding five hundred dollars, and be imprisoned in the jail of the county, not exceeding sixty days, at the discretion of the Court." An effort was made to insert a provision, that such persons "should be punished by imprisonment in the Penitentiary, and be answerable to the party injured four-fold damages."

This submission of Ohio at the foot of the slave power, roused the spirit of incensed justice and freedom in Ohio. The law converted the soil of Ohio, solemnly consecrated to freedom, into a hunting-field for slaves, and made it a penal offense to give a cup of cold water, or a piece of bread to a poor, starving fugitive, on his way to freedom. It made humanity, and a Christian duty, a crime.

> "Alas for freedom! if such fruits as these
> Grow on the branches of her spreading trees.
> Alas for freedom! if the poor oppressed
> Find no sweet sympathy within her breast.
> Alas! alas! when ye, who claim to be
> The great and generous, wise and truly free,
> Scoff at a brother, turn in scorn away,
> Because he wears a robe of darker clay."

Mr. Morris labored for the overthrow of these unjust laws, which, on account of their severity, were stigmatized as the Black Laws of Ohio; and he lived to see them expunged from the statute-book of the State.

On the rendition of fugitive slaves, Mr. Morris had thought profoundly, and anxiously. His views were often boldly expressed, in his public addresses, and in written opinions. The reader is presented with two papers on the subject of the Duties of the States in relation to Fugitives from Labor. The first is as follows:

Dr. BAILY: In the *Philanthropist* of the 14th inst., (May 1839,) you have given to the public, a statement of what you call "another Court House Meeting," in which you suggest that "I advanced the idea, that Ohio, under the Federal Constitution, was not bound to deliver up runaway slaves." This, though correct in the main, does not so fully express what I said on that point as I could wish. I remarked, that the States as parties to the Federal Compact were themselves judges of the time and manner for the performance of those duties which that contract required of each, for carrying on its operations. That the States respectively had reserved to themselves the power to protect, and also to prevent the abduction of any person within their jurisdiction, and from being transported out of the State, without the assent of such State in pursuance of her own laws. That the law of Congress of the 12th of February, 1793, providing, that persons escaping from the service of their masters in one "State, and being found in another State, shall be arrested and delivered to the claimants, was unconstitutional; and in violation of the reserved rights and sovereignty of the States.

That Ohio, nor no other State, was bound by the operation or force of any foreign laws to deliver up any runaway slave or person escaping from the service of their master; that the States were under a moral, Constitutional obligation to do so, but that they were themselves judges when and how they would exercise the power; that if the State should be of opinion that the exercise of the power would tend to the destruction of its independence and sovereignty, or the disturbance of the public peace, or in fact to the detriment of the public welfare, each State had the right, and it would be its duty to refuse such delivery; that it ought to be remembered that the slave States claimed the slaves as a sheer article of property; that we did not permit an article of property, say a horse or an ox, to be taken from our State, but in pursuance of our own laws, much less ought we to permit a man to be taken, whom we acknowledge in our Constitution to be born free and independent: That as a sovereign State, we unquestionably had power to provide by law, the mode and manner of determining a claim to any article of property, before such article could be removed from our State; and the reason was much stronger, that a person, whom we can only know as a free man until the contrary is shown, should be protected by our laws, and that *showing* must be in pursuance of, and in comformity thereto:

That our State ought to provide by law for the reclamation and delivery of runaway slaves I admitted, and that we ought to require from the claimant a strict compliance with such laws, I insisted. I remarked that the principles I had advanced, might, by many, be considered new and dangerous, but with what reflection I had been able to bestow on this subject, my mind was strongly impressed with their truth; however, I might still be in error, and would be extremely glad to meet any gentleman in public discussion who thought me so; that truth, and the safety and peace of the country alone was my object.

I am solicitous to understand the nature and power of slavery in our country, and will add, at this time, one or two suggestions by way of inquiry, which I hope some gentleman will explain. I understand the slaveholders to say and insist, that the United States Government has no power whatever over their slaves; that slavery is a peculiar institution of their own States. The question then is, can a slave commit treason against the United States? or can he be guilty of counterfeiting the current coin of the United States, or any other crime against the General Government? If so, Congress can provide for their punishment, and thus interfere with the system of slavery in the States, and with the right of the master to his slave. Another question is, can Congress provide by law, in any possible case, for the enlistment of slaves into the service of the United States? It seems to me that if slaves are subject to the power of Congress in any one of the foregoing cases, it must follow as a necessary consequence, that Congress have power over the whole slave system as it exists in the United States.

Will you be so good as to obtain an answer from some gentleman in whose candor and legal attainments you have confidence. Yours with respect,

THOMAS MORRIS.

The second paper from the pen of Mr. Morris, on the rendition of fugitives, is lengthy and elaborate. It is in answer to a Report made in the Legislature of Ohio, in 1837, by Mr. Smith of Warren county. The Report is as follows:

The Standing Committee on the Judiciary, to which was referred the memorial of sundry citizens of the county of Clermont, praying the Legislature "to take into consideration the subject of regulating in a more just and effectual manner, the proof and trial in cases of fugitive slaves," report—

The memorialists, who are a numerous body of respectable citizens of the county of Clermont, represent that the enforcement of the Act of Congress, passed the 12th of February, 1793, upon the subject of persons escaping from the service of their masters, "is a source of indescribable mental and physical suffering to its immediate victims, and of painful sympathy and regret to the humane and patriotic citizen, who may be compelled to witness the spectacle."

They complain that by virtue of the provisions of that law, "a *man* may, by the warrant of a single Justice of the Peace, be consigned to interminable *slavery*, no matter how much the decision may have been influenced by interest, ignorance, partiality, or prejudice;" and they ask of the Legislature the passage of a law, by which the persons contemplated in the Constitution of the United States, and law of Congress above referred to, shall be entitled to the right of appeal, and the benefit of our higher courts. They also urge the "importance of taking out of the hands of Justices of the Peace, and city Magistrates, the ability to execute a power so great, and one so liable to be abused and perverted to the worst of purposes, and the placing it in the hands of our higher judicial officers." These views and opinions are urged and sustained by various arguments.

Your Committee have endeavored to give that consideration to these representations, and the arguments urged in their support, which the importance of the subject and the respectability of the memorialists seem to demand. Your Committee are aware, that the topics discussed in the memorial are of a delicate character. Unfortunately for the cause of humanity, there has, for some years past, existed in the public mind a degree of sensitiveness upon this subject, wholly unknown at any former period in the history of Ohio. This is neither the time, nor the place, to discuss the question as to the cause of this excitement, or who are responsible for the consequences; it exists, and its power and intensity are much to be regretted.

For that system of domestic slavery, prevalent in the Southern States of the Union, Ohio has no community of feeling. It is here considered as a great evil, both moral and political; one fraught with more portentous consequences to our existence as a nation than any other. The Constitution of our common country, however, recognizes the existence of this feature in our social system, and the relation of master and servant. Ohio became a constituent member of the Union, with a full knowledge of the fact. Slavery was entailed upon our country during our Colonial state; it existed at the formation of the Constitution; it is a stain upon our National escutcheon, which the existing Government did not create, and for which the present generation are perhaps not responsible.

The formation of the Constitution of the United States was the result of compromise; jarring interests and conflicting claims were to be reconciled. Those States in which slavery existed, would not consent to the adoption of the Constitution, without a provision authorizing them to reclaim their slaves, who should escape from the service of their masters, and be found in a State where that relation did not exist. Hence, it was provided in the third clause of the second section of the fourth article of the Constitution of the United States, that—"No person held to service or labor in one State, under the laws thereof, escaping into another, shall, in consequence of any law or regulation therein, be discharged from such service or labor; but shall be delivered up on claim of the party, to whom such service or labor may be due." Whatever may be our individual opinions as to the question of slavery, we hold it to be our duty as citizens of Ohio, as long as the Constitution remains unaltered, to adhere with the most rigid fidelity to this, as well as every other provision of that hallowed Instrument. In these times of turmoil and excitement, nothing will tend more to our political safety than mutual forbearance, and an unwavering determination in every member of the Union, to respect the Constitutional rights of its fellow-members, and preserve with strict fidelity, the principles of compromise on which the Constitution was formed.

Pursuant to the clause of the Constitution to which reference has been had, Congress, on the 12th day of February, 1793, passed an act entitled —"An act respecting fugitives from justice, and persons escaping from their masters;" by the third section of which it is provided — "That when a person held to labor in any of the United States, or in either of the Territories on the North-West or south of the river Ohio, under the laws thereof, shall escape into any other of the said States or Territories, the person to whom such labor or service may be due, his agent or attorney, is hereby empowered to seize or arrest such fugitives from labor, and to take him or her before any Judge of the Circuit or District Courts of the United States, residing or being within the State, or before any Magistrate of a county, city or town corporate, wherein such seizure or arrest shall be made; and upon proof to the satisfaction of such Judge or Magistrate, either by oral testimony or affidavit, taken before and certified by a Magistrate of any such State or Territory, that the person so seized or arrested, doth under the laws of the State or Territory from which he or she fled, owe service or labor to the person claiming him or her, it shall be the duty of such Judge or Magistrate to give a certificate thereof to such claimant, his agent or attorney, which shall be sufficient warrant for removing the said fugitive from labor, to the State or Territory from which he or she fled."

Your Committee are of the opinion, that the power of legislating upon this subject was conferred upon Congress, that the general provisions of that act were made in pursuance of the Constitution, and constitute a part of the supreme law of the land. It is true, that it may well be doubted, whether Congress under the Constitution, can confer any judicial power on a State officer; and should such power be attempted to be conferred, your Committee are of opinion, that such officer might at his discretion, decline its exercise; and that the State of which he is an officer, might by Legislative enactment, prohibit its exercise. As Congress, however, have deemed it expedient to vest in the judicial officers of the State, where the claim is preferred, jurisdiction in this matter, it seems to your Committee, that it would be alike unwise, uncourteous, and impolitic, for the Legislature to prohibit its exercise; unless the reason for a proceeding of that kind was exceedingly weighty. It would produce relations apparently unfriendly between the General and State Governments; a state of things always to be deprecated. The consequences would be, the vesting of the jurisdiction in matters of this kind, exclusively in the officers of the General Government. This, your Committee believe, would be productive of great difficulty and inconvenience, not only to the claimant, but also to the person sought to be reclaimed. The remote distance at which these officers must reside from various sections of the State, would render it much easier for evil-disposed persons to kidnap the negro or mulatto, and take him beyond the limits of the State, without any judicial investigation, than under our existing regulations: and it is not difficult to perceive, that in a majority of cases, it would be utterly impossible for the alleged fugitive to procure the attendance of witnesses to prove his freedom, at such a distance from his residence.

In reference to that part of the memorial, which prays for the allowance of an appeal from the inferior magistrates to the higher courts in these cases, your Committee would remark, that they are aware of the value of the right of appeal; and were they satisfied of the existence of the power in the Legislature to authorize a review of the proceedings before the inferior tribunal under proper restrictions, it might be difficult to prove its inexpediency. But they believe that under the law of Congress, exclusive cognizance of the matter is given to the officers therein enumerated, and that no appeal is contemplated, or appellate jurisdiction conferred. An *attempt* of a State Legislature to confer this power, they would deem improper, and therefore unwise and inexpedient.

The second object of the memorialists, that is, taking out of the hands of Justices of the Peace, and city magistrates, the ability to exercise this power, has already been virtually anticipated. Your Committee are not aware of any flagrant abuse of the powers conferred by the act of Congress upon Justices and City Magistrates, and it would be a source of extreme regret, if they were forced to the conclusion, that any of their decisions had been influenced by "interest, ignorance, partiality, or predjudice." They hope, for the honor and credit of the judicial officers of State, there is no foundation for such imputation. Unless, then, the reasons for an alteration in our laws, conformably to the prayer of the memorialists, are urgent and imperious, your Committee would deem it inexpedient at this time, when excitement is already ripe, when the feelings of the slaveholding, and anti-slaveholding States are arrayed against each other, any further to fan the flame, or contribute to the existing excitement. Let it be our task to pour oil upon the troubled waters, and restore that comity and kind feeling which should characterize the intercourse between sister States. If Judges of the Supreme Court and Presidents of the Courts of Common Pleas, were the only judicial officers of the State, authorized to adjudicate upon these cases, many of the inconveniencies and hardships before alluded to, would exist: and whatever may be the merits, respectability and integrity of Associate Judges in general, they are not usually technical lawyers. In relation to city magistrates, your Committee would remark, that they consider their jurisdiction in these cases, to have been virtually vested by the second section of the "Act to prevent kidnapping," which provides "That no person or persons shall in any manner attempt to carry out of this State, or knowingly be aiding in carrying out of this State, any black or mulatto person, without first taking such black or mulatto person, before *some Judge or Justice of the Peace*, in the county where such black or mulatto person was taken, and there agreeably to the laws of the United States, establish by proof his or their property, in such black or mulatto person." Your Committee are desirous that not only every citizen of the State, but that every black and mulatto person, may be protected in those rights which are guaranteed by law; but under our existing laws, administered by honest and intelligent officers, and with the habitual reverence of our community for order and law, with the benefit of the writ of *habeas corpus;* we think there is a safe guarantee that the rights of the humblest individual, will be protected. Under these considerations, your Committee believe it would at this time be inexpedient to legislate on this subject, and ask to be discharged from the further consideration thereof.

Mr. Morris, during the recess of Congress, in March, 1837, answered Mr. Smith, as follows:

SIR: In addressing this paper to you, I am in hopes that your standing and character in society, will attract to it public attention, and cause it to be more generally read and considered than it otherwise would be, and I confess I am not without hopes to induce you to enter into a controversy, on the important subject contained in your Report, and the Petition presented to the General Assembly, from a number of citizens of this county, praying the passage of an act for regulating in a more just and effectual manner, the proof and trial of fugitive slaves, and of which Report this paper is designed as a review.

Permit me to assure you, that for your personal and political character, I entertain the highest respect; and the important stations you have filled, both as a legislator and a judge, entitle your opinion to the greatest consideration, and when officially given become public property; and if erroneous, and founded on false premises, are, and ought to be subjected to the severest animadversion. In this light do I view your Report; and for which the public has the right to hold you responsible, and to award to you either their approval or censure, as shall seem meet.

The first great error into which you have fallen, is the presumption that a person of color, found in Ohio, may be the slave of another man; and this error is the predicate of your whole Report. The presumption, however, is directly the reverse; it is, that every human being found in the State is free; that color is not like the form, and want of intelligence in other animals, evidence of property in man; that he who claims that a *person* in our State is subject to any disability, or owes labor or service to another, or is property, must prove the same by some existing law, as well as make proof of the fact of ownership; while a brute animal may be reclaimed by proving the latter fact only. But even if such animal should escape from the service of its master, in any other State, and be found in our own State, it could only be reclaimed in pursuance of our own laws. Yet, strange is the conclusion to which you arrive, that a person who owes service or labor, in another State, and who may be found in this State, may be reclaimed by the operations of a foreign law only; that, in fact, our own Legislature have not the power to defend a free person (and all are free here until the contrary is proven), from being arrested and carried out of the State, or presenting the nature of the proof to be made, and the Courts before which the trial should be had, as well as the mode and manner of such trial—thus degrading the person below the brute, and subjecting him to be adjudged the property of another, in a sister State, by rules which I am conscious you would have spurned with indignation, as a judge, if any such attempt had been made upon you while on the bench, to determine the right of property in a horse or an ox.

We have no measure to test proceedings of such a monstrous character, but the standard which the Creator has implanted in the breast of every man. And ought not we, who have not only this monitor, but all the light which Christianity and Philosophy can afford, feel humbled at the very mention of doctrines, such as are contained in your Report; and if we acknowledge their correctness by practice, to put our hands upon our mouths, and our mouths in the dust, and plead guilty before the Judge of all the earth. "Shall I not visit for these things, saith the Lord, and shall not my soul be avenged on such a nation as this."

You state that the committee were aware that the topics discussed in the memorial are of a delicate character, and "unfortunately for the cause of humanity, there has, for some years existed in the public mind, a degree of sensitiveness on this subject, wholly unknown at any former period in the history of Ohio." I confess I almost doubted the evidence of my own senses on first reading this paragraph. What are the topics discussed? Personal Rights! the right of every human being as secured to him by the Constitution of Ohio; the mode and manner of trial when a claim is laid to a *man* as property; when found within our own jurisdiction; a question which involves the supremacy of our own Constitution as well as the principles of humanity! Yet because the citizens are beginning to awake and inquire into these matters which are of the highest importance, you deem it unfortunate.

Yes, unfortunate to the cause of humanity! Was there ever a sentiment so unjust and so unfortunately expressed. Humanity requires that we do good as well as be just unto all men! Policy requires that we should not permit the foot of the spoiler to tread down either our own Constitution or the liberty of *man*, without showing a paramount authority to do so, and that too in such a way and manner as we may prescribe. In contradiction to your opinion, which rests on assertion only, permit me also to declare, that it is most fortunate for the cause of humanity, for justice, for the preservation of our own institutions, for the honor and dignity of the country, that this degree of sensitiveness of which you complain, exists, and is prevailing throughout the land.

It was prudent in sustaining your Report, that you should avoid discussion as to the cause of the excitement you mention, as a discussion would have shown the fallacy of your Report, and in some degree the deep foundation upon which the prayer of the memorial rested. It would have shown that the civilized as well as the Christian world was against you; it would have proven to you that the deep recesses of the human heart, had been moved in the cause of suffering humanity; that the spirit of light and truth is abroad in the land, and that the dark and hideous form of slavery was receding from before it; inflicting its additional tortures on its unfortunate victims as its power gradually declined, and thus glutting its appetite for cruelty and oppression even in its death struggles. It is, therefore, a matter of rejoicing, not of regret, that it is even now made to feel the power and intensity of public opinion.

You next say, "For that system of domestic slavery, prevalent in the Southern States of the Union, Ohio has no community of feeling. It is here considered as a great evil both moral and political, and fraught with more portentous consequences to our nation than any other." Is this true? It is. And can we for a moment believe that this great truth, which is written on the tablet of every heart will lie dormant in those of the wise and the good? Surely not. And yet you who thus solemnly declare in your Report, the existence in our common country, of this great and alarming evil, should deem it unfortunate for the cause of humanity, that there exists in the public mind an intensity of feeling giving power and energy to its action, is one of those incongruities into which we are all too apt to fall. What do you propose as the reward for supineness? Nothing more than that happiness, which is the result of stupefying medicines given to assuage the pangs of approaching death. You promise us nothing better, and seem even startled in promising us this.

Like an Empyric in physic, who had given over all hopes of the recovery of his patient, you endeavor to find some cause for the fatal disease which is beyond the power of medicines to reach; you consign us to destruction and then sit down, fold your arms under another most fatal error, that the Constitution of our country recognizes the existence of this feature in our social system, and the relation of master and servant.

On this point however, I am at issue with you as to the fact. I deny that the Constitution of the United States recognizes or guarantees the existence of slavery in any of its provisions. You have not pretended to point to such a provision, except that which I shall presently notice, and which does not sustain you, and of course, I conclude that none other exist, on which you can rely with the remotest possibility of success. The very idea of recognizing what shall be property, or the tenure by which property can be holden, is at war with the very nature and object of the Constitution. That instrument is the foundation of all our political as well as personal rights. The Government is made by the Constitution, to rest on *man*, abstract and unconnected with property;

securing to him those valuable and inalienable rights, such as life, liberty, and the pursuit of happiness, with which he is endowed by his Creator; while it has left property as a minor thing, to be formed and provided for by law emanating from the Constitution.

I ask you, sir, as a Lawyer and a Judge, what would be the condition of our own State, if the position you have taken be true, that the Constitution of our common country recognizes slavery, as a feature in our social system? Will you not admit, at once, that slavery can exist in Ohio? It seems to me that the conclusion, from your argument, is irresistible that such would be the case. For if slavery has its existence in our social system, by the Constitution of the United States, then indeed, does it exist everywhere within the jurisdiction of the United States, because the Constitution and laws of each State are subject to the controlling power of that instrument. I can not believe that it is your wish or desire to convert Ohio into a slave State; yet if the doctrines contained in your Report be orthodox, I ask you to escape from the dilemma if you can.

Your next attempt is an excuse for the present existence of slavery, a kind of miserable consolation for the wickedness of its practice, and is at war with your Constitutional recognition of its rights. You say "It was entailed upon our country during our Colonial State, it existed at the foundation of the Constitution, it is a stain upon our National escutcheon which the existing Government did not create, and for which the present generation are, *perhaps*, not responsible. The word perhaps, as used by you, is a word of fearful import. You deplore slavery as a great evil, both moral and political, a stain upon the national escutcheon which the existing Government did not create, and which you say is fully recognized by it, and then find consolation in the idea, that *perhaps* we are not responsible for this great wickedness.

If slavery was wrong in our Colonial State, the change in our political condition, you will not, I am sure, contend makes it right. The wickedness of holding slaves, one hundred years ago, does not prove that it is right to hold slaves now; because our Fathers held in slavery, the fathers of the present race of slaves, it does not prove the practice less criminal or dangerous for that cause. Our fathers have gone to their account, and the present generation must shortly follow, and are equally responsible, both here and hereafter, for the existence of slavery; for slavery is constantly and continually an evil, an evil in all time, under all circumstances, and in all countries; an evil without excuse, and without mitigation — the worst of all possible evils. Yet you would have us shut our eyes on this deplorable wickedness, because we were not the first in the guilt, and content ourselves with saying, perhaps the present generation is not responsible.

That the Constitution of the United States, is the result of Compromise between the different States, is admitted. But I contend that that instrument contains in direct terms all the compromises intended, and that none others are to be inferred. Those agreed to, consist in the formation of the Legislative department, in the mode and manner of collecting revenue, in the grants of power to the Executive and Judicial departments; indeed the whole Constitution of the United States is a compromise between the different States, but it is a compromise in transferring power, which then belonged to the States, and is to be taken and construed, strictly within the letter of the grants made. The power thus granted by the effect of the compromise, I contend, can no longer be exercised by the States. But I deny that the compromises, in any manner affected, or operated on, any of the rights or powers not granted, but the same remains with the States, to be exercised in the same manner, as if no such compromises had been made.

As to the existence of slavery there is no recognition of it in the Constitution. Nor could there be any compromises between the States on that subject, because at the formation of the Constitution, in each and all the States, slavery existed. In your Report, however, you have said, that those States in which slavery existed, would not consent to the adoption of the Constitution, without a provision authorizing them to reclaim their slaves who should escape from the services of their masters, and be found in a State where that relation did not exist. You mean no doubt States of our Union, and if so having mistaken facts, your reasoning is inconclusive.

There were no States, as before said, in which Slavery did not exist at the time of the adoption of the Constitution, and that instrument, instead of guaranteeing the continuance of slavery in the different States, in its whole scope and tendency, has evidently formed the design of terminating its existence at no very remote period. The word slave or slavery was of too base an import to be used in that instrument; and in order to brand with odium, and fix the seal of disapprobation on the practice of slavery, it was agreed as one of the compromises of the Constitution, that the migration or importation, the going out, or the bringing into any of the States *then* existing, such persons as they might think proper to admit, should not be prohibited by Congress, prior to the year 1808; but on such importation Congress might impose a tax or duty, not exceeding ten dollars on each person. It is admitted that the word person, used in this section of the Constitution, evidently means persons of whom slaves have been made by the different States. This provision was clearly intended to vest in Congress a power to prevent the traffic in slaves, either foreign or domestic, and to exhibit it to the public eye as odious, by the imposition of an extraordinary tax.

The restriction upon the power of Congress over the

subject of slavery in this section of the Constitution, is the acknowledgement that the power was ample in all possible cases of a like nature, when not so restricted. And it is a remarkable fact that the power thus restricted, was expressly confined to the States then existing, leaving Congress at full liberty to prohibit the extension of slavery in all new States that might thereafter be admitted into the Union. Yet in the face of all these provisions, is it not strange that a citizen of Ohio, one who has held a high Judicial station, and who is now a member of her Senate, should be willing to join the mercenary slaveholder, who, finding his claims at war with every principle of justice and humanity, is willing to engraft its odium into the Constitution of the country. It is, however, to be hoped that a Constitution whose foundation is laid upon broad principles will never give nourishment to so deadly a shoot, no matter with what skill it may be inserted.

But if you have been unfortunate in your premises, you are still more unfortunate in your proof, and conclusions. You attempt to sustain slavery by the third clause, second Section, fourth Article of the Constitution of the United States, which is in the following words: "No person held to service or labor, in one State, under the laws thereof, escaping into another State, shall, in consequence of any law or regulation therein, be discharged from such service or labor, but shall be delivered up upon the claim of the party to whom such service or labor may be due."

The argument you have drawn from this provision of the Constitution is, that Congress having legislated on the subject, the legislative power of the States on the same subject, is superseded, and that we are bound to recognize the existence of slavery, by virtue of the Constitution of the United States, and to know the slave, not by proof, but by his natural appearance. We are to take the doctrine of the slaveholding States as our guide, that color is, in presumption of law, evidence of slavery, and that the claim arising therefrom must be resisted by proof; and hence, in violation of our own State Constitution, which declares that "All men are born equally free and independent, and have certain natural and inherent rights, among which are the enjoying and defending life and liberty." You are willing to acknowledge the non-existence of those rights as it respects *persons* of color, and permit them to be seized and arrested without an oath, without warrant, and taken and carried before any magistrate of a county, city, or town corporate, wherein such seizure or arrest shall be made. And what is the proof then to be made? That such person is a slave? No. By your theory that is a fact admitted; but to exempt himself from its effects the person arrested will be required to prove his freedom. The only proof, as you contend, as required by the act of Congress, is, that the person arrested owes service or labor to the person claiming him, or her, and on this proof he is surrendered into slavery. And you call this Justice.

I would here ask you to pause and reflect on the consequences of the doctrines you promulgate. I am sure you will not openly deny, that a colored man may not, under our political system, enjoy personal liberty, at least, in the same degree as a white person; and that liberty is as solemnly secured to one person as another by the Constitution of our State. Do you not know colored persons in your own town, whom you are conscious are free, honest, and industrious citizens, subject to no disability but what the laws of our State have created? Could you, as an honest and upright man, feel perfectly satisfied with the justice of your country, to see such persons arrested by a citizen of another State, without oath or warrant, and carried before one of your own upright magistrates, and in a few hours be consigned by him to perpetual and unmitigated slavery, upon proof made by a single person even, unknown to you or the community in which you live, and whether true or false, no opportunity of inquiring; but the magistrate, as you contend, would be bound to deliver over the person claimed, on his own judgment of the proof so made by a stranger, probably a slave-catcher, or more likely a kidnapper, without affording the least opportunity to the person claimed to show that the claim was false, and the testimony untrue. I repeat the question: Would you feel satisfied to see a citizen of Lebanon, though a colored one, carried off in this manner? I answer for you. I am sure you would not. Your sense of justice and right is too strong for that.

I again differ from your conclusions, as to the legislation necessary to carry out the provisions of the Constitution on which you rely. It is evident that many of the provisions of the Constitution of the United States can only be carried into effect by State legislation. Indeed, some of the most important ones are of this character; and to my mind it is clear, that the provision contained in the third clause of the second section, fourth article, to which you refer, is of that description. Have you observed the peculiar phraseology of this paragraph, and with what care it avoids the recognition of slavery as a Constitutional provision. Its power can not begin to operate until a person shall escape from one State into another; he must be held to service or labor in the State only from which he escapes; and, of course, in the State in which he is found, he is, to all intents and purposes, entitled to personal freedom; but such State is prohibited from discharging him from any prior obligation or duty he may be under in the State from which he has escaped; but he shall be delivered up, on the claim of the party to whom such services or labor is due. Every State in the Union has reserved the power of protecting from violation, or insult, the person of any individual found within its jurisdiction.

It would be an anomaly indeed, if the States had given

up this right, this power to preserve the public peace within their borders; no State can do it and claim even the shadow of independence. This is a palpable truth. How then does it happen, that a colored person may be seized and arrested within our State, without the authority of any State law defining the course, or prescribing the mode of arrest, or the form or manner of trial? Are you willing to substitute color, as a ground for the arrest, in lieu of the oath required by the State Constitution, and adopt the act of Congress as the only mode of trial by which persons, however disqualified by the laws of the State, would be competent witnesses under that act.

Fancy yourself again upon the Bench, and a colored man brought before you on a claim to his services or labor by another. What would you think of the knowledge or even the integrity of the Attorney who would contend that color was *prima facie* evidence of slavery, and that the right to the services of the slave by the claimant, should be proven by such persons as he saw proper to introduce, without any regard to the laws of your own State, using the language of your Report, "that the power of legislating upon this subject was conferred upon Congress," and under that legislation alone you must decide? I know you too well to believe that for a moment, you would entertain such a plea. You would at once decide, that no person who was disqualified by the laws of Ohio from being a witness should testify in such a case. Without going further into illustrations, I contend that if the legislation of the State could control your action in one particular, it could regulate it entirely. To me it appears that the law of Congress on which you rely, is an infringement of State sovereignty, and of course, unconstitutional.

Let me not be told, that the long acquiescence of the States, under the provisions of that act, proves the error of my opinions. It has been endured because its operation has been confined to the colored race, that abused and down-trodden population, against whom such strong prejudices exist. But, Sir, its provisions applied in a single instance, to a free white person who might justly owe service or labor in another State, the whole country, at once, I have no doubt, would take alarm and be thrown into a flame of commotion.

But why do I urge upon you the unconstitutionality of this act of Congress? You admit it, in your Report. You say—"It may well be doubted whether Congress, under the Constitution, can confer any judicial power upon a State officer; and should such power be attempted to be conferred, you are of opinion that such officer might, at his discretion, decline its exercise; and that the State of Ohio, of which he is an officer, might by legislative enactment, prohibit its exercise." If Congress had the power Constitutionally to pass the act of the 12th of February, 1793, on which your Report is based, then this latter opinion of yours, carried into effect, would be complete nullification. If you are correct, that a State, by legislative enactment, might prohibit the exercise of a power conferred by Congress; but if, as the latter part of your opinion is, that Congress has not the Constitutional right to confer power on a State officer, then every act of such officer by virtue of a law of Congress, is oppressive, tyrannical and unjust, because it is the exercise of a power without right. Yet to this condition you seem willing to subject a person in Ohio, who has the right to claim protection from her laws, and that too, in order to sustain and perpetuate slavery in other States of the Union.

As I progress with your Report, I find less to approve and more to condemn. After having failed in proving, or entirely given up the right of Congress to require of a State officer the performance of an official duty by virtue of the act of 1793, you say—"As Congress, however, have deemed it expedient to vest in the judicial officers of the State where the claim is preferred, jurisdiction in this matter, it seems that it would be alike unwise, uncourteous, and impolitic, for the Legislature to prohibit its exercise; unless the reason for a proceeding of this kind was exceedingly weighty." Thus, resolve resistance to usurpation into a system of uncourteous policy, and you seem willing that the rights of your fellow citizens should be weighed, not in the balances of justice, but in the scale of interest. This is derogatory to the spirit of liberty as well as to the spirit of independence. This was not the spirit of our fathers, who resisted oppression, not on the ground of the loss of money it extorted, but solely for the principle involved in the issue. And whenever our Government is resolved into a system of convenience, to suit particular cases, there will be an end to all our civil liberty, which consists only in a government of laws emanating from the people themselves, and faithfully and impartially administered, and by which *all* are equally benefited and equally bound.

Your next position is, that under the Act of Congress, exclusive cognizance is given of the matter to the officers enumerated in said Act, and that no appeal is contemplated or appellate jurisdiction conferred; and any attempt of a State to confer this power you deem unwise and inexpedient. Let it be remembered, that the matter is the personal liberty of a human being, who has violated no law of the State, nor done any act by which that liberty has been forfeited. You can not deny but the Constitution of the State guarantees to him the full enjoyment of that liberty, until it shall appear he is not entitled thereto. This is not to depend on a matter of opinion, but on matter of law; and I can not, with you, consent that an Act of Congress shall be exclusively permitted to seize upon the person of an individual, and in violation of the Constitution and law of Ohio, transport him without the State.

You will not, I presume deny, that the very arrest of the person of a fugitive in Ohio deemed a slave, by the laws of a sister State, is a personal injury;—for you have admitted, that slavery as it prevails in the Southern States, is a great moral and political evil; if so, its infliction in any clime, or in any country, is an injury to the person upon whom it is inflicted. Thus, while you admit exclusive cognizance to be given to this matter by the law of Congress, you trample under foot, *nullify* and abnegate, the Constitution of your own State, which expressly declares in the seventh Section, eighth Article "That all Courts shall be open, and every *person*, for an injury done him, in his lands, goods, *person* or reputation, shall have remedy by due course of law, and justice administered without denial or delay."

You nor no other person, I presume, will contend that the Courts here mentioned are any other than the Courts of the States; nor will you contend that the Judges of our Courts, should they attempt to set in judgment, by the authority of any law, but the law of the State, would, for a moment be considered as falling within the description of the aforesaid section, nor can the law mentioned mean any other than the law of the States. I ask you then, what becomes of the Constitution of your own State, if your exclusive cognizance is a correct principle. It is thrown aside as a dead letter, sacrificed upon the altar of Southern slavery, or bartered for political ease and private gain. Establish the doctrine contained in your report, and the debasement of your State is complete, and her pride of independence humbled. Even the slave himself need not envy us; his condition is involuntary, while his mind may remain free and noble, ours would be voluntary and a debasement of the mind itself.

As to the proceedings of Justices of the Peace and city Magistrates in this matter, and the ability with which they exercise the power conferred by the Act of Congress, I am willing your opinion should go to the world for what it is worth. Every man in that case will judge upon facts within his own knowledge. But I confess I do not know what you mean in the conclusion of your report, when you speak of the benefits of the writ of *Habeas Corpus*, as you had previously informed us "that exclusive cognizance of the matter, was by the Act of Congress given to the officers therein numerated. If this be true, then their decision in the matter must be final, and your pretended benefits of the writ of *Habeas Corpus* is only sheer mockery.

I have thus honestly reviewed your Report, and the false premises it has assumed, and the feebleness of the argument by which it is attempted to be sustained, and it has more fully convinced me of the truth of the following propositions:

1. That the Constitution of the United States does in no instance recognize or guarantee the existence of slavery in any of the States.

2. That the Government of the United States has not the power to declare what shall be the tenure of property, or the things of which it shall consist, on the evidence of right to its possession. That this power belongs exclusively to the States.

3. That property is and ought to be, on account of the materiality of its nature, a mere creature of law, and ought not to be taken into the account in the original Constitution of Government.

4. That when property is found in one State, and claimed by a citizen of another State, that the Courts of the State in which such property is, under the laws thereof, are *alone* competent to determine the right of possession, as well as of property, and that in this particular the States are entirely independent of each other.

5. That the claim of property in a human being is contrary to justice and the natural order of things, which is "heaven's first law;" that it is solely permitted and allowed in the States, not guaranteed, or even excused by the Constitution of the United States.

6. That to seize a person, who is found within the jurisdiction of any State, and transport him beyond its limits, without the authority or permission of said State, is a gross violation of State sovereignty, as well as of individual right.

7. That it is the duty of the Legislature of the State of Ohio, seeing that persons are held to service and labor in other of the States, and may escape and be found within this State, to provide by law, in conformity to the Constitution of the United States, the rule of decision by which such persons may be reclaimed.

8. That the provision of the Constitution of the United States on which you rely, is subject to the exclusive legislation of the different States.

9. That the legal, or Constitutional presumption is, that States will faithfully perform their duty in this matter, as they do in the election of Senators and Representatives to Congress.

I am deeply impressed with the incongruity of the act of Congress to which you have given so much consequence. If a murderer, of the deepest dye, shall flee from the justice of the State where the crime was committed, and be found in another of the States, the Executive authority of the State from which he fled, is required to make a demand of the Executive of the State where he is found, and produce a copy of an indictment, or an affidavit charging the person demanded with the crime, and certified as authentic by the Governor of the State from which such person fled, before he shall be delivered up to the demand thus made; while a person, who is held to labor ONLY, in any of the United States, and shall escape into any other State, may be seized, or arrested by any person whatever, carried before a mere Justice of the Peace, and on oral testimony, true or false, or by affidavit, taken *ex parte* in a foreign State, that the person so seized, or arrested does owe labor, or service to the claimant, be consigned by the mere *dictum* of such Justice to a condition worse than death itself—to perpetual slavery; *thus placing the murderer on far more safe and elevated ground, than the unfortunate slave, who is guilty of no crime, but whose condemnation is predicated alone on the color of his skin.*

When I look in the statute book of my country, and find its pages stained with such gross injustice, and continued there for so great a length of time, and find that injustice sustained by men of intelligence and standing, I can not but exclaim with Jefferson, "I tremble for my country, when I remember God is just, and that his justice will not sleep forever."

You admit that slavery is both a moral and political evil, and you place the existence of it, not the commencement of that evil, in the very constitution of your Government. I am not willing to join you, and thus humble our Republican Institutions in the eyes of all mankind. But this is not all. You have sworn to support the Constitution of the United States. Did it ever occur to your mind, that your oath bound you to an active maintenance of slavery in any of the States? If it is proper and right to take an oath to support an entire instrument, I can see no immorality in taking a like oath to support any of its parts. Yet I will not believe, for a moment, that you would, under any circumstances, take an oath to support the existence of the system of slavery, which you pronounce to be a moral and a political evil. We may submit with patience to the evils of government, but to swear to give to those evils an active support, is a requirement which the honesty of the human heart will not submit to, for any place or power the Government can bestow.

It is a strange thought indeed, that the framers of the Constitution of the United States should, by that Instrument, intend to rivet anew the chains of slavery, and guarantee its perpetual existence in all time to come; when the Congress of the United States, by the Ordinance of July, 1787, immediately preceding the date of the Constitution, and while the Convention that framed it were actually in session, gave the death-blow to slavery in the North-Western Territory; it being the first portion of Territory over which the United States had the right of jurisdiction, by providing, in a fundamental article for the government of the country, "that there should be neither slavery nor involuntary servitude in the said Territory, otherwise than in the punishment of crime, whereof the party shall have been duly convicted." This solemn rebuke of slavery was given by the Fathers of the Revolution, the first moment they had the power to act on the subject. The debt of gratitude the people of this portion of the United States owe to the authors and supporters of this Ordinance, can never be paid, nor too often acknowledged.

Yet you would have us believe that the wise and good men of that age who formed the Constitution of the United States, possessing the same feelings and having the same interests as those who framed the Ordinance of the same year, intended to perpetuate slavery as a Constitutional right. It is drawing too largely on the credulity of your fellow citizens, to expect their credence to such a proposition as this. Permit me to ask you, do you expect and believe that slavery as it exists in the United States, is to be perpetuated and concurred in, in all time to come?

Look upon the millions whose rights it has trodden down, and who groan beneath the incalculable load of human suffering it inflicts, and then turn your face to the justice of Heaven, and answer the question.

We have petitioned for some faint alleviation for the evils of slavery. Though at present overthrown, we are not disheartened. Another year will again call your attention to this important subject; and it is hoped that then we may all meet it with greater consideration and a deeper sense of the high obligations it imposes; and that in the pursuit of the object to be attained we will neither do nor suffer wrong, and that the moral power of public opinion will be sufficient to accomplish this work.

Under that belief, we confidently commit the issue to that Being in whose hands are the hearts of our rulers, and "as the rivers of waters, He turneth them whithersoever He will."

New Richmond, March 30*th*. 1837.

CHAPTER XX.

MOBS — Alton Riots — Death of Lovejoy — Mob in Cincinnati, in 1836— Public Meeting — Birney's Press Destroyed — Warned to leave the City — Gazette Threatened — Speech of the Mayor to the mob at midnight — Public sympathy with the mob — Contrast in Public Opinion, Mr. Morris invited to Dayton by the Mayor and others, in 1839 — His Answer — Visited Dayton in 1842 — Mob Violence — His Letter to the Mayor after the mob — Remarks on Mobs — Mob at Lexington, Kentucky, against Cassius M. Clay— His heroism—Mob spirit at Cleves, O. Church closed — Prayer in the public road by Samuel Lewis — Infidel converted — Lane Seminary — Trustees forbid the Students to organize an Anti-Slavery Society — Dr. Beecher's Speech to the Students—Anti Slavery influence of the Beecher Family — Attack on Senator Sumner — Condemned by the North — Approved by the South — Mobs overruled for the extension of Anti-Slavery Sentiments.

REASON and truth are the only legitimate weapons of discussion, the true tribunal before which error is defeated and truth vindicated and established. There is no logic nor light in the use of physical force, or violence; and a resort to them, is a perfidious war on intellect, on right, on every divine prerogative of man's nature. It is the utter annihilation of intellectual manhood, and subversive of the method, which Heaven has ordained for the development and triumph of all truth, and the exposition and overthrow of all error and wrong, and alike destructive to social order and civil Government. Free and thorough investigation, is the right and privilege of all men; and all things are subjected to this searching ordeal. No system is exempted from this universal law, either by the inhibition of the Creator, or in the nature and necessity of things. "*Whatsoever is of the truth cometh to the light*," and desires investigation.

The system of slavery, *alone*, in this free Republic, and in this age of intellectual activity and analysis, demands exemption from the ordeal of thorough discussion. Fearful of the power of truth, it has sought to prevent discussion of its nature, and all its workings, by lawless violence, by the logic of physical force. Almost all the free States, have been dishonored, by the efforts of mobs to silence the voice of freedom, and of a free press, on the subject of slavery. Commercial motives — fears of losing the trade of the South, if the North agitated the slavery question, have been the origin of most of the mobs, that have taken place in the Northern States. Life and property have been sacrificed to the ferocity of mobocratic violence.

Alton, Illinois, witnessed the first blood shed in defense of the rights of freedom. Here, in the press and life of Rev. Elijah P. Lovejoy, was a ruthless mob, triumphant in the destruction of the inalienable and Constitutional rights of American citizens. He was "nursed in storm and trial," and for months nobly contended against a mob, headed by leading citizens, and countenanced by the Municipal authorities of Alton, in the midst of men who thirsted for his blood, and with a courage that was invincible and morally sublime, he waged a warfare against the unholy crusade, that the mob was making on life, and the liberties of the press. Three different times was his press destroyed. Public meetings were called urging him to desist. But he declined, nobly declaring, "I insist on protection in the exercise of my rights. If the civil authorities refuse to protect me, I must look to God; and if I die, I have determined to make my grave in Alton." There, as a martyr to American freedom, he did die. On the night of the 7th of November, 1837, while defending with a few friends, a free Press from the mob, he was murdered. As the blood of the Christian martyrs, was the seed of the Church, so the blood of the martyred Lovejoy, was the seed of freedom.

Cincinnati, in the summer of 1836, witnessed an extraordinary mob. James G. Birney, of Kentucky, convinced of the sinfulness of slavery, became a practical emancipator, by giving the boon of freedom to all his slaves. To aid in the work of general emancipation, through the medium of the press, he attempted to establish a free press in Kentucky. This was denied him, by the slave power of his own State. He came to the free State of Ohio, and under her Constitution, which declared the right "indisputable," of speaking, writing, or printing on any subject, he established in 1836, in Cincinnati, the Philanthropist.

Here also, in the Queen-City-of-the-West — a city which owes all her commercial prosperity and wealth to freedom and free institutions — Mr. Birney met with a strong and unexpected opposition. The city was moved with excitement. The press of the city teemed with inflammatory articles against Anti-Slavery men, and their efforts to publish an Anti-Slavery paper in Cincinnati, declaring that "the citizens of Cincinnati — embracing every class interested in the prosperity of the city, satisfied that the business of the place is receiving a fatal stab from the wicked and misguided operations of the Abolitionists — are *resolved to arrest their course.*" Citizens of the highest respectability and influence, of great wealth and intelligence, "came to the determination, that the Abolition paper *should be put down, peaceably if it could, forcibly if it must.*"

On Saturday, 23d of July, 1836, more than one thousand citizens of Cincinnati assembled in the Lower-Market House, and there resolved — "That nothing short of the absolute discontinuance of the Abolition paper in the city, can prevent a resort to violence."

A Committee of the most distinguished citizens was appointed to wait on Mr. Birney and his associates, requesting them "by every motive of patriotism and philanthropy, to desist from the publication of their paper, and to warn them of the consequences, if they did not." The Chairman of the Committee expressed it as his opinion, that if the Philanthropist was not discontinued, a mob of unusual numbers and respectability would destroy it; that it would consist of four or five thousand persons; and that *two-thirds* of the property-holders of the city would join it. It would destroy any one who should set himself in opposition to it."

Mr. Birney and his associates declined to surrender the freedom of the press. In their answer to the Committee they say:

"It would be a submission to the South, that slavery should never more be mentioned among us; it is an attempt at dictation as insolent and high-handed on the part of the South, as tame submission to it would be base and unmanly on ours. The demand is virtually the demand of slaveholders, who having broken all the safeguards of liberty in their own States, in order that slavery may be perpetuated, are now for the fuller attainment of the same object, making the demand of us to follow their example. The attempt is now first made in our case, formally and deliberately to put down the freedom of speech and of the press; and there is not a freeman in the State whose rights are not invaded in any assault that may be made on us, for refusing to succumb to an imperious demand to surrender our rights."

"Such an attempt to trample under foot the liberties of the people — so deliberate, so carefully matured and backed by such an amount of moral, intellectual, and pecuniary power — has rarely been made in this country." The deed was consummated. Saturday night, July 30th, 1836, to adopt measures to silence the voice of a free press, the mob met on the corner of Main and Seventh streets; and formally and deliberately entered upon their work of destruction. The office was plundered, and the press was taken out and thrown into the river, and Mr. Birney warned to leave the city in twenty-four hours. The Cincinnati Gazette, the oldest paper in the city, then edited by the veteran Charles Hammond, which had discountenanced the proceedings against the freedom of the press, and rebuked the spirit of pro-slavery so rife in the city, was visited by the mob and threatened with destruction. The private residences of several anti-slavery men were also visited by the mob; but no violence was done.

The Mayor of the city, at the hour of midnight addressed the mob in the following speech:

"GENTLEMEN—It is now late at night, and time we were all in bed—by continuing longer, you will disturb the citizens, or deprive them of their rest, besides robbing yourselves of rest. No doubt it is your intention to punish the guilty and leave the innocent. But if you continue longer, you are in danger of punishing the innocent with the guilty. *We have done enough for one night.* [Three cheers for the Mayor]. The Abolitionists themselves, must be convinced by this time, what public sentiment is, and that it will not do any longer to disregard or set it at nought. [Three cheers again]. As you can not punish the guilty, without endangering the innocent, I advise you all to go home."

This was the first deliberate effort to suppress the freedom of the press in Ohio, and, though encouraged by such powerful influences, it signally failed. The *Philanthropist* was issued several years afterward, under the proprietorship of Dr. Bailey, and, instead of a weekly it became a daily Anti-slavery publication, under the title of the Cincinnati *Morning Herald.*

Public sentiment in the city and in Ohio, has *now* so thoroughly changed on the subject of slavery, that it would rally, with an overwhelming power, against any effort to put down the freedom of the press. Truth and light are omnipotent in disarming error and prejudice, and are destined to inaugurate and establish the universal reign of freedom and justice.

Mr. Morris did not escape the honor of being mobbed, for his devotion to the cause of human liberty. In May, 1839, he was invited by the Mayor, and fifty other citizens of Dayton, to visit that city and deliver an address on the important questions connected with slavery. The letter of invitation, and his answer are here inserted.

DAYTON, May 6, 1839.

HON. THOMAS MORRIS—Respected Sir: The undersigned citizens of Dayton, attached to both political parties, admiring the honest and independent course pursued by you, while a member of the United States Senate, in firmly maintaining the honor and dignity of the State against Southern aggression and Northern servility, and in refusing to barter principle for office, solicit you to appoint a time, when it will be convenient for you to visit us and address the citizens of this place, relative to some of those important questions, which, for several years, have been agitated in Congress, in which, in common with the undersigned, you feel a deep and absorbing interest. When your determination shall be made known to us, due notice of the time and place of the meeting shall be given.

ANSWER OF MR. MORRIS.

CINCINNATI, May 10th, 1839.

DEAR SIR: I received this day the invitation from yourself and other gentlemen of Dayton, of the 6th instant, to visit you, and address the citizens of your town, on the deep and interesting question of American slavery; that system that claims to be superior to Constitutions, laws, and rights of the country. It is the fountain and spring, as you justly remark, of "Southern aggression, and Northern servility." I rejoice to find the people everywhere examining the unjust and unreasonable demands of the slave power in our country; that power that is making war upon all political parties and conditions of men who do not render it the homage it demands. It is therefore the duty of all parties to unite to resist its claims. It is, not only the common enemy of our country, but it is the common enemy of mankind.

It claims to rule, or divide and ruin the nation. We must check its onward progress, or it will soon be established in principle, if not in fact, in every State in our Confederacy. My best efforts, feeble as they may be, are at the service of my fellow-citizens, in aiding them in their efforts against the monstrous demands of the slave-holding power. I will shortly inform you when I can visit Dayton, which I shall do with great pleasure.

I am, with respect, yours,

THOMAS MORRIS.

Mr. Morris did not visit Dayton till January, 1841. It was on his return from attending an Anti-Slavery Convention at Columbus, that he, at the request of a number of citizens, attempted to address them on the subject of slavery. He was prevented by a mob. On his return home he addressed the following communication

TO THE MAYOR OF DAYTON.

SIR: Though I address you in your official capacity, yet it is not intended that your character as a gentleman and a citizen is to be overlooked. As the Chief Magistrate of Dayton you are highly responsible for the peace and quiet of the town, not only to the inhabitants thereof, but to the country at large. As an individual, you, in common with your fellow-citizens, have a common duty to perform in the establishment of the power of the laws of the State over the reckless passions of wicked and misguided men. In addressing you, however, I do not intend that you alone shall be the recipient. I wish to be heard and understood by the citizens of Dayton, of the State, and country at large.

You, with many other citizens of Dayton, will recollect, that in May, 1839, I received an invitation, signed by *yourself*, together with a highly respectable number of the inhabitants of Dayton, to visit you and address the citizens. In my answer, it will be seen what I understood you to mean by "Southern aggression, and Northern servility." It was American slavery, to which your letter evidently alluded, that produced this "aggression," and "servility," and on that subject I wished to apprize you, specifically, I intended to speak. I do not remember that I afterward informed you, by letter, when I could visit you; but soon after that time I met and conversed with some gentlemen from Dayton, at Xenia, on this subject, and a desire was still expressed, that I should visit Dayton; but the numerous calls made upon me for a like purpose, probably prevented me. It was not under a belief that mobocracy ruled in Dayton.

On my return from the Anti-Slavery Convention in Columbus, I passed through Dayton, and my friends who were with me, and some gentlemen, residents of Dayton, agreed to call a meeting of the citizens, and requested that I should address them, on the results of American slavery upon the morals, as well as the political and financial concerns of the country. I agreed to do so. Some gentleman, whom I know not, caused to be printed and circulated, the following

NOTICE.

Thomas Morris, formerly United States Senator, will deliver an address, this evening, at the Court House.

January 23d, 1841.

At early evening I repaired to the Court House, not dreaming of any disturbance or violence. I could not suppose that, after what had transpired at the mobs in Cincinnati, and in Alton, and the outpouring of public indignation upon the actors in those scenes, another place could be found in America, much less in Ohio, in which the rude hand of mobocratic violence could overawe the majesty of the law, and trample under its unhallowed feet the lives, liberties, and rights of any portion of the people. But I was, alas! too soon convinced of my error. Soon after my entrance I heard threats of personal violence toward myself. Some said, that if I was in the house I should never leave it alive; and others, that they must wait till I commenced, and then we will give it to him.

I remarked to a friend, that the mob was ruling, and we might as well retire. We did so, unknown, amid their yells and threats. After walking a square, I returned and went into the house, and found them censuring each other for not waiting until I had attempted to speak, then they would have had me in their power. After they found they had missed their prey, I noticed they went into one of those "Ohio Hells," called groceries, where wretchedness, debauchery, and crime of every grade, are sold by measure, and swallowed with greediness. I left Dayton the following day, and, though informed that I was waylaid to be mobbed, escaped personal violence.

The house of the gentleman, Dr. Jewett, whose hospitality I enjoyed, was assaulted during the night, with rotten eggs, and a carriage destroyed. Great and enormous acts of wickedness, have their comcomitants and results. Such attended the mob scene at Dayton. On the Monday evening after my departure, the monthly concert of prayer for the slave, which a few pious persons in Dayton, believed it their duty to hold, was observed in Dr. Jewett's office. The presence of yourself, and other officers prevented the operations of the mob, until the close of the meeting, when the office was attacked, and its contents destroyed. Thus has a religious meeting in

Dayton been set upon by a mob, devoted to the cause of slave-holding in our country, and attempt made to set up that institution above religion, law, and the lives of their fellow men. Such acts as these, if permitted to pass, without condign punishment, will soon destroy the institutions of our country, banish peace and quiet from among us, and compel our citizens to arm in defense of their lives and property. Had I been known to the mob, in the Court House, there can be no doubt, but I would have been instantly murdered, and my blood shed in the Temple of Justice and law, in the town of Dayton. My life was spared, by nothing short of a special interposition of Providence.

I now protest to you and the country, that I had given to the citizens of Dayton no just cause of offense. I was there as an American citizen, and was vested by the Constitution and laws of the country with all those rights, which a portion of my fellow citizens wished me to exercise. I proposed to discuss the subject of American slavery — its evils and aggressions. Have I not, as an American citizen, a right to canvass the demands of this giant system of wrong? What does slavery in fact demand? It demands the overthrow of the religion, the liberties, the morals, the Constitution and laws of the country. It would immolate all the interests of the country upon its bloody altar, except they would bow to its supremacy and obey its behests. Against this foe of God and man we have urged a perpetual and interminable war, and we will teach our children, even at the age of nine years, to lay their hands upon the altar of their country's liberty, and swear eternal enmity and opposition to slavery.

The mind is lost in perfect amazement, that in this Christian land, in this free country which has written Constitutions and laws for its Government, that mobs should be found who endeavor to destroy the freedom of the press, and the liberty of speech. Why should this effort be made in Dayton? Is it because there are slave-holders residing in Dayton, or that more whisky is made in its vicinity than any other portion of the State. May slave-holding and intemperance, the two greatest curses which the world ever saw, be speedily abolished in our country. We believe they are well calculated to bring into action the worst passions of the human heart, and that they have been the moving cause of the mobs and riots which have so often disgraced our State.

These mobs, said Mr. Morris, in a memorial to the Legislature, almost constantly employed their efforts against peaceable citizens, often ending in the destruction of life as well as of property; and that for no other cause than that such citizens were opposed to slavery, and in favor of the repeal of the Black Code of the State. Indeed to such extent, and under such influence, have these outrages been carried on, that safety and protection in the exercise of our clearest Constitutional rights, the liberty of speech and the press, is rendered very problematical, even in our courts of justice.

We claim for all our people, from our public functionaries of the State, protection in the exercise of their rights, and we ask this from our present Legislature. We feel justified in urging this subject upon the special attention of the General Assembly, because we have heard it often suggested, that although the violent proceedings of mobs were by no means justifiable, yet that the doctrines and proceedings of Abolitionists were less so. We will not descend to libel the good sense of the country, in answering such suggestions. We approach the Legislature, however, in the entire confidence of the truth of the declarations, that mob violence in our State has become dangerous to the peace and safety of the community, and ought to be suppressed by penal enactments. If there be an existing cause in the country that produces such violence, and if such cause be more dangerous than the violence itself, suppress that cause; if the doctrines and doings of the Abolitionists be a violation of moral principle, or unconstitutional or dangerous to the public peace and safety of the country, punish the propagators and actors by law; if the freedom of speech and the press, which we claim as our Constitutional right, be also dangerous, punish us for its exercise; or let the Constitution be amended, and this right taken away, if it gives to us a dangerous license. It is the right of every man to be saved from violence; and punished, either in his goods or person, only by the known and established laws of the land, if guilty of any offences. To the laws of the land we owe *submission, but not always voluntary obedience.*

Cassius M. Clay, a native of Kentucky, with a number of slaveholders and others, established in the city of Lexington, in June, 1845, THE TRUE AMERICAN, a paper devoted to "gradual and Constitutional emancipation, and to uphold the Christian morality in ethics, and Constitutional Republicanism in politics." This effort for free discussion met with a powerful resistance from the citizens of Lexington, who through the public press, declared—"That the subject of slavery shall not be discussed, and that violence shall suppress the paper." A Committee, approved by a public meeting, was appointed to confer with Mr. Clay, and urge him to suppress the *True American.*

Mr. Clay met the crisis with heroic courage and chivalry, declaring to the Committee, that—"Your meeting is one unknown to the laws and Constitution of my country; its purposes, its spirit, and its action, like its mode of existence, are in direct violation of every known principle of honor, religion, or government, held sacred by the civilized world. I treat them with the burning contempt of a brave heart and a loyal citizen." Mr. Clay prepared to meet the mob, and determined to die in defense of his birthright, the freedom of the press, and the liberty of speech. He made his will. All his relations believed he would be murdered; and "all but my wife and mother advised me to yield up the liberty of the press; but I preferred to die."

The *True American* was immolated at the shrine of slavery. On the 18th of August, 1845, a Committee of sixty, from a public meeting of twelve hundred, deliberately proceeded to the work of silencing the only press which, in a slave State, gave utterance to the inspirations and thoughts of liberty. The office was dismantled, the press and type boxed up, and sent to Cincinnati. Thus did slavery triumph over freedom and Constitutional right; and in the person and property of this noble champion of liberty, gave a new illustration of the purpose of the slave power to extinguish every light that revealed and exposed the system of slavery.

Mr. Clay is now honored, by the voice of a free nation, as one of the able and intrepid champions of freedom. In the great contest between liberty and slavery, he has been, and now is, active, earnest, and eloquent. Wherever he goes, listening thousands hang on his fervid and inspiring words of freedom. He is a practical emancipator, showing his faith by his works; and in every battle-field of freedom he has fought heroically, and won honorable renown.

This intolerance to anti-slavery sentiments, reached and controlled Christian churches. Notices for anti-slavery meetings were refused to be read from the pulpit, and churches closed against all meetings to deliberate on, and pray for the overthrow of American slavery. The Trustees of Lane Seminary, in 1834, prohibited the formation of an anti-slavery society, and declared that all discussion on the subject was improper. This action, so contrary to the genius of Christianity and of free institutions, compelled the students to leave the Institution, and go where free discussion was tolerated. The Institution itself was threatened with an attack from a mob, if there was not a suppression of the Anti-Slavery Society. The venerable President of the Institution, Dr. Lyman Beecher, whose family have, by their genius and writings, given to the anti-slavery sentiment of the nation and the world, an extraordinary extension and power, said to the students — "*Boys, you are right in your views, but most impracticable in your measures. Mining and quiet strategy are ordinarily better, as well as safer methods of taking a city, than to do it by storm. It is not always wise to take a bull by the horns. You are right; but in your way, you can't succeed. If you should succeed, I will be with you, and swing my hat and shout, huzza!!*" Leading Literary Magazines, and newspapers of Cincinnati, combined to disband this Anti-Slavery Society of Lane Seminary, declaring it "discreditable to the Institution, and calculated to inflict a deep wound on the great interests of education; and the indignation of the public will put it down."

Cleves, in Hamilton county, Ohio, was the scene of violent resistance to free discussion. In the Spring of 1843, the Pastor of the Presbyterian church, Rev. Mr. Scofield, and a majority of his flock, called a meeting for free discussion on slavery. Samual Lewis, Jonathan Blanchard, now President of the Galesburg College, Illinois, and Thomas Morris, whose manly voice for freedom, integrity of principles, and firmness of character, have enrolled his name among the early champions of free speech and free soil, were the speakers.

A mob was organized and a riot threatened. A number of Students from Lane Seminary, went down with the speakers. Landing at North Bend, they passed the mansion and tomb of the lamented General Harrison, on their way to the church. The doors of the meeting house were barred against the friends of freedom. Prominent and influential men were with the rabble, that prevented the Convention from occupying the meeting house. The

Convention, thus forbid to enter the house, occupied the road in front. Rev. S. Lewis, an able and faithful laborer in the cause of freedom, recently gone to an honored grave, kneeled on the ground and offered a most solemn and impressive prayer. For a moment the rioters were palsied in their nefarious operation. One of them often said, "that prayer I shall never forget." An infidel was converted, and "the wrath of man was thus made to praise God," and advance the cause of freedom.

At the invitation of Richard Hughs, a ruling elder in the Presbyterian church of Berea, a mile distant from Cleves, the Convention met at that church and held its sessions two days. The impression of that Convention, abides to this day; fires were kindled that are burning brighter and brighter.

The Cleves rioters, not satisfied with driving the Convention from the village, smashed the windows of the meeting house, mobbed the house of the pastor, threw his buggy into the canal, and shaved the tail of his horse. The perpetrators of these deeds of darkness, chose the covert hour of night for their mob performances; they were of the baser sort in the community, but were instigated and backed by quite a number "of those of reputation." These mob scenes, created an era in the history of that region and will be long remembered.

Mob violence also transpired in the Temple of National Legislation, on the floor of the Senate of the United States, where Thomas Morris had stood, twenty years before, to defend the Constitutional liberty and the rights of his countrymen.

Charles Sumner, a finished scholar, a brilliant orator, a ripe Christian Stateman, and a Senator from Massachusetts, had devoted his genius and powers to the cause of human Liberty.

In May, 1856, in the Senate Chamber, he made a masterly and logical speech against the slave power, for its infliction of grievous and multiplied wrongs, on the free people of Kansas Territory. This truthful expose of wrong, and manly vindication of right, created great excitement in both Houses of Congress, and slavery must have revenge.

Preston S. Brooks, a member of the House, from South Carolina, was the selected champion of the South, and of the club law. While Mr. Sumner, was seated at his desk in the Senate engaged in writing, Brooks covertly went up to him, and, with a heavy cane, smote Senator Sumner to the floor, his blood staining the Temple of Legislation, and crying from that spot for vindication from an insulted and an indignant Nation. Mr. Sumner was dangerously wounded, and carried insensible from the Senate.

This nefarious and deliberate plot, to strike down free discussion in the person of the noble Senator from Massachusetts, electrified the country with a profound and startling sensation. The North, inspired with a general and generous impulse, in a multitude of meetings, where thousands met, denounced the great crime, and demanded the expulsion of Brooks. The South, with even more unanimity, approved the deed as chivalrous and right, and thus made the act of Brooks the symbol of their own faith, purpose, and practice.

A Committee of the House, of which Lewis D. Campbell, of Ohio, an able and faithful defender of freedom, in Congress, was Chairman, was appointed, who brought in a resolution of expulsion against Brooks, and which, after a lengthy debate, was adopted by a majority vote of one hundred and twenty-one against ninety-five. Brooks, however, was not expelled, it requiring a vote of two-thirds of the members present. The moral power of the vote compelled him to resign his seat, and appeal to his constituents. He was unanimously re-elected; thus proclaiming to the world that his violent purpose, and act, were approved and applauded by the South. This resort to mob-law in the Halls of the National Legislature, is painful evidence of the violent spirit of the slave power, and of its determination to rule or ruin.

These outrages on the rights of American citizens, and in the destruction of the freedom of the press, and of speech, were overruled for the diffusion of light, the extension of anti-slavery sentiments, and the re-awakening of public opinion against the designs of the slave power. Every effort made to suppress discussion, either in the halls of legislation, or by the violence of mobs, gave an intenser glow to the unconquerable spirit of freedom, and multiplied, by tens of thousands, the friends and advocates of human liberty, ready to resist the aggressions of the slave power. This fact is evidence of a Providential government over the affairs of men, overruling evil for good, and is prophetic of progress and final victory. The voice of millions, now in the battle-field of freedom, responds to the noble words of Whittier, the Poet of Freedom and Truth,

> Think ye, one heart of man or child
> Will falter from its lofty faith,
> At the Mob's tumult, fierce and wild—
> The prison cell—the shameful death?
> No! nursed in storm and trial long,
> The weakest of our band is strong!
> We can not falter! Did we so
> The stones beneath would murmur out,
> And all the winds that round us blow
> Would whisper of our shame about.
> No! let the tempest rock the land,
> Our faith shall live—our truth shall stand.
> We bate no breath—we curb no thought;
> Come what may come, WE FALTER NOT!

CHAPTER XXI.

ANTI-SLAVERY Publications — Mails Examined — Post Office in Charleston Mobbed — President Jackson's Recommendation — Incendiary Bill — Speech of Mr. Morris.

THE slave power, in 1836, made a strong effort to exercise a censorship over the public press of the country. The Post Office, the common property of the people, was used as a medium for the transmission of Anti-slavery publications, to some of the citizens of the South. The exercise of this Constitutional privilege, awakened great indignation, and efforts were immediately made, to arrest it. The Northern Mails when they arrived in Charleston, South Carolina, were guarded as the passed through the city to the Post Office, and, after undergoing a thorough search, all Anti-slavery publications were taken out of the mails, and consumed in a bonfire, in the streets, in the midst of a general rejoicing of the citizens. Similar acts were commited in other portions of the South.

President Jackson, at the opening of Congress, in 1836, recommended in his Annual Message, "the passage a law, that will prohibit, under severe penalties, the circulation in the Southern States through the Mail, of incendiary publications, intended to instigate the slaves to insurrection." Mr. Calhoun reported to the Senate a Bill, prohibiting Postmasters from delivering, "any pamphlet, newspaper, handbill, or other printed paper, or pictorial representation touching the subject of slavery, in any State, in which their circulation is prohibited by law."

Against this Bill, Mr. Morris, on the 14th of April, 1836, made the following

SPEECH.

Mr. President: I am opposed to the Bill; it contemplates the exercise of new power or powers, in a new form, over the Post Office and mails of the United States; and if the power contemplated be not unconstitutional, it is, to my mind, a most dangerous abuse. "Congress shall have power to establish post offices, and post roads." Those words, as used in the Constitution, have an evident reference to an existing state of things, and the use for which post offices and post roads was intended—for the purpose of a free intercommunication of thoughts and opinions between the citizens of different parts of the country; and was deemed of so much importance, that the power to provide for its safety was vested in Congress; and the words "to establish" were used to denote, that Congress had the power to fix, unalterably and immovably, beyond the interference of any State power, the entire operations of the Post Office, and the traveling of the mail throughout every part of our extended Republic. The Post Office establishment was not intended as an attribute of the power of Government, but as a means by which that power should be exercised for the benefit of the citizens individually, by providing a channel of free and full communication between them, though residing in different sections of the country; and that their letters, papers, or pamphlets, should pass without any hindrance or molestation from State authority. This principle has never been considered as a proper charge on the revenue of the country, but Congress have provided that it shall be supported and paid for by those who use it; Congress being vested with its management, and guaranteeing its safety and fidelity. The use of the mail, then, is in the nature of a reserved right, with which no law ought to interfere. It is not, then a Government machine exclusively, which Congress can withdraw at pleasure, or render nugatory by the acts of its officers; but Congress have the power to regulate the expenses of the Department and fix its income, so that the Government shall at no time be subject to, or chargeable with, any expense of the establishment; and the postage has, from time to time, been regulated accordingly.

It is true that the mail is a great convenience, and probably a necessary appendage to the Government; but I consider this not to be the first and most important object; it is second to the safety of intercommunication between the citizens of this extensive Republic. Though this was the primary object, yet Congress has, in the regulation of the mail, levied a tax on those who make use of this privilege to the full extent of all the purposes of Government, by the exercise of the franking privilege. I somewhat question the correctness of this franking power, while the Government contributes nothing toward the support of the Post Office establishment, because it is in the nature of a direct tax in the rates of postage, which is levied upon those only who use the mail, while all such taxes ought to be apportioned among the States according to their respective numbers. But, Sir, it is not necessary for the purpose I have in view, to examine this point. That Congress have power to regulate the mail, and prescribe what shall be carried therein, I do not deny; but I insist that this power is confined to the material, not the moral matter to be conveyed. Congress can prescribe the weight, the bulk, and the kind of material which shall not be conveyed by mail, but the material must be judged by its outward appearance alone, and not by breaking any envelope or seal for the purpose of ascertaining this fact; for instance, no postmaster would be bound to put into the mail a piece of sheet iron or tin of the shape and size of a common letter, even on the payment of postage according to established rates; and why not? because it is the usual means of conveying mental property only, and because its very texture would tend to the destruction of papers and documents which the mail was designed to convey, and which is its legitimate business; but if even an article of the above kind was carefully folded in the usual paper envelopes, sealed, directed, and put into the Post Office, it would be a dangerous exercise of power indeed, to permit a deputy postmaster to refuse its conveyance in the mail, because he should judge it contained improper matter. But, Sir, I would say to the Senator from Connecticut, that his amendment affords no redeeming quality to the dangerous principles of this Bill, by confining its operation to postmasters in the slaveholding States.

Can we, can Congress, take from any citizen in such State any personal right or privilege, or regulate under any circumstances the manner of this engagement? I should think not. Suppose a letter, package, or even a pictorial representation, folded and directed in the usual manner, and put into any Post Office in the United States: I would ask the gentleman whose property that letter or pamphlet is? Does it remain the property of him who deposited it? I think not. And though postmasters might as a mere act of courtesy, permit the depositor to take it back from the mail, yet he would not be bound to do so, because it is his sworn duty to forward all packages, which, in their common outward appearance, are such as are commonly sent by the mail. Is a letter or package, when left in a Post Office, the property of the United States or Post Office Department? Surely not; no one will contend for this. It is then the property of the person to whom it is directed, and the United States have given a solemn Constitutional pledge that they will convey it to him, without permitting its contents to be inspected or suffering it in any degree or manner to be detained or injured, beyond what must necessarily take place in its passage.

Sir, what would be thought of the honor, or even honesty of an individual, who would receive a letter or printed document, under a general or special promise that he would deliver it safely to the person to whom it was directed, and should afterward retain or destroy it, because he should be of opinion it contained offensive matter? Every honorable mind can furnish a ready answer. And what, Sir, shall be thought of the honor of this Government, which, after having declared that "The right of the people to be secure in their persons, houses, PAPERS, and effects, against unreasonable searches and seizures, should not be violated," and that no State shall pass any law impairing the obligation of contracts; who, after having received into its possession, for the purpose of carriage and safe delivery, the PAPERS and property of one of its citizens (for printed publications and letters are property, as well as papers), suffer this property to be seized and detained, by the most unreasonable of all means, that of the belief of a postmaster that it contained something touching the subject of slavery? or permit the States, by any law or regulation therein, to violate, or rather *impair* the obligation of the contract on the part of the United States for the delivery, as well as that existing between the person who sent, and him who has paid for the publication or document, and for its transportation? Sir, the very thought that this Government is, or ever will be, disposed to listen to a regulation of this kind, must, in my humble judgment, meet with the most decided disapprobation of the great majority of the American people. We, Sir, frequently lose sight of our argument, by attempting to extend it too much into generalities: the mind, by attempting to embrace too many ideas, is apt to become confused. I will, then, make a single case for an illustration of the subject; and I will take one as strong as the honorable Senator from South Carolina could desire. Suppose I and a citizen of the gentleman's own State should see proper to subscribe and pay for a New York Abolition paper, or the proceedings of an Abolition society. These tracts, by the laws of New York, are legitimate property, and he would violate no law, either human or Divine, in making such purchase. The United States has an establishment, the Post Office, by which the Government has given a general notice that all property of this kind shall be conveyed for a given price; he pays that price, and his property, thus purchased, is sent to the Post Office in New York for that purpose; and, according to the gentleman's theory, this property is to be seized by an officer of this Government, without warrant, detained on mere suspicion, or with a knowledge of its contents, I care not which, and without the knowledge of the person to whom it belongs, and finally destroyed; and that, too, in the very face of these sacred pledges, given in the Constitution for the inviolability of its contracts, and the security of papers thus sent. I should tremble for the liberties of my country, could I suppose for a moment that Congress would adopt a principle of this kind; the very suggestion, coming from the quarter it does, is sufficient to give alarm.

But, Sir, permit me to turn the tables on the gentleman. He, too, has had within his State a proceeding which caused much excitement, both within and without the State; I mean the attempt to nullify acts of Congress on the subject of the tariff. I assure the gentleman I do not mention this with any unkind feelings whatever. If, in that excitement, societies had been formed, and publications made in the State, for instance, in which I reside, in aid of the doctrine contended for by the gentleman and his friends in South Carolina; I ask the gentleman what he would have thought and said, if an act of Congress had been passed to prevent the proceedings of those societies, and such publications in newspapers, from being sent by the mail to any citizen of South Carolina? Sir, I have no doubt he would have condemned the Government in the most strong and emphatic manner, for the bare attempt thus to embargo public opinion; but we are now called on in the most impressive manner to sustain a like measure, by the provisions of the bill now before us; a bill new in its character, unthought of by any former Congress, and in my opinion, well calculated to produce more excess and wide spread discontent throughout the country, than any measure that has been submitted to the consideration of this body, since the existence of the Government. And pray upon what ground is this extraordinary call made upon our judgment, addressed to our feelings, and I had almost said, in despite of our patience? It is upon the ground that the General Government is bound to respect the laws of the States, to aid in their execution, and to permit its own officers, in the discharge of their duties, as required by acts of Congress, to be subject to the control of State laws, and liable to punishment for the performance of those very duties. And it is further insisted, that slavery is a domestic or State regulation; and that the property of the master in his slave is guaranteed by the Constitution of the United States; and that it is the duty of Congress to provide by law, in obedience to the wishes of the slaveholding States, or any one of them, that no pamphlet, newspaper, handbill, or other paper, printed or written, or pictorial representation, touching the subject of slavery, shall be sent into any State, Territory, or District, where by the laws of such State, Territory or District, their circulation is prohibited.

Sir, the whole doctrine is founded in error; that fatal error, which would subject the laws of Congress to the different policy of twenty-four States, and thus entirely destroy the usefulness and benefits which this Government was intended, and is calculated to administer. In support of this strange, wild, and visionary doctrine, we, (the free States I mean,) are called on to put the gag into the mouths of our citizens, to declare that they have no right to talk, to preach, or to pray on the subject of slavery; that we must put down societies who meet for such purposes; that we shall not be permitted to send abroad our thoughts or our opinions on the abstract question of slavery; that the very liberty of thought, of speech, and of the press, shall be so embarrassed, as to be in many instances denied us, and if not entirely prohibited, rendered in a great degree useless. All this is required to be done by an act of this Government, out of respect to laws of one or more of the slaveholding States. Sir, I deny the whole argument, and all its inferences, with but one single exception; and it is that which declares that slavery is a domestic or State regulation. While I freely admit this as my opinion, as my vote on the admission of Arkansas into the Union will prove, and although I may view slavery both as a moral and political evil, yet while we assure our brethren of the South and slaveholding States, in the spirit of truth and candor, that we have no power to interfere with their domestic regulations, and that our sense of the moral wrong can not cause us pain for a breach of our political duties imposed on us by our own consent, with a full knowledge of their condition; and that under our social compact, we would be bound to aid them in the suppression of any insurrection, whether servile or free, that should become too powerful for their own laws; if, after all these assurances made by us — and I repeat it with the utmost candor — I think it unkind, if not unjust toward us, that gentlemen should not be satisfied, but still require of us another condition, that we should acknowledge that slavery is guaranteed by the Constitution of the United States; and though I have heard that doctrine often repeated, I have heard no express denial, a denial which I now venture to make in this Senate, and before the American people; and on behalf of the State I in part represent here, as well as myself, I enter my most solemn protest against it. This is the important point in this whole controversy, and on it I wish so to express myself, not only that I may be understood, but that it may be, as far as I am able to make it, impossible to misunderstand me. I deny that the right of property is guaranteed by the Constitution of the United States, or that the right of the master to his slave as property, is founded on, or arises from, that instrument. Property in slaves, as well as other things, is a mere creature of law, and in this country is entirely the creature of State laws. The word slave or slavery, is not to be found in the Constitution of the United States; and by a bare perusal of that Instrument, without a knowledge of the past, no one would suppose that slavery existed in any form in this Republic. Yet I am willing to admit, that the Constitution was formed with a knowledge existing in its framers, that slavery did in fact exist in the different States; yet the slave is treated as a person, not a thing; and as a person, not as property, is represented in Congress. Hence provision is made in the Constitution of the United States, that no person who is held to service or labor in one State, under the laws thereof, escaping into another, shall, in consequence of any law or regulation therein, be discharged from service or labor, but shall be delivered up on the claim of the party to whom such service or labor is due. This provision of the Constitution of the United States only recognizes the existence of a person held to service or labor, under the laws of a State, and in its application would as well be understood to mean a white as a colored person, and one held to labor for a term of years, as well as a slave for life; and I can not consent that this provision disproves the position I assume, that the Constitution of the United

States does not guarantee the right of property in slaves; yet I have heard this so often and so earnestly asserted, that I begin to feel some concern, that should this doctrine remain much longer without being contradicted, it might become the settled doctrine of the country, and produce the most mischievous consequences to the non-slaveholding States; for if it be true, and can be maintained, the honorable Senator from South Carolina, or any other gentleman, may bring his hundreds or thousands of slaves into the State of Ohio, cause them to labor there as long as shall suit his convenience, and withdraw them at pleasure; and no law or regulation of my State—no, not even the Constitutional prohibition against slavery—could reach his case, or afford us any security against this innovation; for the Constitution of the United States, and the laws of Congress made in pursuance thereof, shall be, or is, the supreme law of the land, and the Judges in every State are bound thereby; anything in the Constitution or laws of any State to the contrary notwithstanding. It seems to me, that the free States have a thousand times more just cause of fear and alarm, while gentlemen so strongly assert their Constitutional right to their slaves, that they will attempt to introduce slavery into the free States, than the slaveholding States have that we shall attempt to interfere in any manner with the question of slavery, as settled by the laws of their own States. They are attempting to overwhelm us by the power of this Government, while we deny the right of Congress or the Legislature of any State to interfere with the internal regulations or police of another State; but while we deny this power of legal action, we contend that no institution of any State, or of this Government, can or ought to be exempt from the moral power of public opinion; that power by which the whole fabric of our institutions ought to live, move, and have its being. If the argument as to the Constitutional question of the right of property in persons be sacred and inviolable, it is certainly much stronger and more forcible when applied to property in things; and although a State might by penal enactments endeavor to prevent any person from bringing into its jurisdiction, for use or for sale, playing cards, or gambling machines of any description, yet as these articles might be considered property, and the right of the owner secured under the Constitution of the United States, such penal enactments would be vain and useless attempts. A state of things of this kind would be most deplorable indeed, and one to which, I think, the people of the United States would not long and tamely submit. Yet if these things were manufactured in a sister State, held and recognized as valuable property there, our condition would be far worse. Should Congress, by the exercise of its power, attempt to prevent us from speaking, writing, printing, publishing, and forming societies, for the exercise of all our moral power, in order to induce the people of our sister States to refrain from such practices; and of sending by mail all such proceedings, in order to induce them to abandon their pursuits, by proving that they were both moral and political evils? Yet such is the doctrine of the bill now before us; a plain exposition of which is its best refutation.

There has been another topic constantly connected with this subject, that if Abolition societies and papers were not put down, and incendiary publications (as they are called here,) prevented from being sent into the slaveholding States, the Union must and would be dissolved, and that the South would take care of her own interests, and that she was sufficiently able to do so. I regret, as I have before expressed myself, on another subject, that I so often hear this threat of a dissolution of the Union; it is, however, a vain and idle threat, calculated to affect no good, but may do some mischief. We are sometimes spoken of as a family of States, and the allusion is not an inappropriate one. What family, I would ask, could long continue in harmony, if any one of its members, on the least dissatisfaction with the general economy pursued, should always be found declaring that he or she would dissolve the union of the family, or secede from it altogether? No family could long continue happy and prosperous under such a state of things; nor could partners in business ever be successful, or labor together in peace, if one of them should, on every slight occurrence, which he did not approve, make a like threat. For my own part, I should always be disposed to believe, that persons who make such threats, desire what they threaten, and that their continuance in the family or firm, instead of being a benefit, is always an injury to the remaining members. Dissolve the Union? Who has the right to do this? No State or individual has either the moral or Constitutional right to dissolve or secede from the Union for any cause. A man may attempt revolution, and may commit treason against his country, but whether he may finally receive the reward of the traitor or the patriot, may depend on the final issue of the contest. The union of these States *can not* be dissolved but by the consent of the people to a change in their Government, in the manner provided by the Constitution of the country. States or individuals will never be permitted to do it; for if there exists in the American bosom one principle of patriotism, more strong than another, it is that of attachment to the Union. This principle is so deeply-seated in the hearts of our countrymen, that it can not be shaken, and the Union must and will be preserved. All threats of dissolution, as I before said, are vain and illusory; they never can, they never will be carried into effect.

This question, like most others agitated here, has not been suffered to pass by, without an allusion to party. We have been told that such is the influence of party discipline, that in the very eye of the gentlemen rests one, who, by raising his finger, could muster the party to vote. Insinuations of this kind, I, for one, cast behind me; the country will judge of their correctness. It is said, however, that the President in his annual message, recommended a measure of this kind; and it is strange that his party should now falter. I follow party where the Constitution and principle lead; and when men attempt to take their place, I halt. I support the administration party, because I am a firm believer in the great principles which govern them; and I endeavor to sustain them in all minor and formal points. For the sake of these principles, I sustain the President to the best of my abilities, because I believe he has done more for the liberty of his country, and to place his administration upon the basis of the Government and public opinion, than any man living. That he may sometimes err, is human. That his most ardent friends may sometimes think him in error, when, in truth he is not, is natural to expect. But that this honest difference of opinion should divide them, his opposers need not hope for; that he has recommended that postmasters and officers of this Government should arrest the passage through the mail of publications of any kind, as contemplated in this Bill, I do not understand, but he suggests the propriety of passing such a law as would prohibit, under severe penalties, the circulation in the Southern States, through the mail, of incendiary publications intended to instigate the slave to insurrection; not barely a publication touching the subject of slavery. With great respect to this recommendation, or rather suggestion, I can not give it my support; to punish injuries done to individuals, belongs exclusively to the States; they have ample security in their own power to punish any person in their jurisdiction, who may read or distribute any publication which their laws may prohibit, but they can not reach the post office or the postmaster for its delivery as directed, because such act is under a paramount authority. I, for one, doubt, strongly doubt the power of Congress to provide by law for the punishment of any act, as a criminal offense, but for those especially enumerated in the Constitution; and I can find but few such grants, such as counterfeiting the securities and current coin of the United States, the punishment of piracies and felonies committed on the high seas, offenses against the law of nations, and treason against the United States. It will readily be perceived that I confine my doubts to punishments to be inflicted in consequence of judgments by the civil tribunals of the country, rendered in courts of justice. Whatever is my course here, or elsewhere, on this or any other measure, I can not suffer the Senator from South Carolina to be my sole judge. There is another and a higher tribunal before which I must and am willing to answer; and to whose just judgment I will most cheerfully submit for my opposition to this Bill.

This Bill, designed to fetter the freedom of the press, and the circulation of thought, was rejected by a small majority in the Senate.

CHAPTER XXII.

FORMATION of parties—Their nature and results—Politics and morality—The necessity of their union—Opinions of Washington—His views need a new application to parties—Mr. Morris's views on this subject—The platforms of the two great parties on slavery—Necessity of a new party—Liberty party formed—Its platform—Birney and Morris nominated—Free Soil party—Its platform—Van Buren and Adams nominated—Hale and Julian nominated in 1852—The platform—Republican party—Fremont and Dayton nominated—Its platform—Letter of Mr. Morris on his nomination—Address of the Liberty State Convention—Votes cast for the party of freedom in 1844, 1848, and in 1852.

THE formation of parties is a natural result of a republican form of Government. The freedom of thought, created and protected by Democratic institutions, gives rise to varied political opinions and policies, and these become the nucleus around which different parties gather and rally. The wisdom and beneficent influences of parties, based on the great landmarks of true political science, admit of no doubt. They are the symbols of political faith, and the index of political action. They classify men according to their various views, and allow them to act with energy and unity in that line of policy congenial to their principles. Parties produce conflict of opinions, and collision of intellect, both of which contribute to a healthy national and individual growth.

They act as a conservative power on each other, and thus tend to a clearer vision of political truth, and to a purer and more patriotic course of action. The danger of parties in a Democratic Republic is not in their distinctive organizations, but in their rigid exclusiveness, and clan-ship. This abridges the free expansion of thought, compresses conscience into party platforms, and transfers the judgment and actions of men to party-chieftains, who, often selfish and ambitious, are liable to make, and do often make, a shipwreck of freedom and morality to purposes of personal aggrandizement.

If "Parties in free countries are useful checks upon the administration of the Government, and serve to keep alive the spirit of liberty," yet there is great danger in a Republican Government, that parties will lose sight of great moral and political principles, and absorb their independence and manhood, not in devotion to the interests of their country, but in men and parties. The evils of this are great. It tends to corruption in public men, and to the subversion of the pillars of national strength and prosperity, by disintegrating political science from moral truth. The philosophy of politics ought ever to have an indissoluble connection with moral principles. The true end of all wise legislation, and of true political science, is, not to enunciate new moral truth, but to give sound political principles, and true morality, a vital power *through* the fabric of society and civil government.

Politics is a noble science, combining the great political truths of civil government with the truest moral principles. Webster, the lexicographer, defines politics, or the science of government, "That part of ethics which consists in the regulation and government of the Nation or State, for the preservation of its safety, peace, and prosperity; comprehending the defense of its existence and rights against foreign control or conquest, the augmentation of its strength and resources, and the protection of its citizens in their rights, with the *preservation and improvement of their morals.*"

This view of the science of politics, elevates it into a system of morality, and imparts to it the dignity of truth, and the sanctity and importance of Christianity. It involves the whole interests of the nation, and is interwoven with all that constitutes a true State. Moral truths, therefore, and the life-giving and *life-preserving* elements and inspirations of religion must mingle with politics, and create and govern every system of political policy. This union is ordained of Heaven, and carries the moral sap of Christianity through all the tree of liberty, watering its roots, giving life and growth to its trunk, strength to its branches, beauty to its foliage, richness to its fruits, and perpetual preservation to its existence. To divorce politics from morals and religion, is to girdle the tree of liberty, planted by the fathers of the nation, and let it die in convulsive spasms, or by a lingering disease.

Washington gave in his Farewell Address to the nation, a solemn utterance to these cardinal truths, in saying: "It will be worthy of a free, enlightened, and at no distant period, a great nation, to give mankind the magnanimous, and too novel example of a people always guided by an exalted justice and benevolence. Who can doubt that, in the course of time and things, the fruits of such a plan would richly repay any temporary advantage which might be lost by a steady adherence to it. Can it be that Providence has not connected the permanent felicity of a nation with its virtues? The experiment, at least is recommended by every sentiment which ennobles human nature. Alas! it is rendered impossible by its vices."

"Of all the dispositions and habits which lead to political prosperity, *Religion* and *Morality* are indispensable supporters. In vain would that man claim the tribute of patriotism, who should labor to subvert these great pillars of human happiness—these firmest props of the duty of men and citizens. The mere *politician*, equally with the pious man, ought to respect and cherish them. A volume could not trace all their connection with private and public felicity. And let us, with caution, indulge the supposition that morality can be maintained without religion. Reason and experience both forbid us to expect that national morality can prevail in exclusion of religious principles."

These fundamental principles, need a re-confirmation and a fresh application to the *regime* of parties among the American people. The doctrine is *now* proclaimed, in party Conventions, that religion and morality must be disconnected with politics ; for when united it is said " It withdraws attention from the great political principles upon which the Government is founded, and is dangerous to the perpetuity of our Republican form of Government."

Mr. Morris firmly believed, that all lasting National prosperity, had its existence and growth, in the principles of Christianity. Two years before his death, he declared " *That one of the worst signs of the times was, the fact, that politicians and men high in public favor, were in the habit of sneering at the morality of the Bible. If the morality of the Bible, said he, is rejected in politics, and in the affairs of Government, it would have but little influence in private life, and the consequences would be disastrous to the character and happiness of the people and the country.*"

In view of the unsoundness of the two great parties of the United States, Democratic and Whig, and to restore the action of the Government, in regard to slavery, to the policy of the Patriots of the Revolution, and to bring politics under the benign influences of Christian morality, the friends of freedom resolved to form a new party, and make their principles known and felt, through the ballot box.

The ballot box, in the United States, is the prerogative of freedom, the palladium of American liberty, and the effectual Panacea for the political and social evils, that may afflict the country. It rules men in and out of office, and directs the whole policy of the Government. It places the power of the Government into the hands of the people, and through their sovereignty, the vital organic principles of the Government, are made efficient and powerful. Its legitimate domain, covers all that enters into the honor, the prosperity and well-being of the nation; not only the principles of politics, but the religion and morals of the people of a Republican Government, are closely identified with the right of suffrage. If "*When the righteous are in authority, the people rejoice, but when the wicked beareth rule, the people mourn,*" then the people, who, by their votes, place them in authority, must be affected in all their interests, by the Ballot Box. As all political policies and all civil Legislation are directed by the people, in the exercise of the elective franchise; and as all National prosperity, must be connected with, and supported by religion and morality, the power and influence of the Ballot Box, is under a Democracy, omnipotent.

It must be applied to the correction and eradication of all the political, social, and moral evils, that are chronic in the Body Politic. It would fall immeasurably below the dignity and sublime functions of the Ballot Box, to confine it to the petty business, of putting men into and out of office, and making it the mere engine to drive on the well-constructed machinery of *mere* Party, independent of moral principles. "Government is ordained of God," and "Rulers are the Ministers of God to be for the punishment of evil-doers, and for the praise of them that do well." And since "there is no power (civil government) but of God;" and since civil Rulers, "are God's Ministers" attending continually to be "Ministers of good," the great purpose and use of the Ballot Box, ought to be to place in power, those, and *those only*, who will give practical efficiency to the principles of a Christian morality, and so promote all that is good, and extirpate all that is evil, in society, or in civil Government.

Senator Morris saw its relations and power to the destruction of American Slavery, and pronounced upon the ballot box a noble eulogy. He said that "The moral power of the ballot box is sufficient to correct all abuses." "Moral power must work by means; and the elective franchise is the great, if not the only means to make it effectual." "Political action is necessary to produce moral reformation in a nation; and that action with us, can only be effectually exercised through the ballot box." "If the ballot box, then, is honestly and independently used, it alone will soon produce the extinguishment of slavery in our country. Resist slavery by the ballot box."

> "It executes a freeman's will,
> As lightning does the will of God."

The necessity of a new, and third party, to resist through the ballot box, the aggressions of the slave power, had its origin in the practice of the two great political parties in discountenancing all agitation of the slavery question. Their platforms, in both National and State Conventions, contained explicit resolutions against all agitation of the subject. The resolutions they adopted are presented in chronological order.

The Democratic Convention that nominated Lewis Cass, of Michigan, for President, in 1848, put the following resolution in their platform:

"1. That Congress has no power, under the Constitution, to interfere with, or control the domestic institutions of the several States, and that such States are the sole and proper judges of every thing appertaining to their own affairs, not prohibited by the Constitution; that all efforts of the Abolitionists or others, made to induce Congress to interfere with questions of slavery, or to take incipient steps in relation thereto, are calculated to lead to the most alarming and dangerous consequences; and that all such efforts have an inevitable tendency to diminish the happiness of the people, and endanger the stability and permanency of the Union, and ought not to be countenanced by any friend of our political institutions."

The Democratic Convention, in June, 1852, met in Baltimore, and nominated Franklin Pierce, of New Hampshire, for President, and William R. King, of Alabama, for Vice President. That Convention passed the same resolution on the subject of slavery, as in 1848, and these additional ones:

"*Resolved*, That the foregoing proposition covers, and was intended to embrace the whole subject of slavery agitation in Congress; and therefore the Democratic party of the Union, standing upon this National platform, will abide by and adhere to a faithful execution of the Acts known as the Compromise Measures, settled by the last Congress—the Act for the reclaiming of fugitives from service or labor, included; which act being designed to carry out an express provision of the Constitution, can not, with fidelity thereto, be repealed, or so changed as to destroy or impair its efficiency.

"*Resolved*, That the Democratic party will resist all attempts at renewing, in Congress or out of it, the agitation of the slavery question, under whatever shape or color the attempts may be made."

In June, 1856, the Democratic Convention met in Cincinnati and nominated James Buchanan, of Pennsylvania, for President, and John C. Breckenridge of Kentucky, for Vice President. This Convention put the same resolutions into their platform as in 1852, with these additional ones:

"1. *Resolved*, That claiming fellowship with, and desiring the co-operation of all who regard the preservation of the Union under the Constitution as the paramount issue —and repudiating all sectional parties and platforms, concerning domestic slavery, which seek to embroil the States and incite to treason, and armed resistance to law in the Territories, and whose avowed purposes, if consummated, must end in civil war and disunion—the American Democracy recognize and adopt the principles contained in the organic laws establishing the Territories of Kansas and Nebraska as embodying the only sound and safe solution of the 'slavery question' upon which the great National idea of the people of this whole country can repose in its determined conservatism of the Union—NON-INTERFERENCE BY CONGRESS WITH SLAVERY IN STATE AND TERRITORY, OR IN THE DISTRICT OF COLUMBIA.

"2. That this was the basis of the Compromises of 1850—confirmed by both the Democratic and Whig parties in National Conventions—ratified by the people in the election of 1852—and rightly applied to the organization of Territories in 1854.

"3. That by the uniform application of this Democratic principle to the organization of Territories, and to the admission of new States, with or without domestic slavery, as they may elect—the equal rights of all the States will be preserved intact—the original compacts of the Constitution maintained inviolate—and the perpetuity and expansion of this Union insured to its utmost capacity of embracing, in peace and harmony, every future American State that may be constituted or annexed, with a Republican form of Government.

"*Resolved*, That we recognize the right of the people of all the Territories, including Kansas and Nebraska, acting through the legally and fairly expressed will of a majority of actual residents; and whenever the number of their inhabitants justifies it, to form a Constitution, with or without domestic slavery, and be admitted into the Union upon terms of perfect equality with the other States."

The Whig National Convention, in 1848, nominated General Taylor, of Louisiana, for President, and Millard Fillmore, of New York, for Vice-President. A member of the Convention (Mr. Tilden, of Ohio), offered for adoption the following resolution:

Resolved, That while all power is denied to Congress,

under the Constitution, to control or in any manner to interfere with the institution of slavery, within the several States of this Union, it nevertheless has the power, and it is the duty of Congress to prohibit the introduction or existence of slavery in any Territory now possessed or which may hereafter be acquired by the United States.

This resolution was refused, by a vote of the Convention, to be put into the Whig Platform.

In June, 1852, the Convention of the Whig party nominated Winfield Scott, of New York, for President, and William R. Graham, of North Carolina, for Vice-President. That Convention put the following resolution into their Platform;

Resolved, That the series of acts of the thirty-first Congress (the act known as the Fugitive Slave Law included), are received and acquiesced in by the Whig party of the United States, as a settlement in principle and substance, of the dangerous and exciting questions which they embrace; and, so far as they are concerned, we will maintain them, and insist upon their strict enforcement, until time and experience shall demonstrate the necessity of further legislation, to guard against evasion of the laws on the one hand, and the abuse of their powers on the other, not impairing their present efficiency; and we deprecate all future agitation of the question thus settled as dangerous to our peace; and we will discountenance all efforts to continue or renew such agitation, *whenever*, *wherever*, or *however* the attempt may be made; and we will maintain this system as essential to the Nationality of the Whig party, and the integrity of the Union.

This subserviency of the two great parties of the country to the slave power, having its increasing development during the Senatorial term of Mr. Morris, demanded the formation of a new and third party, to resist slavery by the ballot box. Accordingly, in 1840, the friends of freedom organized themselves under the name of the LIBERTY-PARTY OF THE UNITED STATES. A Convention was called, in April, 1840, at Albany, New York, to discuss the question of an independent nomination of Abolition candidates for the two highest offices in our National Government, and if thought expedient, to make such nominations for the friends of freedom to support, at the next election. This Convention met, and nominated James G. Birney for President and Thomas Earle for Vice-President.

In August, 1843, the Liberty-Party met in a mass Convention, in Buffalo, New York, to nominate their National candidates. Every free State but New Hampshire was represented, and more than a thousand delegates were in attendance. Hon. Leicester King, of Ohio, an able and veteran friend of freedom, presided over that Convention of freemen.

The Convention proceeded to nominate their candidates; and James G. Birney, of Michigan, was unanimously selected as their candidate for President, and Thomas Morris, of Ohio, for Vice-President.

The following Platform was adopted, as the principles and policy of the Liberty-Party:

1. *Resolved*, That human brotherhood is a cardinal doctrine of true Democracy, as well as of pure Christianity, which spurns all inconsistent limitations; and neither the political party which repudiates it, nor the political system which is based upon and controlled in its practical workings by it, can be truly democratic or permanent.

2. *Resolved*, That the Liberty-Party, placing itself upon this broad principle, will demand the absolute and unqualified divorce of the General Government from slavery, and also the restoration of equal rights among men in every State, where the party exists, or may exist

3. *Resolved*, That the Liberty-Party has not been organized for any temporary purpose, by interested politicians, but has arisen from among the people, in consequence of a conviction, hourly gaining ground, that no other party in the country represents the true principles of American Liberty, or the true spirit of the Constitution of the United States.

4. *Resolved*, That the Liberty-Party has not been organized merely for the overthrow of slavery. Its first decided effort must indeed be directed against slaveholding, as the grossest form, and most revolting manifestation of despotism; but it will also carry out the principles of equal rights into all its practical consequences and applications, and support every just measure conducive to individual and social freedom.

5. *Resolved*, That the Liberty-Party is not a sectional party, but a National party; has not originated in a desire to accomplish a single object, but in a comprehensive regard to the interests of the whole country; is not a new party, or a third party, but is the party of 1776, reviving the principles of that memorable era, and striving to carry them into practical application.

6. *Resolved*, That it was understood in the times of the Declaration of Independence and the Constitution, that the existence of slavery in some of the States, was in derogation of the principles of American liberty, and a deep stain upon the character of the country; and the implied faith of the States, and of the Nation, was pledged, that slavery should never be extended beyond its then existing limits; but should be gradually, and, yet at no distant day, abolished by State authority.

7. *Resolved*, That we believe intelligence, religion and morality, to be the indispensable supports of a good government.

8. *Resolved*, That we regard voting, in an eminent degree, as a moral and religious duty, which when

exercised, should be by voting for those who will do all in their power for immediate emancipation.

9. *Resolved*, That we especially entreat the friends of liberty in the slave States to reflect on the vast importance of voting openly for Liberty and Liberty men, and to remember and adopt the words of the illustrious Washington, who said—"There is but one proper and effectual mode by which the abolition of slavery can be accomplished, and that is by legislative authority; *and this, as far as my suffrage will go, shall not be wanting.*"

10. *Resolved*, That it is a principle of universal morality, that the laws of the Creator are paramount to all human laws; or, in the language of the Apostle, that "we ought to obey God rather than man."

In August, 1848, a Convention of the friends of freedom met in Buffalo, as the Free-Soil party of the country, opposed to the extension of slavery. This Convention nominated Martin Van Buren, of New York, for President, and Charles Francis Adams (a son of John Quincy Adams), for Vice-President. The Platform of Resolutions was as follows:

Resolved, That we the people, here assembled, remembering the example of our fathers in the days of the first Declaration of Independence, putting our trust in God for the triumph of our cause, and invoking His guidance in our endeavors to advance it, in opposition to the sectional Platform of Slavery.

Resolved, That slavery in the several States of this Union which recognize its existence, depends upon State laws alone, which can not be repealed or modified by the Federal Government, and for which laws that Government is not responsible. We therefore propose no interference by Congress with slavery within the limits of any State.

Resolved, That the Proviso of Jefferson, to prohibit the

existence of slavery, after 1800, in all Territories in the United States, Southern and Northern; the votes of six States and sixteen Delegates in the Congress of 1784, for the Proviso, to three States and seven Delegates against it; the actual exclusion of slavery from the North-Western Territory, by the Ordinance of 1787, unanimously adopted by the States in Congress; and the entire history of that period—clearly show, that it was the settled policy of the Nation not to extend, nationalize, or encourage, but to limit, localize, and discourage slavery; and to this policy, which should never have been departed from, the Government ought to return.

Resolved, That our Fathers ordained the Constitution of the United States, in order, among other great national objects, to establish justice, promote the general welfare, and secure the blessings of liberty, but expressly denied to the Federal Government, which they created, all Constitutional power to deprive any person of life, liberty, or property, without due legal process.

Resolved, That in the judgment of this Convention, Congress has no more power to make a slave, than to make a king; no more power to institute or establish slavery, than to institute or establish a monarchy, — no such power can be found among those specially conferred by the Constitution, or derived by just implication from them.

Resolved, That it is the duty of the Federal Government to relieve itself from all responsibility for the existence or continuance of slavery, wherever that Government possesses Constitutional authority to legislate on that subject, and is thus responsible for its existence.

Resolved, That the true, and, in the judgment of this Convention, the only safe means of preventing the extension of slavery into territory now free, is to prohibit its existence in all such territory by an act of Congress.

Resolved, That we accept the issue which the slave power has forced upon us, and to their demand for more slave

States, and more slave Territories, our calm but firm answer is; no more slave States, and no more slave Territories. Let the soil of our extensive domains be ever kept free, for the hardy pioneers of our own land, and the oppressed and banished of other lands, seeking homes of comfort and fields of enterprise in the new world.

Mr. Van Buren, in accepting the nomination, declared in a public letter, "I have examined and considered the platform adopted by the Buffalo Convention, as defining the political creed of the "Free Democracy," with the attention due to the grave subjects under which it is presented. It breaths the right spirit, and presents a political chart which, with the explanation I am about to make, I can in good faith, adopt and sustain. The present movement, in the public mind, said he, in the non-slaveholding States, upon the subject of slavery, is caused mainly by an earnest desire to uphold and enforce the policy in regard to it, established by the founders of the Republic."

It is a singular fact illustrative of the changes that politicians have made on the subject of slavery, that Mr. Van Buren, once the idol of the Democratic party, and by it elected to the Presidency in 1836, and who in his Inaugural Address, discountenanced the agitation of slavery in Congress, declaring he would veto any Bill passed for the abolition of slavery in the District of Columbia, became the Presidential candidate of the Free Soil party, in 1848, and was the chief cause of the defeat of Mr. Cass, who was the candidate of the Democratic party, then in unnatural alliance with the slave power; and it is even more singular, that Mr. Van Buren, and his friends in the great State of New York, renouncing their free soil principles of 1848, should, in 1856, commit themselves, to a platform of principles, that gives no restriction to the extension of slavery. Such changes in men and parties, are sad illustrations of the power of slavery over the brightest intellects, and the most sagacious Statesmen of our country.

In 1852, John P. Hale, of New Hampshire, one of the earliest, and ablest advocates of freedom, and who, like Mr. Morris, stood firm, in resisting the slave power in Congress, in the darkest hours of opposition, was, by the friends of freedom, put in nomination for the President, and George W. Julian, of Indiana, for Vice President. The Platform on which they stood in that contest, was as follows :

"That no permanent settlement of the slavery question can be looked for, except in the practical recognition of the truth that slavery is sectional and freedom national; by the total separation of the General Government from slavery, and the exercise of its legitimate and Constitutional influence on the side of freedom, by leaving to the States the whole subject of slavery and the extradition of fugitives from service.

"That slavery is a sin against God and a crime against man, the enormity of which, no human enactment or usage can make right, and that Christianity, humanity, and patriotism alike demand its abolition.

"That the Fugitive Slave Act of 1850, is repugnant to the Constitution, to the principles of the common law, to the spirit of Christianity, and to the sentiments of the civilized world. We therefore deny its binding force upon the American people, and we demand its immediate and total repeal.

"That the doctrine that any human law is a 'finality,' and not subject to modification or repeal, is not in accordance with the creed of the founders of our Government, and is dangerous to the liberties of the people."

On the 17th of June, 1856, in Philadelphia, the city where the Declaration of Independence was adopted and read, from the steps of the Old State House, by one of its immortal Signers, to the multitudes assembled to hear, and who responded to its sentiments of liberty with loud and enthusiastic greetings, a large Convention of freemen, met to nominate candidates, to represent the sentiments of liberty and the political policy, which the freemen and patriots of Revolutionary memory had roused, on the subject of slavery. Every Free State was largely represented, as well as delegates from the slave States of Virginia, Maryland, Delaware, Kentucky and Missouri. It was a great assemblage convened to promote a great and noble cause. This Convention unanimously nominated John Charles Fremont, of California, for President, and William L. Dayton, of New Jersey, for Vice President. The platform adopted by the Republican Party, in this important Presidential canvas was as follows:

NATIONAL PLATFORM OF THE REPUBLICAN PARTY.

The Convention of Delegates having assembled in pursuance to a call addressed to the people of the United States, without regard to past political differences or divisions, who are now opposed to the repeal of the Missouri Compromise; to the policy of the present Administration; to the extension of slavery into free territory; in favor of the admission of Kansas; of restoring the action of the Federal Government to the principles of Washington and Jefferson, and for the purpose of presenting candidates for the offices of President and Vice President, therefore,

Resolved, That the maintenance of the principles promulgated in the Declaration of Independence, and embodied in the Federal Constitution, are essential to the preservation of our Republican institutions and the Federal Constitution: the rights of the States and the Union of the States must and shall be preserved.

Resolved, That with our Republican Fathers, we hold it to be a self-evident truth, that all men are endowed with the inalienable right to liberty and the pursuit of happiness, and that the primary object and ulterior design of our Federal Government, was to secure these rights to all persons within its exclusive jurisdiction. That as our Republican Fathers, when they had abolished slavery in all our National Territories, ordained that no person shall be deprived of life, liberty, or property, without due process of law, it becomes our duty to maintain this provision in the Constitution against all attempts to violate it, for the purpose of establishing slavery in the United States, by positive legislation, prohibiting its existence or extension therein. That we deny the authority of Congress, of a Territorial Legislature, of any individual or association of individuals, to give legal assistance to slavery in any Territory of the United States, while the present Constitution shall be maintained.

Resolved, That the Constitution confers upon Congress sovereign power over the Territories of the United States for their government, and that in the exercise of this power it is both the right and duty of Congress to prohibit in the Territories those twin relics of barbarism, polygamy and slavery.

Resolved, That while the Constitution of the United States was ordained and established by the people in order to form a more perfect Union, establish justice, insure domestic tranquillity, provide for the common defense, promote the general welfare, and secure the blessings of liberty, and contains ample provisions for the protection of the life, liberty and property of every citizen — the dearest Constitutional rights of the people of Kansas have been fraudulently and violently taken away from them; their territory been invaded by an armed force; spurious and pretended legislative, judicial and executive officers have been set over them, by whose usurped authority, sustained by the military power of the Government, tyrannical and unconstitutional laws have been enacted and enforced; the right of the people to keep and bear arms has been infringed, test oaths of an extraordinary and entangling nature have been imposed as a condition of exercising the right of suffrage and holding office; the right of an accused person to a speedy and public trial by an impartial jury has been denied; the right of the people to be secure in their persons, houses, papers and effects against unreasonable search and seizure has been violated, and they have been deprived of life, liberty, and property without due process of law; the press has been abridged; the right to choose their own representative has been made of no effect; murders and robberies encouraged, and the offenders have been allowed to go unpunished; that all these things have been done with the knowledge, sanction, and procurement of the present administration, and that for the high crime against the Constitution, the Union, and humanity, we arraign the Administration — the President, his advisers, agents, supporters, apologists and accessories — either before or after the facts — before the country and before the world, and that it is our fixed purpose to bring the actual perpetrators of the atrocious outrages and their accomplices, to a sure and condign punishment hereafter.

Resolved,. That Kansas should be admitted as a State into the Union, with her present Constitution, as at once the most effectual way of securing to her citizens the enjoyment of the rights and privileges to which they are entitled, and of ending strife now raging in the Territory.

Resolved, That the highwayman's plan, that might makes right, embodied in the Ostend Circular, was in every respect unworthy of American diplomacy, would bring shame and dishonor upon any Government or people that gave it their sanction

Resolved, That a railroad to the Pacific ocean, by the most central, practicable route, is imperatively demanded by the interests of the whole country, and that the Federal Government ought to render immediate and efficient aid to its construction, and as an auxiliary thereto the immediate construction of an emigrant road to the line of the railroad.

Resolved, That the appropriations of Congress for the improvement of rivers and harbors of a National character, required for the accommodation and security of our existing commerce, are authorized by the Constitution and justified by the obligations of the Government, to protect the lives and property of its citizens.

Resolved, That we invite the affiliation and co-operation of men of all parties, however different from us in other respects, in supporting the principles herein declared; and believing that the spirit of our institutions as well as the Constitution of our country, guarantees to us liberty of conscience, and equality of rights among the citizens, we oppose all legislation impairing their security.

The great issue in the political contest of 1856, is the extension, or non-extension of slavery. Banks, Tariff, Public Lands, and all issues involving the financial or material interests of the country, have been settled in favor of the policy of the Democratic party.

The Whig party, embracing a large proportion of the intelligence, wealth, and moral influence of the nation, have disbanded and passed away.

A new party, designated as the American, or Know Nothing party, arose, in 1854, to sudden and great political influence, and its policy was based on resistance to Popery and the Catholic religion, as a politico-religious system. A National Convention of this party, met in Philadelphia, on the 22d of February, 1856, and nominated Millard Fillmore, of New York, for President, and Andrew Jackson Donnelson, of Tennessee, for Vice-President. It refused to take decided ground against the extension of slavery, and a large majority of the Northern delegates seceded. This purpose to avoid the absorbing question of slavery, lost the party the prestige of its power in all the free States, and will, most probably, in a short time prove its political extinction. These facts in the history of parties, confirm what Daniel Webster, the great American Statesman, declared in a speech made in Faneuil Hall, Boston, in 1852. He said:

"New parties may arise, growing out of new events and new questions; but as to these old parties which have sprung from controversies now no longer pending, or from feelings which time and other causes have now greatly changed or allayed, I do not believe they can long remain. Efforts, indeed, made to that end, with zeal and perseverance may delay their extinction; but, I think, can not prevent it. There is nothing to keep alive these distinctions in the interests and objects which now engage society. New questions and objects arise, having no connection with subjects of past controversies; and present interest overcomes and absorbs the recollection of former controversies. All that are united on these existing questions and present interests, will not likely weaken their efforts to promote them, by angry reflections on past differences. If there was nothing in things to divide about, I think the people not likely to maintain systematic controversies about men. They have no interest in doing so. Associations, formed to support principles, may be called parties; but if they have no bond of union but adherence to particular men, they become factions."

The providence of God, and the dominant sentiment of freedom in the free States, produced by the continual aggressions of the slave power, forced the issue on the American people. The South admits and accepts it. It says through its press:

"It is vain to disguise it, the great issue of our day in this country is, slavery or no slavery. The present phase of that issue is the extension or non-extension of the institution, the foundations of which are broad and solid in our midst. Whatever the general measure, whatever the political combinations, whatever the party movement, whatever the action of sections at Washington, the one single, dominant, and pervading idea, solving all leading questions, insinuating itself into every polity, drawing the horoscopes of all aspirants, serving as a lever or fulcrum for every interest, class or individuality—a sort of directing fatality is that master issue. As, in spite of right and reason—of organism and men—of interest and efforts, it has become, *per se*, political destiny—why not meet it? It controls the North, it controls the South—it precludes escape. It is at last and simply a question between the South and the remainder of the Union, as sections and as people. All efforts to give it other divisions, to solve it by considerations other than those which pertain to them in their *local* character and fates, to divert it, to confound it with objects and designs of a general nature, are rendered futile. It has to be determined by these real parties, by their action in their character as sections—inchoate countries."

This great issue rises into unsurpassed importance and dignity, and the result decides the great question, whether the American Government and people will commit themselves, and all their institutions of freedom, civilization, and christianity, to the mission of extending slavery over the American continent, or return to the ancient, and the only wise and safe policy, the policy of the statesmen and patriots of the Revolution, to restrict and arrest slavery, and direct all Constitutional and moral means for its final extinguishment—a consummation that would be the crowning glory of the American nation, and remove the only hindrance to the perpetual peace and prosperity of the country. The great Republican party, inviting all of every party, and receiving its existence and growth, and its present great and permanent political influence, from an unalterable purpose to arrest the extension of slavery over the broad and free domain of the country, has intrusted to it this great mission of freedom.

Thomas Morris, in this political and moral work, was early honored, with a prominent position. His steadfastness, and loyalty to freedom and principle, secured, in the summer of 1841, his nomination for Vice President, on the Liberty Ticket, formed by the friends of freedom, in the State of New York. This nomination being only for a single State, he suggested through the following public letter, that his name be withdrawn, until a Convention from all the free States could meet and deliberate.

Dr. Bailey: — Domestic affliction, occasioned by the illness of a part of my family, and which is yet continued, has required my attention and presence within the family circle. I have thus been, in a good degree, prevented from noticing the important events that are almost daily taking place, in the great enterprise in which we are engaged, by endeavoring to restore to a large portion of our fellow men, their lost humanity and their rights, of which they have been robbed by sheer despotism.

In this enterprise, my name has been placed by my fellow citizens in New York before the country, in a very conspicuous situation, as a candidate for the Vice Presidency of the United States. This nomination was not only unsought, but unlooked for, by myself; but I can say, with perfect sincerity, that I then received it, and still view it as the highest honor ever conferred on me by any portion of my fellow citizens. Was I desirous of posthumous fame, (which I believe all men are more or less) I had rather have my name inscribed upon the most obscure record of the friends of liberty, in the present struggle, than to be placed in the highest seats of power in opposition thereto. The liberty for which we contend, is that which *like the Star of Bethlehem, leads to the salvation of men.*

As the progress of our cause and principles have been rapid beyond all calculation, (at least mine,) and as I know and feel that many men, far more able and worthy than I am, to lead in this noble cause, have of late been added to our ranks, though I can not admit that any are more desirous of its success and ultimate triumph than I am, yet I thought it due to the cause, and to the country, to afford an opportunity to all our friends to review the nomination. I, therefore, gave notice to our last Liberty Convention, at Columbus, that it was my intention to decline, and wait for further developments in regard to duty.

I have, within a day or two past, seen, in some of our Eastern Liberty papers, remarks on the course I thought it my duty to take. Permit me to say to our friends, in every part of the country, that no abatement of my zeal in the cause of human liberty has taken place; and that my hopes, and my expectations, were never brighter than they now are, of the speedy and ultimate triumph of our principles. I feel a strong desire, and I trust some faith, advanced as I am in life, that I shall yet be spared to see the day, when the soil of our beloved country, shall no where be cursed with the foot-prints of a slave. I shall then leave the world, believing I have left my posterity a legacy beyond all price.

I would not have taken the step which I have, had I not fully understood that a General Convention of liberty men, from all the States, would be held during the ensuing summer. When that Convention shall have met, they may dispose of my name as they shall judge best. All I ask is, that the friends of liberty will believe me, when I assure them, that I am engaged in this cause, under a full conviction, that it is just and right; and that on its success depends, not only the prosperity but the salvation of the country ; and no matter where I labor, my enlistment and my promise of service are not for years but for life.

I write this hasty communication for fear a wrong construction may be put upon the position I now occupy. I hope soon, to find time to address the Executive Committee at NewYork on the subject more at length.

THOMAS MORRIS.

Cincinnati, March 20th, 1843.

He was renominated as a candidate for the Vice Presidency on the Liberty ticket, by the General Convention at Buffalo, August 30th, 1843.

Ohio met in Convention, at the Capitol of the State, in October succeeding the National Convention, to ratify the nominations. After presenting the claims and services of James G. Birney, their candidate for the Presidency, the Address of the Liberty Convention to the people of Ohio, says of the candidate for the Vice-Presidency:

"Thomas Morris, our candidate for the Vice-Presidency, is one of the oldest citizens of this State. Whether as Representative in your State Legislature, or Senator in Congress, he has ever been known as the fearless, independent, consistent politician. That most eloquent speech, delivered by him in 1839, amid the sneers and frowns of servile and slaveholding Senators; in defense of human liberty, and in vindication of its advocates against the assaults of him, who is now the recognized leader of the Whig party ; delivered too, without a word of encouragement from those whose principles and characters he vindicated; in the face of the policy of his own party, and with the certain prospect of losing its favor; that speech, and the heroic love of liberty it evinced, have endeared him FOREVER to the friends of freedom. Ohio will remember *hereafter*, with delight, that the only voice which broke the stillness of the Senate Chamber of the United States, for fifteen long years, in rebuke of despotism, was the voice of her undaunted son, Thomas Morris."

Western Virginia, whence Thomas Morris had emigrated in 1795, had a Spartan band who held to the ancient liberty doctrines of Jefferson, and one county (Ohio), had in 1843, a Liberty ticket, and issued an Address, in which they speak of Thomas Morris as follows:

"They have selected, as their candidate for Vice-President, Thomas Morris, of Ohio, a native of Western Virginia, who has been from his boyhood a consistent advocate of equal rights. This distinguished citizen, when a few years since, he represented the State of his adoption, in the Senate of the United States, stood up *alone* in that Body, uncheered by the sympathies of political associates, and unsupported except by a noble confidence in the justness of his cause, to vindicate the principles of liberty, against the assaults of Henry Clay, who then stood as the champion of perpetual slavery. By that most *signal service* to the cause of the people, Thomas Morris forfeited the support of party, but *endeared himself forever to the lovers of liberty.*"

The following votes for the candidates representing the sentiment of freedom, will show the progress of the party devoted to freedom and the American Nation:

In 1840, seven thousand; in 1844, sixty-two thousand one hundred and sixty-three; in 1848, two hundred and ninety-one thousand three hundred and seventy-eight; in 1852, one hundred and fifty-five thousand eight hundred and forty-nine; and in 1856, the date of the present writing, the free States are anxiously waiting to cast their hundreds of thousands of votes for the Republican candidates, and confidently expect to carry the country in favor of freedom.

> "Who can tell how vast the plan
> Which this day's incident began?
> And it may prove, when understood,
> The harbinger of endless good."

CHAPTER XXIII.

Territorial Expansion of Slavery—Missouri Compromise—Her Admission—Agitation—Sentiments of Daniel Webster on the Admission of Missouri—Admission of Arkansas—Remarks of Mr. Morris, in the Senate, on the Admission of Arkansas—Republic of Texas—Remarks and Resolution of Mr. Morris on Texas—Acquisition of Territory from Mexico—California—Repeal of the Missouri Compromise—Agitation through the country—Manifesto of Chase and others — Ministers Remonstrate — The act done — New Territory opened to Slavery — Kansas—Its Slave Laws—Struggle between Freedom and Slavery—Results of the Expansion of Slave Territory—Shall Kansas be Free or not?—Its effects on Labor—Opinions of Slaveholders on Labor—Its effects on Society and on White Laborers—Slavery Demonstrated to be a Curse.

The expansion of the area of slavery has ever been a leading purpose with Southern Statesmen. The great motive was the increase of their political power, and its permanent supremacy in the Government of the Nation. Every new State added to the Union, not only aided in the preservation of a political equilibrium between the free and slave States, but continued to the slave power, its political ascendency. The Constitution provides that the members of the House of Representatives, shall be proportioned to the free inhabitants of the States they represent, *except* that in each State, three-fifths of the slave population, shall be for this purpose considered as free inhabitants. According to this proviso, every five slaves are to be counted as three white persons. If by law, every sixty thousand free inhabitants may elect a Representative, a district containing forty-five thousand whites and twenty-five thousand slaves, is by the *Federal ratio* entitled to a member. This Constitutional stipulation, has through all the political history of the American Government, given the slaveholders a prepondering weight in the National Councils. Hence the fact, and it is a political anomaly, that at the present time, the slaveholding interest, has a representation of thirty members in *addition* to the equal representation of the free inhabitants. This is a property Representation—for slaves in the South are but property in the eye of the law—which is denied to every species of property in the free States; and this fundamental law of the Government operates unequally.

In the Senate of the United States, there is an equality of political power in the States, each State, however small or great, being entitled to two Senators in Congress, so that, a small slave State, like Delaware, has, in the Senate, a political power equal to the great State of New York, with her immense population and wealth. The preservation and the increase of this power in the Government, has been, and is now, the great motive that prompts the South to seek the extension of slavery. A brief historical expose of this extension is here presented.

The first efforts, subsequent to the purchase of Louisiana in 1803, from France, under the Administration of President Jefferson, made by the slave power, to extend slavery, was in the case of Missouri. In 1820, Missouri sought admission into the Union, as an independent State. Her Constitution admitted the existence and perpetuity of slavery; and when she came to ask for admission as a new State, into the Union, it was earnestly resisted by the free States, both by the people and their Representatives in Congress. It was a most memorable struggle between freedom and slavery, and agitated the whole country profoundly. After a postponement of a year, Missouri was admitted into the Union, on condition that, "In all that Territory ceded by France to the United

States, under the name of Louisiana, which lies North of thirty-six degrees, and thirty minutes of North Latitude, not included within the limits of the State of Missouri, *slavery and involuntary servitude shall be and is hereby forever prohibited.*" The admission of Missouri as a slave State, under this compromise, was the first great expansion of the slave power. President Monroe, before he signed the Missouri Act, of 1820, required a written opinion of each member of his Cabinet, as to the proposition whether "Congress has a right, under the powers vested in it by the Constitution, to make a regulation prohibiting slavery in a Territory." All the members of the Cabinet, including John C. Calhoun, and John Quincy Adams, answered in the affirmative.

Daniel Webster, in 1819, drew up an able memorial against the admission of Missouri as a slave State, which he, and others of Boston, signed and sent to Congress, and from which the following extracts are taken :

"Your memorialists would most respectfully submit that the terms of the Constitution, as well as the practice of the Government under it, must, as they humbly conceive, entirely justify the conclusion, that Congress may prohibit the further introduction of slavery, into its own Territories, and also make such provision a condition of the admission of any new State into the Union. We have a strong feeling of the injustice of any toleration of slavery. But to permit it in a new country, where yet no habits are formed to render it indispensable, what is it, but to encourage that rapacity and fraud, and violence, against which we have so long pointed the denunciations of our penal code? What is it but to tarnish the proud fame of the country? What is it but to throw suspicion on its good faith, and to render questionable all its professions of regard for the rights of humanity and the liberties of mankind. If the extensive and fertile fields of the Missouri Territory shall be opened as a market for slaves, the Government will seem to become a party to a traffic, which, in so many acts, through so many years, it has denounced as impolitic, unchristian, and inhuman."

Arkansas, in 1836, was admitted into the Union, with a Constitution making slavery perpetual. Mr. Morris, was then called upon as a Senator of the United States to vote on the question of the admission of another slave State. His views are presented in extracts from his speech found in Benton's "Thirty Years in the United States Senate," "Mr. Morris," said Mr. Benton, "spoke more freely on the objectional points than other Senators. He said:

"Before I record my vote in favor of the passage of the Bill under consideration, I must ask the indulgence of the Senate for a moment, while I offer a few of the reasons which govern me in the vote I shall give. Being one of the Representatives of a free State, and believing slavery to be wrong in principle, and mischievous in practice, I wish to be clearly understood on the subject, both here, and by those I have the honor to represent. I have objections to the Constitution of Arkansas, on the ground that slavery is recognized in that Constitution, and settled and established as a fundamental principle in her government. I object to the existence of this principle forming a part of the organic law of any State; and I would vote against the admission of Arkansas, if I believed I had power to do so. The wrong, in a moral sense, with which I view slavery, would be sufficient for me to do this, did I not consider my political obligations, and the duty, as a member of this body, under which I now act, clearly require of me this vote.

"I hold that any portion of American citizens, who may reside on any part of the Territory of the United States, whenever their number shall amount to that which would entitle them to a representation in the House of Representatives in Congress, have a right to provide for themselves a Constitution and State Government, and to be admitted into the Union whenever they shall so apply; and they are not bound to wait the action of Congress in the first instance, except there is some compact or agreement requiring them to do so. I place this right upon the broad, and as I think, indisputable ground, that all persons living within the jurisdiction of the United States, are entitled to equal privileges; and it ought to be a matter of high gratification to us here, that in every position, even the most remote of our country, our people are anxious to obtain this high privilege at as early a day as possible. It furnishes clear proof that the Union is highly esteemed, and has its foundation deep in the hearts of our fellow citizens.

"By the Constitution of the United States, power is given to Congress to admit new States into the Union. It is in the character of a State that any portion of our citizens must apply to be admitted into the Union; a State Constitution and Government must be first formed. It is not necessary for the power of Congress, and I doubt whether Congress has such power, to prescribe the mode by which the people shall form a State Constitution; and for this plain reason, that Congress would be entirely incompetent to the exercise of any coersive power to carry into effect the mode they might prescribe. I can not therefore, vote against the admission of Arkansas into the Union, on the ground that there was no previous act of Congress to authorize the holding of her Convention. As a member of Congress I will not look beyond the Constitution that has been presented. I have no right to presume it was formed by incompetent persons, or that it does not fully express the opinions and wishes of the people of that country. It is true that the United States shall guarantee to every State in the Union a Republican form of Government: meaning, in my judgment, that Congress shall not permit any power to establish in any State, a Government without the assent of the people of such State; and it will not be amiss that we remember here, also, that that guarantee is to the State, and not as to the formation of the Government by the people of the State; but, should it be admitted that Congress can look into the Constitution of a State, in order to ascertain its character, before such State is admitted into the Union, yet I contend that Congress can not object to it for the want of a Republican form, if it contains the great principle that all power is inherent in the people, and that the Government draws all its just powers from the governed.

"The people of the Territory of Arkansas, having formed for themselves a State Government, having presented their Constitution for admission into the Union, and that Constitution being Republican in its form; and believing that the people who prepared and sent this Constitution, are sufficiently numerous to entitle them to a Representative in Congress; and believing, also, that Congress has no right or power to regulate the system of police these people have established for themselves, and the Ordinance of 1787 not operating on them, nor have they entered into any agreement with the United States that Slavery should not be admitted into the State—have the right to choose this lot for themselves. Though I regret that they have made this choice, yet believing that this Government has no right to interfere with the question of slavery in any of the States, or prescribe what shall or shall not be considered property in the different States, or by what tenure property of any kind shall be holden, but that all these are questions of State policy, I can not, as a member of this body, refuse my vote to admit this State into the Union, because her Constitution recognizes the right and existence of slavery."

Similar views were expressed by John Quincy Adams, in the House. He said: "I can not, consistently with a sense of my obligations as a citizen of the United States, and bound to support their Constitution, object to the admission of Arkansas into the Union as a slave State. It is written in the bond, and however I may lament that it ever was so written, I must faithfully perform its obligations."

The next successful movement of the extension of the slave power, was the admission of the Republic of Texas, on the 29th of December, 1845.

Mr. Morris foresaw, in the Senate of the United States, that the recognition of the independence of Texas had an ulterior object in reference to slavery. He said, in 1836, after presenting memorials from Cincinnati, requesting Congress to acknowledge the independence of Texas, and in answer to a Southern Senator, Mr. Walker, that "The recognition of Texas involved *a question which did not meet the eye*, and which was beyond the mere recognition of her independence—a question which would convulse *this Union from one end to the other.*" That prophecy has been fearfully fulfilled. Since the annexation of Texas, the Union has been in a state of intense excitement, almost of continued convulsion. That event led to a war with Mexico, and the war with Mexico resulted in a cession to the United States of New Mexico and California.

Mr. Morris offered for the consideration of the Senate, the following resolution:

"*Resolved*, That while we hail with joy the events in Texas, which seem to look to an emancipation in that country, we fear there is increased reason for believing that a desperate effort will soon be made by the slave power to annex Texas to this Union, and we therefore earnestly implore our fellow-citizens of every party to use all lawful endeavors to avert such a calamity."

In 1854, another wide field was opened, into which the slave power might extend its dominion. The Missouri Compromise Act was canonized by a sacred compact, and by all the forms and sanctions of solemn legislation, and was regarded with the strongest affection by the American people, both North and South. This, however, was not sufficient to guard it against the covetousness and the aggressions of slavery. It was a restraint, a prohibition to the expansion of slavery, which could no longer be tolerated. The repeal of the Missouri Compromise was deliberately meditated, and deliberately done. In the month of March, 1854, the Senate, by a large majority, consummated its repeal, and the House, by a decisive majority concurred, and the approval of the President of the United States, Mr. Pierce, completed its legal repeal. It opened an immense territory, a territory that had been for a generation consecrated to freedom, and ample enough to form twelve States as large as the great State of Ohio, to the evil inroads of slavery. The repealing clause of the Bill, designated as the Kansas and Nebraska Bill, declared the prohibition of slavery over those broad and fertile regions "inoperative and void."

Mr. Chase, then a Senator from Ohio, with other Senators and Representatives from free States, issued from the Capital of the Nation, a Manifesto to the people, warning them of the purpose of the slave power, and the peril of freedom. The public sentiment of the North was roused to active resistance, and numerous and large public meetings were held, to remonstrate against the measure, and to protest against the great wrong.

The religious sensibilities and conscience of all Christian denominations, were awakened into intense activity. The pulpit of the free States, as in Revolutionary times, vindicated the cause of freedom, and denounced the measure as a wrong to Christianity, to humanity, and to the plighted faith and integrity of the nation. Three thousand clergymen of New England, representing the sentiments of their respective congregations, with their names on one large memorial, sent up their petitions to the Senate of the United States, against the act of repeal, declaring that it was "a great moral wrong, a breach of faith, and eminently injurious to the morals of the community, and calculated to bring down upon the nation the curse of God." Clergymen in almost all the free States, sent to both branches of the National Legislature, similar remonstrances. Senators from the free and slave States, charged all such clergymen with "prostituting the sacred desk to the miserable and corrupting influences of party politics;" of "neglecting their holy religion, and violating its principles;" "as political preachers, meddling with matters of which they were ignorant." Slavery, through the subserviency of Northern Congressmen, obtained the triumph, and the gate was opened for its entrance.

The repeal of the Missouri Compromise converted Kansas into a field of contest between slavery and freedom; into a trial of the nature and forces of the two opposite systems. In this great contest, on which the entire nation looked with deep sympathy and attention, freedom, as it had always done, outrivaled the efforts of slavery—in enterprise, in numbers, in all the institutions of a Christian civilization; and Kansas gave promise that freedom and its blessings should yet be the rich inheritance of the millions who were to live upon her soil.

The time came for the Territory to assume an organized form of civil government. In the election of members to the Territorial Convention to form a Constitution, the settlers from the free States were driven from the polls, by several thousand men from Missouri, and no man was permitted to cast his suffrage, unless he would vote for making Kansas a slave Territory and State. The Convention elected were all, but one or two, pro-slavery men; notwithstanding the free State voters—the actual citizens of the Territory—outnumbered the pro-slavery men five-fold.

This Convention, elected by Missourians, passed a Code of laws, marked by the greatest injustice and cruelty, and which were (in Congress and throughout the country), denounced as a disgrace to the age. They enacted that:

"Every person who should write, print, or publish any book, paper, argument, opinion, advice, or in words, calculated to produce disaffection among the slaves in the Territory, or induce them to escape from their masters, should be deemed guilty of FELONY, and be punished by imprisonment at hard labor, for a term not less than five years; and if he should publish anything even denying the right of persons to hold slaves in the Territory, he should be punished by imprisonment at hard labor for two years." It was also enacted, that—"Every person who should raise an insurrection among the Negroes; who should aid in enticing away a slave, with intent to procure his freedom; or who should aid in enticing away a slave; or who should entice and bring from any other State in the Union, a slave into Kansas, with the intent to set him free, upon conviction should suffer DEATH." These and similar acts were passed by the Territorial Legislature of Kansas.

Freedom, however, did not yield the contest. The interests and issues were too great to be lost, without an earnest and laborious struggle. The free and actual citizens of the Territory held their own election, and sent members to another Convention, to form a free Constitution, and organize a free Government. Under this State Constitution, they organized and came before Congress asking admission into the Union. The House of Representatives, by a majority of three, accepted of the Constitution, and voted to admit Kansas as an independent State; the Senate, however, rejected it, by a large majority.

This contest in Kansas, between slavery and freedom, was marked by the most inhuman atrocities against the free settlers. They were invaded by armies from Missouri, and South Carolina; their towns were burned;

their houses plundered, and their property destroyed; their printing-presses demolished; their free citizens, for defending freedom and establishing free institutions, were imprisoned and murdered; and almost every act of injustice and inhumanity was perpetrated. In this great contest the free State men stood firm, and acted and said—"Give us liberty or death;" and the free women of Kansas, like their mothers of Revolutionary memory, rallied with their husbands and sons, to the defense of freedom, and laid their offerings and themselves upon the altar of liberty.

The struggle is still in progress, and the issue is with Him who ruleth among the nations; and who created, not only all men to be free, but gave the earth, as a rich patrimony to men, to be cultivated as a free soil, and by free labor. Of Kansas, let every freeman ask, in the words of a poet.

Shall the free winds, that sweep her grassy vales
Be burdened with the groan of sad despair?
Shall the free waves, that wash her fertile shores
Blush with the blood that runs from furrowed backs?
Shall her tall mountains, crowned with sparkling snow,
Become red altars for the slaughtered slave?
Shall her green valleys be the early grave
Of Freedom, or the cradle of the Free?
Shall her broad rivers, rolling to the deep,
Shout Liberty's inspiring song for aye,
Or slink to the old Ocean's arm to hide
Their stains behind his ample cloak of waves?
Shall her vast plains and prairies, filled with flowers
As glorious night is filled with gleaming stars,
Be cleared, and ploughed, and hoed, and reaped by slaves?

Not only Christianity, the genius of our free institutions and of the age, but humanity and the interests and dignity of Free labor, demand that the soil of our nation, every acre of it, should be preserved free from slavery.

Slavery is a system that puts dishonor and disgrace on labor, which has the seal of honor instamped upon it by the Creator

The free States of the North, where free labor, has wrought out all their splendid achievements of enterprise, are described, by the Southern press, as "rioting in the excesses of an indiscriminate freedom, prodigal in liberty, bankrupts in law;—where labor is elevated to political power, and enjoys the same political privileges with the capital that employs it." "All society," says a Southern politician, "settles down into a classification of capitalists and laborers. The former will own the latter." "If laborers," said Mr. McDuffie, "obtain the political power of a country, it is, in fact, in a state of revolution. The institution of slavery supersedes the necessity of an order of nobility." Slavery is by the South declared to be a "National blessing;" "a Patriarchal Institution;" "The corner stone of our Republican Edifice." "In a few years the blasphemous Reformers, who curse the Constitution for legalizing, and the Bible for consecrating slavery, will curse Heaven, that it did not bless the North with African slavery, the only antidote to a crowded, motley, foreign and native population."

Slavery is not only the antagonism of free labor, dishonoring it, and the free laborers of the North, but it is a system that operates most injuriously and debasingly, upon the poorer classes of the non-slaving South. Of the six millions of people in the slaveholding States, and of the 876,243 voters in the same section, there are but 347,000 slaveholders, leaving 528,000 voters in the South, and more than five millions of persons, who have no personal interest or complicity with slavery. They are in the technical language of the slave system, the "Poor Whites of the South." Though not able, or not willing to be the owners of slaves, yet this immense preponderating population of the slave States, are dishonored by the system that surrounds them. They have but little influence in political affairs, and are so under the surveillance of the slave Aristocracy, that freedom of opinion is stifled, and an independent course of action prevented. Social as well as political disfranchisement, and debasement, is the condition of this class, who are numerous and worthy in the South. Schools for popular education, are not provided, and Free Schools, are unknown, and thus ignorance, the natural result of slavery, aids in the work of degradation.

The soil also of a slave country, soon becomes, under the working of the slave system, unproductive. In this aspect it is a perfect contrast with the results of freedom and free labor. Consecrate a soil to perpetual freedom; let the genius of freedom, breathe its air of inspiration and purity over the soil, and the soil under its power will produce an abundant harvest. Freedom will replenish, too, the waste and worn out soil, with a new life and a fresh reproductive vitality. Not so with slavery.

Governeur Morris, a statesman of the highest order of talents, in the Convention that formed the Constitution, in 1787, said, "Compare the free regions of the Middle States, where a rich and noble cultivation marks the prosperity and happiness of the people, with the misery and poverty which overspread the barren wastes of Virginia and Maryland, and other States having slaves. The moment you leave the free States and enter the slave States, the effects of the institution become visible. Every step you take through the great regions of slaves, presents a desert, increasing with the increasing proportion of these wretched beings." This contrast, ages of experiment, the whole history of the world, and the philosophy of cause and effect, confirm; thus demonstrating, that slavery is a curse, blighting and destroying every true interest of a nation, and ought not to extend and establish itself anywhere among a free people, or over a free soil.

CHAPTER XXIV.

SLAVES brought to Ohio—Mr. Morris memorializes the Governor against it—Slaveholders in office in free States—Mr. Morris's views on it—A Judge refuses to license a colored Clergyman to perform the Marriage Rite—Mr. Morris obtains a writ to compel him to grant it—A memorial to the Legislature of Ohio, in 1844—Extracts from a Letter—Appeal to Christians—Poem, descriptive of his course and principles.

THE Constitution of Ohio, and of all the free States, secures personal freedom to every slave, voluntarily brought by his master within their jurisdiction. The noble truth, uttered by Cowper, the Christian poet of England, is the doctrine incorporated into their charters of freedom:

"Slaves can not breathe in England; if their lungs
Receive our air, that moment they are free;
They touch our country, and their shackles fall.
That's noble, and bespeaks a nation proud
And jealous of the blessing."

Ohio, in her Constitution, does not permit slavery, or the foot-prints of a slave, to pollute her soil. Notwithstanding this prohibition, and in defiance of the public sentiment and moral sense of the citizens of the free States, slaveholders, in their social visits, or on their way to a Southern market with their slaves, have brought them into free States, and during their transit or stay, have virtually converted free into slave territory.

The free States, also, not unfrequently, are represented in their State and National interests, by virtual slaveholders. Marriage, or inheritance, puts into their possession, or under their control, Southern plantations, well stocked with slaves. Interest and sympathy are then transferred to the slave power, and thus Northern politicians become the most subservient and devoted friends of the slave power. A potent evil influence, from this source, has spread through the free States, and tended to vitiate the public sentiment of the North on the subject of slavery. In reference to these two subjects, connected with slavery, which involved the free States in indirect complicity with the system, Mr. Morris addressed a memorial to the Governor of Ohio, containing the following sentiments:

"The violation of our laws by slaveholders bringing, or sending their slaves into our State, is productive of more injury to, and creates more disgust and heart-burnings among our citizens, than any other violation of the laws known among us. Ought we not then to be protected by Executive proclamation, as to what the law is, and encouraged to carry it into faithful execution? Ought not our people to be honored in securing liberty to every man upon whom our laws confer it, instead of the constant attempts to disgrace them, by heaping upon them opprobrious epithets, as "negro thieves," etc., to which the public press, if not the pulpit, sometimes basely descends.

"For myself I go for the law, the whole law, and nothing but the law, in which the liberty of my fellow-man is concerned; and as a citizen of the State I call upon its Executive officer to do the same. If we have no sympathy for the slave, no feeling for his sufferings, let us take care that a power, arising out of his condition, does not rule and govern us. To talk of security and peace in Ohio, while our laws are trampled under foot by the slave-hunter, is vain and idle. Even the slave-trade is carried on through Ohio, with entire impunity; coffles of chained slaves have landed on our wharf, while numbers are almost daily within our jurisdiction, on steam-boats, on their way to Southern markets; and yet we talk about our opposition to slavery, while we permit the cursed traffic in slaves thus to be carried on in our midst; and if any of our citizens shall inform those slaves, that by our laws they are free, they are indicted and found guilty of riot. Call you this a faithful execution of the laws?

"Permit me, Sir, to suggest to you the propriety of obtaining full and correct information on this subject, and give to the General Assembly such information, and recommend such measures to their consideration as will in future entirely prevent the slave trade from being carried on through our State. Nothing short of this will preserve the public quiet among us.

"Another consideration I beg leave to mention. Ought not persons who own slaves in another State, be prohibited from holding any office in this State? Such persons are inimical to the principles of our Government, and it is solemn mockery for them to take an oath to support our Constitution, while they are violating its very essence, in sight, probably, of the very spot where they take such oath. Is not the legislative power competent to prevent this evil, and cause our Government to be administered in good faith, and thus define our position, by which alone peace and good will can be restored between us and our sister slaveholding States? 'Let not them pass over to us for our hurt, and we will not pass over for their hurt, and then there will be no strife between us.' This is a consummation devoutly to be wished."

An incident, illustrative of his sense of justice as well as his benevolence toward an oppressed people, is here recorded. A colored clergyman of the Methodist Episcopal church, applied to a certain Judge of a Court, in Brown county, Ohio, having proper jurisdiction, for a legal license to perform the marriage rite. The prejudice of the Judge was so strong against the color of the applicant, that in the exercise of his "little brief authority," he peremptorily refused to grant to the clergyman his legal right. Mr. Morris, perfectly conscious of the injustice and illegality of the act, took the case up to the Supreme Court of the State. There he obtained justice. That Court ordered a writ of *Mandamus* to the lower Court, to grant the applicant a license to marry those who desired his services in that way.

The following memorial was written in November, 1844, a short time previous to his death. It was designed as a form for circulation among all opposed to the extension of slavery, and to the exercise of its power in the free State of Ohio. It is brief and comprehensive:

To the Honorable the General Assembly of the State of Ohio.

In approaching the Legislature, we know that it is our Constitutional right, and while it is our desire respectfully to address the General Assembly, we hope to do so in the language of freemen. We intend to make Truth our guide, Equity and Justice our object, and the Common Good our ultimate aim; and we ask Legislative action on the following subjects:

WE PROTEST against the annexation of Texas to the United States, as unconstitutional, unwise, impolitic, and dangerous to the peace and safety of our country; and we pray the General Assembly, without delay, to pass a resolution against such annexation, and transmit the same immediately to Congress.

We further ask the Legislature to repeal all the Black Laws (commonly so called), that are now in force upon the Statute Book. And we make this request, because those laws are of no benefit to the white man; while they are unjust and oppressive to the black man, without cause.

We also ask the passage of a law prohibiting the use of the jails within this State, for the purpose of detaining, in any manner whatever, any person who may be claimed as a fugitive slave.

And we further ask the passage of a law, punishing under severe penalties, any officer holding his office under or by the authority of this State, from aiding in his official character, in any manner or form whatever, to return or send out of the State any person who may be claimed as a FUGITIVE SLAVE. And further, to punish in like manner any citizen of Ohio, or any person within her jurisdiction, who shall aid or abet, (or who shall attempt to do so,) any other person to take or carry without the State, any such claimed fugitive slave, except the person be a citizen of another State, his agent or attorney, by whom the labor or service of such fugitive slave may be claimed, under the law of the State from which he or she fled, or by an officer of the United States.

We have often heard it said, that "Ohio is a free State, that slavery does not exist here, and that we ought to let slavery alone." That Ohio is Constitutionally a free State is admitted; but that many of her citizens and the administration of her Government is under the influence and control of the slave power, is equally clear; that her citizens and officers ought to "let slavery alone," is not denied; but as this is not the case, we pray the Legislature to provide by law for the attainment of this desirable object.

A distinguished laborer in the cause of freedom, and an Elder in one of the New-School Presbyterian churches of Ohio, in a recent letter, says of Mr. Morris:

"My recollections of him are very vivid and very pleasant. I met him at several State Conventions, and always listened to him with great interest and profit. In those days, when politicians of all parties united in opposition to the anti-slavery movement, it was as remarkable as it was gratifying to find one honest, earnest, influential public man, willing to lay himself upon the altar of liberty; and we young men could but respect and revere him, who almost alone made the sacrifice.

"The last time I had the pleasure of hearing him was at Bloomingsburgh, when with remarkable plainness and force, he called on professors of religion to wipe out the reproach which their complicity with slavery brings upon the cause of true Christianity; and I shall never forget with what feelings of pain and grief, a few of us Presbyterians met and discussed, what we hoped would prove the initiatory steps to a complete reform in the New-School church. The death of the lamented George Beecher, which occurred soon after, broke up the Committee, to whom the matters had been referred, for the purpose of giving them shape and direction.

"His integrity of character, and devotion to the great Democratic principles, are worthy of all honor, and are unlike his compeers, who recognize, as do too many modern Democrats, only the doctrine as applied to classes?"

The following poem, giving a just description of his course and principles, on the great cause of human rights and freedom, is here inserted; it was written on the eve of his retirement from the Senate of the United States, by an unknown friend, and addressed to

THOMAS MORRIS.

Free Senator! accept the lay
  The unknown muse attunes for thee:
Not for the valorous display
  Of martial feats and chivalry:
Or for the blood-stained laurels won
  By knightly deeds of daring done.

Not for the palm of high renown,
  The price of blood, and chains and tears;
Nor for the talents vainly shown
  In windy war with thy compeers;
But for a deed more nobly brave—
  The pleading for the outcast slave.

For this thy name shall live in song,
If song of mine itself shall live;
And living, bear the meed along
Thy deeds have earned, and faithful give
To future time thy moral worth,
When cold thy ashes rest in earth.

And when thy proud compatriots lie
Forgotten, 'neath the silent sod;
And when their words and memory die,
Scathed by the blighting curse of God—
Thy deeds shall gain immortal fame,
And men unborn revere thy name.

Ah! yes, the ransomed slave shall bless
Thy name, when thou art laid at rest,
And pointing to thy tomb express:
"There lies in peaceful slumber blest,
"The advocate of the oppressed,
"Friend of the poor and the distressed."

Intrepid Statesman! when the tongues
Of Northern Senators were hushed,
And despots triumphed o'er the wrongs
Of minds debased and spirits crushed;
When even Webster's spirit quailed,
And firm John Quincy's ardor failed—

'Twas then thou rose to breast the storm,
And throw thyself as in the breach—
To raise the captives bleeding form,
And with undaunted manly speech,
To show his wrongs—the sighs and tears
That preyed upon his soul for years.

Thou spake, and on the opppressor flung
  The burden of thy strong rebuke,
Who quite alarmed and conscience stung,
  With rage and consternation shook;
And haughty Southrons, awe-struck hung
  Upon the thunders of thy tongue.

Firm and erect thou stood'st alone,
  And slavery's haughty champions met;
Not the stern brow of fierce Calhoun,
  Nor Patton's gag, nor Preston's threat,
Thy dauntless spirit could dismay—
  Thou fear'dest not *the face of Clay.*

Let fiery Rhett and Campbell roar,
  And woman's weak petition spurn—
Let Waddy Thompson—slavery's slave—
  With fury rage and anger burn—
Let Pinkney, Wise, and Atherton
  Reap all the fame their deeds have won.

But thou shalt gain immortal praise,
  Thy country's blessing rests on thee;
The bondman freed his voice shall raise,
  And link thy name with Liberty:—
For lo! thy monuments shall be
  Raised in the hearts of slaves made free.

CHAPTER XXV.

MISCELLANEOUS reflections during his Senatorial term—Calls on the President—The President's Levee—Bank Excitement—Removal of Deposits—Violence of Party Spirit—McDuffie's Oratory—Funerals of Members of Congress—Their pageantry and expense—Departure of the Government from Republican simplicity—Letter Writers at Washington, etc.

IN this chapter the reader will find various extracts from letters written by Mr. Morris, to his eldest son, in a free and familiar manner. They are interesting as reflections on the political condition and parties of the country; and as the opinions of an observing man, himself a veteran politician of the times in which he lived.

WASHINGTON, November 30, 1833.

YESTERDAY spent most of the time in visiting the President and Heads of Departments, according to the etiquette of this city. I found the President (Gen. Jackson), a man less in stature than I expected. The constant crowd around him would not permit any one to stay but a few minutes. A tedious and stormy session is expected, and party lines are to be more distinctly drawn here, if I am not mistaken, than in Ohio. It is said that more members have brought with them their ladies, than was ever known before. This, to my mind, shows they expect a long session.

The Capitol is, I presume, one of the most extravagant buildings for the same purpose in the world, though both the House and Senate Chamber are small, and to my mind, not very convenient. I have taken a seat next to Mr. Calhoun, between him and Mr. Mangum. You see I am in the midst of the Nullifiers. Col. Benton is upon the same tier; as is Mr. Clay, on the opposite side of the chamber; but though surrounded by these great men, I trust I shall be able to think and act for myself. I shall, I trust, not give a single vote, or do a single act, I thought was not right, before I left Ohio.

DECEMBER 2, 1833.

Both Houses this day, at 12 o'clock, formed a quorum. In the Senate a question arose on the Rhode Island case, which caused considerable debate, and what I suppose is very unusual on the first day, the yeas and nays were taken.

When the certificates of the new members were presented, Judge White, the President *pro tempore*, called on them to take their oath; as we were walking from our seats to the chair, Mr. Clay rose and remarked, that there was another member, whose name had not been called. Judge White remarked he was aware of that fact, but he thought as the two members from Rhode Island were both present, the action of the Senate was necessary to give either a seat. So soon as we had retired from the chair, Mr. Poindexter moved, that Mr. Robbins, who was the first elected, be permitted to take the oath. This motion brought on considerable debate, in which Mr. Poindexter, King, of Alabama, Clay, Kane, Wright, Benton, Chambers, Ewing, and Mangum, took part. It appeared that Mr. Robbins had been elected by the Legislature of Rhode Island, in January last, and had obtained the usual certificate. In October the Legislature passed an act declaring the election of Robbins void, and proceeded to elect Mr. Potter. Under these circumstances the question was whether either should be admitted to a seat, until the subject was examined by a committee, and we had all the facts officially before us.

I was much disappointed at the debate I heard. It was certainly much less dignified and orderly than I expected, and if I should say far less wise and forcible, I should say the truth. There was too much of the small arts of the County Court Lawyer in it. I know I have heard stronger and more orderly debates in the Ohio Senate than I heard to-day. The disorder of the Senate during the debate was surprising; Mr. Benton remarked, unusual.

DECEMBER 17th, 1833.

Yesterday, the Vice-President (Mr. Van Buren) took his seat in the Senate. You will see his Address delivered on the occasion, in the papers; it was handsomely done. He is rather rapid in the dispatch of business, but will, I think, preside with dignity. He is a fine, erect man in his gait, and is, I should think, about fifty-five years old. With all the hue and cry against him, I have no doubt he will be the next President. A majority of the Senate are decidedly oppositionists, and they have appointed all the Committees, bearing the same complexion. There has been some speculation here, that Mr. Webster is about to leave Mr. Clay, and join the Administration. I am half inclined to think so myself; but it will be done by degrees, and this session, I think, you may look for him between the parties. It is idle to talk of party spirit, in the Ohio Legislature, when compared with the feeling of the opposition here; but they are entirely overpowered in the House.

I am a good deal disappointed in the appearance and management of the great men. McDuffie is far from the man I expected to find him; he is violent in his gestures, and dogmatical in his statements. The Senate may well be termed, the aristocratic branch of the Government, for it is truly so at present. It is even whispered here, that Mr. Taney, as Secretary of the Treasury, is to be rejected. I hope not, for the honor and dignity of the Senate.

Is the rejection of Mr. Van Buren already forgotten, and will the Senate destroy their usefulness by their capriciousness?

A number of bills have been reported to the Senate, all asking for money to some individual purpose. In looking over the appropriations of last year, when applied to their individual objects, I did not believe it possible that human ingenuity was capable of inventing as many schemes for the laying out of money. This city lives upon the bounty of Congress, and wishes to claim it as a right.

The Senate continues in session rather less than three hours each day; the House somewhat longer.

December 22d, 1833.

I expressed to you, in some of my letters, that the North and East were coming round to correct principles, while the South was receding. I am still more and more, of that opinion, from what I see and hear daily. I sent you the first part of Mr. McDuffie's speech; you see the tone which it displays; yet it speaks the language of the Southern majority. We have here a great deal of combustible matter and discordant materials. I have far less hopes of a lasting Union between the States than when I left home. I hope that I may, before the Session adjourns, find I am in error; but of this every day lessens my hope. If this Government will confine its action within the strict letter of the Constitution, and exercise even then, as little power as possible, so as to fulfill the design of the Constitution, all will yet be well.

My fears of consolidation are subsiding, as to the exercise of the civil powers of this Government. Congress can not put down the State authorities by the operation of law — that sentiment, I feel certain, is gaining ground. The States can, and will, govern here, if they make the effort, and are united; and an attempt on the part of the General Government, to oppress any State, will, as every other act of oppression does, eventually create sympathy for its fate.

Matthew Carey, in his New Series of the Olive Branch, tells the people of the South, that he would willingly part from them, if the tie could be broken without shedding blood; that, although the course they are pursuing is an evil to the country, yet their separation would be a still greater one.

DECEMBER 24th, 1833.

I mail you the *Telegraph*, of this morning. You will see renewed evidences of the bitter feeling of the Nullifiers, in that paper, and in McDuffie's speech. With him the Bank is everything, and the Government nothing; Biddle his idol, and Jackson his Devil. I went into the Hall of the House on yesterday, while he was speaking. You know that the members sit with their hats on; but one-half or more, had left the room.

McDuffie is not the orator that we used to think he was. While speaking he throws his hands very awkwardly, picks up and then puts down his handerchief and papers before him, has rather a squealing and disagreeable voice, is small, and leans forward. If he is the great intellectual champion of Nullification, I think its props will soon give way.

I have as yet sat still in my place. I am endeavoring to learn what sort of stuff the Senate is made of. I have heard some speeches here not so good as I have heard in the Ohio Senate. The Reporter here makes the speech as printed. It is delivered not half as correct, and frequently so low as to be scarcely audible. I sat near the center of the room, and I could not correctly hear Mr. Webster.

DECEMBER 29, 1832.

The Bank and Bank-men are in dreadful agony. We hear their groans daily; all will not do. The House have settled the question. No one of the majority there can now go for the Bank, without a total loss of his reputation, both public and private.

JANUARY 1, 1834.

I have just returned from the President's Levee. The house was so filled that it was irksome to be there; to the President it must be splendid misery. Such I thought was his situation the other day when I dined with him; his visitors, however, have the advantage, as they can leave as they please. It is only imagination that men here are greater than elsewhere.

The Bank party find themselves in a minority in the House. They pretend to wish a speedy discussion on the Deposit question—but this is mere pretense. It is plainly perceivable that they bend their whole course to create as much excitement here as possible, in order to create a corresponding excitement in the country, in hopes that a state of things will be produced which will terrify or induce men to vote for the Bank. This complied with, the money influence is now their only hope. They act in perfect concert. This plan of operation, which is no doubt designed to affect the public mind, is prepared by the master spirits out of doors.

Mr. Polk, of Tennessee, has begun his reply to McDuffie, in the House. It will be a most triumphant refutation, and will completely vindicate the President and Secretary in the removal of the Deposits. It will disabuse the public mind, and set matters in their proper light. But this is to be procrastinated by the arts of the Opposition, as long as possible. Never has any curse fallen on this Republic equal to the Bank. If it triumph now it will rule for ages. I trust the majority of the House will stand firm. Should corruption find its way into the Capitol Gen. Jackson will be found safe. But I do wish and hope the venerable chief will be spared this further trial.

JANUARY 3d, 1834.

Col. Benton is now engaged in replying to Mr. Clay. He has so far, in my opinion, completely prostrated all the arguments and assertions that have been used against the President and Secretary, on the removal of the Deposits. He has stated some facts showing the most unjustifiable and illegal conduct of the Bank, and which ought at once to close the mouths of its advocates.

One of these facts is, that the Bank had issued orders to its several Branches, to dishonor each other's notes; that in fact notes on Branches have been received on account of the Customs, and refused by the Branch where the Custom was collected; that individuals owing at Branches, could not pay their debts with the notes of other Branches; that this order had been lately issued, and this is one cause, and among the greatest, of the pressure upon the money market in the commercial cities. The Bank and its friends are no doubt doing all in their power to distract the country.

Col. Benton has given notice, to-day, that he will offer a resolution to call President Biddle to the bar of the Senate, to answer under oath, together with others, respecting the conduct of the Bank. This resolution will, no doubt, be offered, and I can not see upon what principle the Bank-men can vote against it. It will be a scene indeed, to see "Old Nick" marching up to the bar of the Senate, to give an account of his evil deeds. Will he come? I doubt it. It is said, and appearances are in favor of it, that Mr. Webster is courting the West; looking, probably, beyond Mr. Van Buren's time, and the opinion or resolution of our General Assembly will have much weight with him.

JANUARY 24th, 1834.

The rage for speech-making is not in the least abated. Colonel Preston, of South Carolina, finished his speech to-day. It was a most inflammatory and theatrical one; but containing assertions repugnant to every American feeling. It will be extolled to the skies by the Nullifiers. Men of sense however, will and already do, condemn it.

I visited the President last evening; he is firm, and in good heart. Every day brings him fresh assurances of increased confidence among the people, in his administration. And I have not at present, a doubt, but he is fully, if not more popular now than at any former period; although in the Senate, he is every day, if any of the opposition speak, called over and over again, a usurper, a tyrant, a violator of the Constitution, and totally disregarding any law, he heedlessly follows the blind impulses of his own mind. Indeed this abuse is moderate, as to what is sometimes said. But all this thunder is lost on the walls of the Capitol, or only cheers a few Bank dependents that surround the Halls.

I am fearful we shall not adjourn before next harvest. Mr. Webster said on yesterday, that we ought not to adjourn until we did something to regulate the currency; that a Bank of some kind must be had; that for his part, he was in favor of a re-charter of the present Bank. I thought when he said it, and I still think, if we stay until that time, we shall not be at home after the fourth of next March a year. Indeed, I have but little doubt, that in five years time, Congress will continue in session the whole time after their first meeting, until the end of the two years, unless the people and the State Legislatures express themselves strongly on the subject.

FEBRUARY 7th, 1834.

I have just returned to my lodgings, from the Hall of the House. The long agony is over. The House has taken the vote on the preliminary question which has been debated for more than two months past—130 against the Bank, 98 in favor of it. The country now I think, will settle down; and men, instead of depending on borrowing, will look to their own industry for support — at least it ought to be so.

FEBRUARY 13, 1834.

I have just returned from the funeral of Judge Boulden, of Virginia, the successor of John Randolph in the House of Representatives. The time, place, and manner of his death, you will see in the *Telegraph.* It is an extraordinary circumstance, and one no doubt, that will cause considerable political speculation.

The manner of burying a member of Congress here, is a piece of vain pageantry, costing I have no doubt, not less than ten thousand dollars. The very hacks that went out from the Capitol to the graveyard (I have no doubt), will amount to more than five hundred dollars, paid out of the contingent fund of the House. But so it is, and so it will be, till the people of the States are more attentive to what is done in small things, as well as great.

Bank petitions from the cities still come in; the country however, is on the other side. Some of the opposition papers talk of a civil war. Yes, even in the State of New York, is this vain and wicked threatening made, when their own Legislature, by more than two to one, voted against the restoration of the Deposits and a renewal of the Charter.

JANUARY 20th, 1834.

We have had for some weeks past, petitions from the Bank Gentry pouring in upon us, by thousands and tens of thousands, but we now begin to hear from the great mass of the people. Pennsylvania will no doubt stand firm against the Bank; both her Senators and I believe a majority of her Representatives, are for the people and against the Bank.

The corruptions of that Institution are horrible; and could we get a Committee to examine and make a faithful Report, the public would be astonished. I have been told to-day, that in the Folding room of the House, there are now twenty thousand or more of the different speeches of the members of Congress, and other documents, in favor of the Bank, that have no doubt been printed by its order, and sent here to be folded and franked by members of Congress; thus the folding paper, the time of the officers of the House, the postage that is saved by the frank, amount to many thousand dollars, of which the Bank thus defrauds the people by their friends in Congress. There are a number of young men and boys employed by each House, who fold all the public documents for the members, and a room is appropriated in the Capitol for that purpose. This is what I mean by the folding room, and it is thus prostituted to the service of the Bank.

I see that in some places in Ohio, movements are making in favor of the Bank; it has produced here considerable effect. If the people were called to act in a Presidential Election, under the present excited state of feeling, it would, in my opinion, be doubtful if the Bank would not be sustained. It has evidenced much prudence and foresight in the President, that the Crisis has been brought on *now* by a removal of the Deposits. The public will have time to examine, reflect, and judge; and they will discover in time only, the dangerous power of the Bank.

Mr. Wirt, late Attorney General, was buried to-day. He died the evening before last. He had attended Court until a few days before his death.

From all I can learn, there appears to be no doubt, that Van Buren and Johnson are to be taken up by a National Convention. They will succeed.

MARCH 1st, 1834.

A rather unpleasant and curious circumstance took place in the Senate, yesterday. Mr. Poindexter had made some serious and unfounded remarks against the Secretary of the Treasury, saying, that he had issued an order to remove a million of dollars or more, from the Bank at Natchez, which had been deposited on account of the United States, to New York, to prevent the Safety Fund Banks, in that State from failing. Mr. Forsyth received from the Treasury department, a certificate, that no such order had been issued, or even thought of, and he charged the matter home on Poindexter, by telling him on the floor that he had stated a falsehood.

Poin—— in a passion, demanded to know if Forsyth intended to impeach his veracity, saying, at the same time, no man should do this but at the hazard of his life. Forsyth, with much dignity, said, "what he had said was said; he despised the threat of the gentleman, and would not answer his questions." You can easily see, in what a position this answer placed the parties. The Senate, however, before they adjourned, and with closed doors, had the matter compromised, much to the satisfaction of both Poindexter and his friends; for he found in Forsyth he had caught a Tartar.

MARCH 12th, 1834.

We are now threatened by Mr. Webster, that we must stay here until the country is relieved, that is, the Bank must be re-chartered, and this is to be effected by operating on members by keeping them in Session by force of the majority in the Senate, until the agitation of the country shall be such, that fear and not duty shall do the work.

Mr. Clayton, of Delaware, said, a day or two since, the people would obtain redress by petitions and remonstrances if they could, if these would not do, they would resort to other means, that of revolution; that his constituents had strong arms and stout hearts. Other Senators had used still more threatening language than this. The Bank partisans adopted the same idea, and by this kind of operation, worse than folly itself, they hope to succeed. As far, however, as I can learn, a reaction is now begun in the country, and I feel certain that the President would be sustained, if the question was put at this time. A new election will, however, show the state of public feeling, and this, I believe, is what they most fear; and hope before that evidence is taken, to carry their project by storm.

MARCH 25th, 1834.

Mr. Webster has reported a bill to extend the Bank charter six years. The question was leave to introduce it; a debate had begun on the bill to-day; he moved to lay his motion on the table; a few of us tried to keep it up for debate but were outruled.

The distress party here, are in real distress themselves; they have cried wolf so long that no one cares for it, and now when public opinion against the Bank is coming in from almost every quarter, in such force, as to leave no doubt that the country will sustain the President, their own cries of distress will not avail them. The Virginia elections come on next week, and no doubt is entertained here but they will sustain the President, and that Mr. Rives will be returned to the Senate next winter.

Pennsylvania, too, will be found against the Bank. Resolutions to that effect have already passed the Senate, and no doubt will pass the House; a sufficient number of States in that event, will have declared against the Bank, to carry the next Presidential Election. The Bank men may hang their harps on the willows.

April 29th, 1834.

No possible good can come of this session, is now admitted by all parties here; yet we are to be kept in Session by the majority of the Senate, for the purpose of producing effect on public opinion, which is to operate on the next October elections, in some of the most important States.

May 20th, 1834.

Though the Bank party here are still apparently in good spirits, yet it is evident their cause is on the decline, in every part of the country. The whole object seems now to be, to induce some friends of the Administration to propose to the present Congress, a bill for a new Bank, and have hope that the scheme will come from R. M. Johnson. If the Col. should take this step, it will, in my opinion, prostrate his hopes in the Western country.

The investigating Committee have not yet reported. If the American people can submit to the conduct of the Bank toward that Committee, they may well be considered not only slaves, but fit slaves of the Bank.

There are more falsehoods fabricated here and sent abroad by letter writers, than from any other spot in the United States. They are a set of hangers on about

Congress, who live by misrepresentations and falsehoods. They are constantly striving to keep up the present excitement in the country, and to procure memorials in favor of the Bank to be sent to Congress. Ohio has so far escaped their wiles.

I have begun a calculation on the public printing, showing the amount of printing only. I have no doubt but it will be found that each member of Congress requires ten dollars per day for Contingent expenses alone, independent of the officers of each House, which will amount during the present Congress, to nearly nine hundred thousand dollars. I confess I am astonished at the result. Can this Government be continued under such abuses? *The country is too large; we are too far from our Constituents.*

This Government in money matters is becoming more corrupt than any other on the face of the earth, yet we talk of Republican simplicity. It is in the power of the States, in the formation of a Senate, to do more for the preservation of our liberties than any other branch of the Government. If the States, in their sovereign character will not take charge of, and keep this Government in proper bounds, I predict its total change, either by a separation of its parties, or an amalgamation of them; and in this opinion, I know I am not alone. Many of the most sober minded men in Congress, think the same.

We are now near the close of the Session, without having done anything but vote money, lands, etc. No news yet from France. I am confident the country will sustain the President, in his proposed actions against France, though I would willingly forbear as long as possible; yet something ought to be done, before our adjournment. I am for a non-intercourse Act. This, I think will do for the present.

CHAPTER XXVI.

EXTRACTS from Various Speeches — Extravagance in Public Printing — Contingent Expenses of Members of Congress — Cost of their Snuff, and Horse Hire, etc. — Speech on the Safe Keeping of the Public Moneys — Extracts from it — Its Just Views — Speech on the Land Bill — Speech on the Ohio and Michigan Boundary Line.

As a Senator in Congress, to whom was intrusted, in part, the special interests of Ohio, and the common interests of the country, Mr. Morris felt his responsibilities, and was active and faithful in the discharge of his duties. His manly position and defense of freedom, and his vigilant labors against the aggressions of the slave power, did not exclude from his attention other important interests of the country. As an independent politician and legislator, he acted, and voted, in the Senate Chamber of the United States, on all subjects, in accordance with the matured convictions of his judgment. A Democrat from principle, and not for party — he was always found advocating the doctrines of Democracy, on the great financial questions that came up for examination and settlement. A Southern Democratic Senator, in familiar greeting, said to him — "Morris, you are right on *all subjects but slavery.*"

In this Chapter will be found extracts from various elaborate speeches he made on the Currency of the Country; the Land Bill; the Boundary Line between Ohio and Michigan; and on the Extravagance of the Government, in the use of Public Moneys. They are worthy of the reader's attention.

The first extracts are from a Speech on the Extravagance of Congress in Printing Documents and Books.

Mr. Benton, on the 28th of December, 1838, made a motion, that thirty thousand copies of certain voluminous documents, printed by the British Parliament in 1818, in reference to salt duties, be reprinted by Congress, for the use of members, and for information to the country. The motion was carried. Mr. Morris, a day or two subsequent, moved, that the resolutions to print these documents, be rescinded; and offered, among others, the following remarks, on the practice of extravagant printing by Congress:

"He thought the printing of books by order of Congress, a very unjustifiable use of the public money, and if Congress took a few steps more in this business — indeed, if they persisted in the order for printing thirty thousand copies of this book — it might well be said, that instead of a legislative body, Congress would soon convert themselves into a great National Book Concern. A Methodist Book Concern, a Presbyterian Book Concern, or that of any other religious or political association, was a commendable thing; but it was a private affair, by which individuals at their own expense, undertook to promulgate through the country and among the people, their own peculiar opinions and doctrines; and all they asked of the Government in the exercise of this, their undoubted right, was protection and safety for their persons and property, from mobs and unlawful violence. But he had seen with regret and alarm, Congress as a public body, ordering the printing of documents and papers calculated to promote the peculiar views and doctrines of individuals and parties in Congress.

"The fact was, and he well knew it, those Public Documents, printed by order, were seldom read; and if the thirty thousand of these Salt Documents should be printed, not one-third of the members of Congress themselves would read one, and they would be read by a far less proportion of the community at large. There was another objectionable view of this matter.

"These Books and Documents were always made with a *professed* view of circulating information among the people. And how was this done? We tax the people at large, say two hundred thousand dollars, yet books and papers when printed, become *ipso facto*, the private property of the members. A fair division of the plunder, he admitted, was always made. The members could either sell them or send them to their friends, as each one thought best; or leave them in their boarding rooms, to be used as waste paper.

"These documents were frequently printed for political effect; for the purpose of advancing the private and political views of individuals, and he did not believe that the people would be willing to be taxed for this purpose. Let any Senator collect together one hundred thousand of his constituents, and inform them that he would lay and collect a tax, to which each should contribute fifty cents, and that with this sum of fifty thousand dollars he would cause to be published, thirty thousand documents—these British documents—and that he would select thirty thousand from among the number, to whom, if it should suit his pleasure, he would bestow as a gratuity, and under his own frank too, one copy each, to become the private property of such individual. He did not believe any portion of the American people would consent to be taxed in this manner, and for such a purpose as this; yet such were the facts in the case, and such the results of voting books and documents to ourselves. We tax the whole people, and then put our hands into the public Treasury, apply the tax to the purchase of books to distribute among our friends, which may enable them to sustain us at all future elections. He would much rather let the fifty thousand dollars, which the printing of these books would cost, remain in the pockets of the people, to purchase such books as their judgments or fancy should suggest. There is a still more pressing objection to the printing of these foreign books.

"The extravagance of the Government has become proverbial, and the corruption which such a system was introducing throughout the country was alarming. The astounding defalcations which had lately taken place among collecting and disbursing agents, was a part and parcel of this system of extravagant and improper appropriations; and in these piping times of talking about economy and reform, our declarations were but in mockery of our doings.

"What was the amount of contingent expenses of the other House of Congress, the last session (1838)? $272,-245.84! Yes! *only two hundred and seventy-two thousand, two hundred and forty-five dollars and eighty-four cents!* The contingent expenses of the Senate, for the same session, was $112,992.20—*one hundred and twelve thousand, nine hundred and ninety-two dollars and twenty cents!* A man of common sense and prudent habits, in looking over the items to make up this enormous amount of expenditure, for the mere contingencies of Congress for one session, must feel amazed at the ingenuity of men in devising means to waste the public money. He had looked hastily over the items, and found one hundred and fifty-two dollars for making *pens*, thirty-nine dollars and fifty cents for *snuff*, and one thousand six hundred and forty-one dollars for *horse-hire* for the House of Representatives, and three hundred and fourteen dollars for an *hostler;* in the Senate for the same hire, one thousand six hundred and thirty-three dollars. It would seem to a plain, upright man, if he were informed that this sum of three thousand two hundred and seventy-four dollars and ninety-two cents for *horse-hire*, and three hundred and fourteen dollars for an *hostler*, was expended during one session, that this Congress actually legislated for the greater part of the time on horseback. Sir, it is mockery, cruel mockery, to talk here about favoring the laboring classes, the agriculturists—those from whom you draw all the means for the extravagance around us; some thousands of dollars, Mr. President, for the very drapery over and around your chair, while every part of the Senate chamber presents equal extravagance. The money expended yearly, within your iron-bound enclosures, which surround your Capitol, was more than the yearly expenses of the Government of the State of Ohio, which he had the honor, in part, to represent.

"He did not wish now to look into the expenditures of the public money in the different departments of the Government; that stupendous mass of extravagance, corruption and fraud, which he feared existed; the fault of which was, mainly, if not altogether, in the legislation aud acts of Congress. He had confined his view to the household economy of the body, to their furniture, the dress of their chamber, and their *pin-money* alone; and he hoped they would begin the work of reformation and retrenchment at home. The people had been "*salted*" quite sufficient in this branch of the public expenditure, without adding to the amount fifty thousand dollars for printing these British salt documents.

"He hoped Senators would pause, and look back at what they had done. The amount paid for printing had been enormous. The Post Office Report—some thirty thousand copies, or more—had been printed at about fifty thousand dollars cost, with a view of enlightening the people, as to the alleged corruptions of that Department; and what had this printing done? Furnished—a fat job for the printer—and the whole story is told. He had heard of their being used as wadding for cannon, fired to celebrate Democratic victories! He thought this an effectual mode of *distribution*, and commended the inventor for his wit. In his part of the country, this document, with others, under which the mails groan, franked by members of Congress, was distributed in country stores, and used for wrapping paper for tea, and other articles.

"Thus we had gone on, printing and distributing books and documents, until the practice had become a serious drain upon the Treasury, and almost a nuisance in the country; they were used, not for information, but as weapons for political warfare, by contending parties."

The extravagance of Congress, in public printing, and in other things, as here described by Mr. Morris, has greatly increased since he was in the Senate. The cost of three publications, during the Congress of 1853 and '4, "Perry's Japan Expedition," "The Pacific Railroad Survey," and "Ellis's Report," cost over one million of dollars; and the present Congress of 1856, voted each member over a thousand dollars worth of books, printed at the expense of the people.

EXTRACTS FROM HIS SPEECH ON THE CURRENCY, AND SAFE KEEPING OF THE PUBLIC MONEYS.

What, Mr. President, is the question before us? It is, does there exist a vital, inherent power in this Government, that Congress can call into action, for the purpose of preserving, and keeping safely, the money contributed by the people, for the purpose of carrying on the functions of Government, between the times of its collection and disbursement in pursuance of law, and that, too, without any foreign or extraneous aid? To a plain and honest man, unacquainted with the intrigues of office, or the wiles of speculators, to ask this question would be to answer it.

The position assumed is, that Congress is bound to provide a currency for the country. I can by no means admit this argument, in the sense in which it has been urged in this debate. Congress furnish, in fact, a currency for the country! If so, from what source is that power derived, and in what form is it to be exercised? Congress, by the Constitution, has power to coin money, and regulate its value, and the value of foreign coins. This provision of the Constitution by no means authorizes Congress, to make or increase the currency, by the mere act of Government, either for its own use, or the use of individual citizens. It would be a dangerous practice, and at war with every principle of our Government, for Congress to exercise or possess a power like this.

I admit, that in despotic or monarchical Governments, where power is claimed not to be derived from the people, but *jure divino*, the power to supply their own Treasury, by their own authority, is claimed and exercised. It is the peculiar prerogative of the crown to make its own money. That power, in this country, belongs to the people. The Government can have no money, but by their permission. The people have in their Constitution provided, that gold and silver shall be the material of which money shall be made; and they have given the power to Congress to coin it, and regulate its value. Congress has declared by law the shape and size of money, and the inscription it shall bear. They have also caused to be erected a mint, a great national workshop, where money shall be made; they have erected machinery and employed workmen for this purpose, all at the public expense, and the operation is called coining; but Congress have no power to dig the ore or purchase bullion, in order to make money for the use of the Government. The mint belongs to the people; it is for their use; it is to make money for them, free of personal expense, out of their own metal, and for their own benefit; and how much, or how little they will have, like all other articles of property, depends on themselves, and will be regulated by their means, their industry, their fancy, and their taste; and the Government is under no more obligation to afford aid to individuals in this pursuit, than it is to aid them in rearing cattle, or in acquiring any other species of property. It would be as dangerous to public liberty to permit the Government to enter into competition with individual enterprise, in this particular, as it would be to enter into competition in the trade, commerce, manufacturing, or agricultural pursuits of the people.

Hence the wise men who framed our Constitution, have prescribed that the Government shall have no other income for its support, but what the people shall contribute, by taxes, duties, imposts, excises, the sale of the public domain, and the borrowing of money. If I am correct in the positions I have assumed, and upon which I have no doubt, what becomes of the argument—that Congress is bound to furnish a currency for the country? It is lost, having no foundation whatever on which to rest.

Gentlemen urge on us another system, which they call the credit system—a concentrated and corporate credit, which circulates in the form of bank notes, and which they contend, is the purifier of our morals, the reformer of the age, and whose benign influence scatters peace and smiling plenty on the country, and without which we would retrograde in a short time, at least to a semi-barbarian age. Permit me Sir, to examine for a moment, this credit system. Gentlemen say that the Government is making war upon that system, and thus destroying confidence, upon which the whole prosperity of the country depends. Sir, in my opinion, we have too much, instead of too little credit; too many of our citizens are endeavoring to live on credit, instead of industry. These consist of the trading and speculating classes. And they are asking the aid of the Government, to enable them to seize upon the property of the laboring and production, classes, and appropriate it to their own use, by virtue of this credit system. Credit belongs to man.in his individual character, not in his corporate capacity; and it is the essence of oppression and tyranny for the Government to bestow upon it a fictitious existence, in order to give them a credit which they never could otherwise have, and for which, in that character (their individual character), they are not responsible. It is to my mind impossible for the Government to lend its support to the credit of any man or set of men, without producing injury to others. The Government has nothing of its own intrinsically: what it bestows upon one, it must wrest from another; and it would be as highly impolitic, unjust, and despotic, for the Government to seize upon the individual credit of the country, and force it out of its natural channel according to its pleasure, as it would be to seize upon the entire property of the country for the same purpose. No country can be free, where the Government thus interferes with the private concerns of individuals, for the purpose of adjusting the balance of wealth among them.

On first taking my seat in this body, I was surprised to hear that the practice had been to permit those who had the public money in their hands, to use it in trade or speculation, between the time of its collection and disbursement. Large sums were then being paid into the treasury, for which the Government had no immediate use. I was asked if I would permit those sums to lie idle until expended by operation of law? Surely I would. I thought then, and I think now, that it would be better for the country that they should have been entirely lost, even burnt in the streets of Washington, rather than be used for the corruption of the people. But, Sir, other counsels prevailed, the money was ordered to be deposited in the State Bank, a measure to which I gave an unwilling assent. The banks were told to loan liberally on those deposits. And what has been the consequence? A host of borrowers were immediately found at the banks, who, in the pursuit of fancied wealth, neglected the ordinary and substantial pursuits of life. Loans were obtained, and many estimable young men, who otherwise would have been valuable and useful citizens, became speculators in practice, and gamblers in principle. The Government thus tempted them to leave the sober, honest walks of life, for the uncertain pursuit of riches; and they forgot that excellent prayer, the best ever put into the mouth of man, "Lead us not into temptation." Thus, this valuable class of our citizens were prevented from adding to the permanent wealth of the country. They became borrowers, dependants upon the banks; they forgot that word of truth, "That the borrower is the servant of the lender," and it seems to be forgotten here. A gentleman near me, Sir, says that *slave* is the original word; yes, Sir, the borrower is the slave of the lender! Who, Sir, will dispute this? Thus, that manly independence of mind that should mark the American character, is exchanged for a miserable dependence on soulless corporations, and in the midst of this wild course of extravagance, the banks themselves become involved, they close their doors, refuse to refund to the Government the money deposited, or to discharge their other liabilities to individuals. What a monstrous picture of corruption.

Born, Sir, and cradled in the lap of the Revolution, my infant mind received its first impressions of Government from that Constitution under which we now live, formed by the wise and good men of that day. I was taught to believe that the great object of the Revolution, and the end proposed by the Constitution, was the security of the individual liberty — not the promotion of individual aggrandizement, or the means of procuring individual wealth. It was to secure the blessings of liberty, of equal rights to each and to all, to themselves and their posterity forever. All we ask from the Government, is protection, security from violence, and the administration of impartial justice; that the domestic fireside may be safe from either internal or foreign aggression; that the bounties of Providence which we have gathered through the day by the labor of our own hands, may be safe from the midnight robber; in fact, that we may all sit with safety under our own vine or our own fig tree, and none be suffered to make us afraid.

We claim neither the vine nor fig tree of Government; nor do we wish the power or means of Government to enable us to avail ourselves of the labor, or possess the vineyard, of another. Riches and wealth should be the reward of individual industry, frugality, and economy — and not acquired by the favor or patronage of Government. Yet the whole of the arguments against this bill, are based upon this principle — the principle that the Government is bound to furnish the means to the citizens, not only for obtaining a livelihood, but of accumulating a fortune. Sir, this is the language of tyranny and despotism — to promise the people much, for the purpose of gaining sufficient power to rob them of *all.* I heartily agree in the sentiment expressed by the President — "That all communities are apt to look to Government for too much. Even in our country, where its powers and duties are so strictly limited, we are prone to do so, especially at periods of sudden embarrassment and distress. But this ought not to be. The powers of our excellent Constitution, and the people who approved it with calm and serious deliberation, acted at the same time on a sounder principle. They wisely judged, that the less the Government should interfere in private pursuits, the better for the general prosperity. It is not its legitimate object to make men rich; or to repair by direct grants of money or by legislation, in favor of particular pursuits, the losses not incurred in public service. This would be substantially, to use the property of some for the benefit of others; but its real duty — that duty, the performance of which makes a good Government the most precious of human blessings—is to enact and enforce the system of general laws commensurate with, but not exceeding the objects of its establishment; and to leave every citizen and every interest to reap under its benign influence, the rewards of virtue, industry, and prudence."

The President further says—"I can not doubt that on this as on all similar occasions, the Federal Government will find its agency most condusive to the security and happiness of the people, when limited to the exercise of its conceded powers. In never assuming for a well-meant object, such powers as were not designed to be conferred upon it, we shall in reality do most for the general welfare. To avoid every unnecessary interference with the pursuits of the citizens, will result in more benefit than to adopt measures which could only assist limited interest."

Sir, these are the sentiments of our Republican citizens, and of that eminent man whom they have called to preside over the affairs of the country; they are sentiments in the belief of which I have grown up, and they now form the creed of my political faith, and in the belief of which I expect to die. But, Sir, this is not the political doctrine which the opposers of this administration inculcate. Their doctrine teaches a servile dependence of the people upon the Government for the promotion of individual or local interest; a doctrine which makes the people nothing within themselves, and the Government everything for the promotion of their pecuniary interest. This is the doctrine of despotism, and the means by which tyrants have always seized upon power. Establish it here, and your boasted liberty will be but an empty sound, a mere delusive phantom, of which you will soon lose even the sight.

It has been thundered in our ears, that the great question is, whether the people shall have bread or no bread? This sound was first heard from the consuming classes of our great commercial cities; it originated with those who not only lived upon their own credit, but had sold that credit to their laborers and dependents, and when it failed and became worthless for want of a "*basis*," they came forward and asked the Government to sustain it in its sinking condition, by permitting them to amalgate it with the credit of the Government; and because this unjust application is refused, they raise the cry of bread or no bread, and declare that the Government is withholding bread from the people; indeed this false and groundless position is assumed on this floor. Gentleman have asserted the same thing—indeed, they have gone still further. It has been said (but I do not deem it necessary to designate gentlemen by reference), that "the duty of the Government, as I understand it, is to provide bread for the people."

"The duty of the Government to provide bread for the people!" Clothing also, I suppose! This idea of providing by the Government for the private wants of the people, has in it nothing new. It has been long practiced by men whose object was the overthrow of their country; and we find this scheme resorted to, in almost every age of the world.

When the unnatural son of the Jewish King wished to dethrone his father, he made use of this same principle. He told every man who had any application to make to the Government, that his matters were *just* and *right*, but there was no one deputed to hear him; and he, also, told all such, that if he were made Judge in the land, that he would do every man justice. I fear, Sir, the same disposition is felt and breathed from many a heart in this our day. "Oh! that I were made President of these United States, then should every man have bread." I trust the last scene of Absalom's career will not be theirs. And Watt Tyler, too (if I mistake not the name), promised the people of England, in his attempt to break down the Government of that country, that when he obtained rule, a four-penny loaf should be sold for two pence, and the price of ale should be reduced. He also endeavored to make the people believe, that a change in the Administion would give them abundance of bread. In every age and in every country, in which the people have not relied for their support and comfort upon their own individual industry, but have consented like cattle, to be fed from the public crib, the downfall of freedom has been sure, and the establishment of despotism certain.

I have always believed that the happiness of a country, and the safety of Republican institutions, were to be found in an industrious and rich population, with a poor and just government. All the public works executed and owned by any Government, have a tendency to strengthen its powers, and make it arbitrary and despotic, by reducing the people to the condition of its laborers, dependants, or tenants. It has also the direct effect to increase official stations, and the arrogance of office; and I am well satisfied, that if the Government now owned all the canals, railroads, and turnpikes in the United States, and should reduce the fare, it would not be to the advantage of the country, because it would soon change the nature of our Republican institutions—except we prefer a Government to rule over the people, instead of a Government to be ruled by the people, we might then put off the honest garb of home-industry, and glitter in the livery of power.

The following are extracts from his speech on the Bill to appropriate, for a limited time, the Proceeds of the Sales of Public Lands, and to grant Lands to other States; delivered in the Senate, April, 1836.

" The Committee assume in their Report, that there is a vast surplus of revenue in the Treasury; that this state of things is not desirable, because its natural tendency is to produce extravagance in appropriation, and wastefulness in the expenditure of the public money. This is a truism, in part, not to be controverted; but if it be true that this surplus actually exists, it is strange that the Committee, after having discovered this wasteful disease, and its cause, instead of recommending a radical cure, should propose to extract the infectious matter from this Government, and diffuse it into the State Governments, and thus innoculate the entire body politic. To prevent its effects here, this political empiricism would be productive of the most fatal results. The reduction of the customs, which would be a complete and effectual cure, the Committee believe can not, or rather ought not to be resorted to, because it would awaken, as they say, feelings dangerous to the peace and harmony of the country. And the reason assigned for this strange conclusion is, that the tariff law now in force, is the result of compromise of the opinions of citizens in different sections of the Union, and ought not to be disturbed, unless a strong political necessity calls for some new modification. The first position assumed by the Committee, I believe to be founded in error, and calculated to mislead the public mind.

"The tariff, as it now exists, is not the compromise of the opinions of the citizens in the different sections of the country, because it is too evident to require proof, that the citizens of the United States have constantly been opposed to a protective tariff, and to the collection of taxes either directly or indirectly, to a greater amount than would be necessary for the support of the Government; and on this ground have they constantly opposed the whole doctrine of internal improvements by Congress. The present tariff law is rather the result of a compromise between individual members of Congress, representing different sectional interests of the country, and was entered into for the advancement of those interests, independent of any consideration of results, as operating upon the citizens generally, in each and every section of the

Union. The measure was a foul conception, and produced an unnatural offspring. Its first born was an attempt to bind the hands of any future Congress from legislating on the subject, for a given term of years: its next has been to accumulate money in the Treasury, which may be used to corrupt this Government, or be used for corrupting the Governments of the States, as may best suit the interest or convenience of those who have, for the time being, the power of its disposal. And under this unnatural state of things, it is said that the present rate of duties must be continued, and kept up for the proper regulation of commerce, and may be necessary for the ordinary wants of Government. If this last be true, then indeed ought not the customs to be reduced? and if sufficient for the ordinary wants of the Government is to be raised by the customs, then the public lands ought no longer to be considered as a source of revenue; but I confess I am unable to see either the truth or force of the former part of the argument. Duties for the proper regulation of commerce, does not depend on the amount, but on their equality in the different ports of entry in the United States. If this be correct, and I deem it an undeniable position, then the whole argument, on this point, falls to the ground; for surely the customs can be so lessened as to reduce entirely the whole surplus revenue in the Treasury. The attempt to tie up the hands of a future Congress, by the mere operation of a law, is still a more palpable error. The legislative power of the country is at all times equal; it has no bounds but the Constitution, and ought to have no other guide but the public will: where that leads it ought always to follow. It is essential to the welfare of the country, as well as the maintenance of equal rights, that the legislative power should constantly be free and unencumbered; but this never would be the case if its deliberations could be prevented from being had on any subject by existing laws, over which it ought not to exercise any control. It would establish this dangerous principle, that the power of the people is not always competent for the maintenance of their rights. The proposed measure of increasing the appropriations for fortifications, the navy, and general defense of the country, is not by the Committee attempted to be directly negatived; but it is said that large and liberal appropriations of money for these purposes, though just and proper in itself, can not be well applied, and ought not to be made, because it is not in our power to supply proper materials, and skillful engineers for this purpose. This is, at least, the force of the argument; and on account of this exigency, no more than ordinary appropriations ought to be made. I am at loss for words to express my surprise at this argument; nor can I, for a moment, admit its correctness; I can view it in no other light than as a libel upon the American people, and an imputation on their skill and industry; that people, whose inventive faculties and mechanical genius have not only surpassed former ages, but is the wonder of our own, and who have subjected the very elements to the condition of a laborer in their employ; that this people should be told by their representatives that they have not sufficient knowledge to erect forts, build ships, and other public works to any extent, and in the best possible manner, is an assertion as new as it is unjust.

"The reducing the price of the public lands, or the ceding them to the States in which they lie, is next considered by the Committees. The first objection to a reduction of price is, that it would tend to reduce the price of real estate generally. This objection is not well founded; the price of an article is a relative term, wanting both stability and uniformity: it is the effect, not of reason or justice, but frequently of caprice or whim, and not unfrequently of taste, convenience, or necessity. But as to the public lands, justice, reason, convenience, and necessity, all seem to unite in requiring Congress to reduce the price; and if this argument of the Committee be valid, it applies with equal force against the introduction or erection of any new machinery, or the establishment of any new trading house; for those now in existence will be lessened in value thereby, a position which I believe the Committee themselves would not contend for.

"The next objection to a reduction of the price of the public lands, is, that it would operate to the injury, not the benefit, of the country in which the lands are situated. This argument is attempted to be sustained on the same grounds as the former, but making its application more local, by the assertion, that it would reduce the price of all land in the neighborhood, *pro rata* with that of the public land. In reply to this argument, I beg leave to remind the Committee, that the united voice, and almost unanimous opinion of the people, in all the States in which the public lands are situate, is against them, as well as the opinion of every intelligent and unbiased citizen who has any correct knowledge of the new countries. They all well know, that the Government which secures the greatest quantity of happiness and comfort to the people, is unquestionably the best; and that the surest means to accomplish this desirable end, is to enable every man to become a freeholder, so that he can have the satisfaction of saying, that some spot, however small, is his own; that the Government of this country is bound to protect him in its quiet enjoyment, and that, when he shall return from his daily labor to his hearth and his fireside, none shall be suffered to make him afraid: the sleep of such a man will be quiet, and his repose sweet: and no matter how coarse his fare may be, his love of country will never fade nor languish. Such men as these are the true riches of Government, and will always be found ready to defend their country for their country's sake. It ought to be our most ardent wish, and constant policy, to provide means by which every man in the United States might become a freeholder, if that freehold did not consist of more than twenty-five acres; indeed, it matters not so much as to quantity, if a right to the soil be the lot of every citizen.

"Another objection, made to a reduction of the price of the public lands by the Committee, is, that it would encourage speculation, and throw the whole of the public domain into the hands of sharp sighted capitalists, who would be enabled to retail it at advanced prices to actual settlers. This objection is more showy than solid, for every day's experience teaches us, that speculation in articles of high value is more common than in those of low; when the Government lands were sold at two dollars per acre, speculation was as much complained of then as now. It is the relative, not the actual value of an article, that induces speculation. But this objection is easily obviated by providing for the sale of the public land to actual settlers only, and in limited quantities.

"The last, and which the Committee consider the most important objection to the reduction of price in the sale of public lands, or ceding them to the States in which they are situate, is, that the several States, by their deeds of cession to the United States, vested only a trust power, and that the Government of the United States is only the mere trustee of the several States, bound to carry into effect the grants made by the States for the specific purposes intended by the grantors; and when those purposes are fulfilled, the residue of the grant does, and of right ought to revert to the States; and extending the trust power further than I believe it has ever been extended in equity, they give the trustee the power to change the nature of the trust, and convert the land into money, and distribute that among the States. And one further stretch of the imagination leads the Committee to conclude, that lands acquired by the United States by virtue of treaties made since the adoption of the Constitution, have been paid for by money had from the sale of lands ceded by the States, and, according to the rule laid down, they subject the proceeds of these lands to the like disposition.

"My first objection to this fine-spun and subtle theory is, that I have serious doubts that the sovereign power of a country, at least the sovereign power of this Government as vested in Congress by virtue of the Constitution of the United States, can, in any case, become a mere and naked trustee; though it may be said the idea is borrowed from monarchical power, yet it is no less correct, that the sovereign power of a country, be it vested in whom it may, is supposed to be constantly employed for the public good, and that no partial care can enter into its composition. It can not subject itself to control by any part of those over whom its constant duty is to watch for the welfare of all; nor can it act in subordination to any other power; for, in either case, it would be an abrogation of sovereignty. But it is not absolutely necessary to sustain the argument that I should rely exclusively on the general doctrine that the sovereign power, where it is primary, original and confined in its operation only by Constitutional limits, as in the case with the Legislative power of the States, can not be a trustee; yet in a Government like that of the United States, where its whole action exists and is brought into operation by grants, the exercise of its power must be limited and brought expressly within those grants; and I contend, that in no part or clause of the Constitution of the United States, is the power granted to Congress to become a trustee in any case; no, not even for the purpose of diffusing knowledge among men. But if such power can be inferred from the Constitution, it must be from some general grant in that instrument; and if so, by virtue thereof, the United States can not only act as trustee for the several States, but may be the trustee of any foreign gentleman or State whatever.

This Government, if this position be correct, can become the trustee of the Barings or Rothschilds in the management of any money concern they may think proper to establish in this country, whether it be for the diffusion of knowledge among men, or of buying men for political purposes without knowledge, or at least, without virtue. Under this general trust power, as it is presented to my mind, and as admitted, and, indeed, contended for by the Committee, Congress can become the trustee of the Bank of England; the trustee of the East India Company, or of any foreign Government whatever; and thus act in the double capacity of an American Legislature, and as agent or trustee for another power, however inimical that power may be to our own. Indeed, I can not see but Congress, by becoming trustee, can effect any object they wish, no matter what that object is, whether within the granted powers of the Constitution or not. Congress may have in view a favorite object of an internal improvement, for the benefit of two or more favorite States; they may bestow upon, or, in the language of the bill, distribute to these States millions of the public revenue; and it may be well understood that the States are to create Congress a trustee for the express purpose of expending this money according to their own wish. There can be no end of abuses of this kind if Congress can act as trustee, and accomplish that which they can not do by direct acts of Legislation. I contend, in the next place, that the deeds of cession made by the States to the United States, did not create a trust, nor were they so intended; they contain no words of limitation, but such as are applicable to the exercise of power by Congress in every other case.

"Take, for example, as the Committee have, the deed of cession made by Virginia. The only words of limitation mentioned by the Committee, and they are the only ones in the deed, are, that the land ceded shall be considered a common fund for the use and benefit of the United States, members of the federal alliance, and shall be faithfully and bona fide disposed of for that purpose, and for no other use or purpose whatever. These words, which are now to operate as a talisman, and change the money received for public lands from the character of revenue, into that of property held by the Government in trust for the States, are nothing more, nor can they rightfully receive any other construction, than to place the avails of the public lands on the same footing as the proceeds of taxes, duties, or customs. The money received from all or either of these sources, is the revenue of the country, and Congress is bound in good faith to consider it a common fund for the use and benefit of all the United States, as a joint confederacy, and not as a fund belonging to the States severally; and Congress have power only to apply the whole, or any part thereof, to such objects as are exclusively within the power of this Government, and to no other use, intent, or purpose, whatever.

"But there is an inconsistency in the views of the Committee, which they seem to have entirely overlooked. They contend that this Government, as trustee, ought to distribute the proceeds of the public lands to the States in severality, while the very words of the trust which they claim, are, that the land shall be a common fund for the use of the States as a joint confederacy. This very inconsistency proves the fallacy of their whole system.

"That the United States acquired a full and absolute title to the lands ceded by the States, I think is clearly evident, because Congress have granted portions of these lands to States, as well as individuals, without any compensation given for the same; and titles made in pursuance of such grants are unquestionably valid in courts of law, and the power of Congress in this particular, as being rightfully exercised, has never been questioned in public opinion.

"In my own mind, I am perfectly satisfied that the public lands of the United States may be granted by Congress to the individual States in which they lie, or to individual persons, with or without compensation, as the safety or security of the United States shall require; but when converted into money, and paid into the Treasury of the United States, they assume a different character; they are revenue; and that Congress can apply the revenue of the country to internal improvements, or make a donation of it to States or individuals, has been constantly denied by a great majority of the American people.

"If we are to consider the distribution contemplated by the bill as a mere gratuity on the part of this Government, and that Congress has no power to define the purposes to which the States shall apply it — and this principle seems to be admitted by the bill itself — I should be glad to know what could prevent Congress from distributing to twenty-four individuals, or any other number, this money, instead of a distribution among the States. I can see no difference in the principle governing the two cases; and the exercise of power, in my view of the subject, is as clearly unconstitutional in one case as the other; though a distribution to individuals would so shock the moral sense of every man that, with one united voice, it would be declared that Congress had most grossly violated the Constitution, as well as being guilty of an act of moral turpitude.

"There is another view of this subject still more appalling. It is true that Congress, by the Constitution of the United States, have no power to make any law respecting an establishment of religion, or prohibiting the free exercise thereof; but if Congress have power to create a surplus revenue, and power to make a distribution of the same, they can in effect render null and void this provision of the Constitution; they can distribute this money to any church or sect they please, and thus as far as money and the favor of the Government will answer, give such church or sect the ascendency, whether the same be Protestant or Catholic. It is said money answers all things. Congress can then, by its use, make an establishment of religion. There can be no doubt on this subject, if Congress possesses the power to make the distribution contemplated by the bill, I feel confident that I have not extended the argument further than the premises will warrant; and I now seriously put the question to every member of this Body, if he is prepared to say, that by virtue of the power vested in him by the Constitution of the United States, he has the right to vote an appropriation of money to be paid out of the Treasury of the United States, for any of the purposes which I have mentioned? I do not believe there is one Senator who will openly and positively avow such right.

"As you lessen the necessity for the States relying on their own means and exertions for their support, you destroy their ability to do so; their increasing weakness becomes the strength of this Government, and thus enables it to supply additional means to make the States still more weak. The very money you bestow, although it may make the State rich in a pecuniary point of view, yet those very riches will be the bane of equality and freedom. Suppose the money you bestow should be sufficient to enable the State to become the owner of every canal and leading road in its jurisdiction, and to hold the same as Government property; the first result would be a host of officers to 'eat out the substance of the people, and destroy their living;' the next to bring into existence a class of men who would of course become the tenants, laborers, and dependents of the Government, instead of being free citizens of the State. When Government is a large property holder, the inevitable consequence must and will be distinctions in society. The wealth of the country will be found in the lesser number, and power will be more secure in the hands of those who are intrusted with the management of public affairs, until the very condition of landlord and tenant will be found to exist between the officers of Government and laborers for the State. It is, in my opinion, a perfect absurdity to suppose that the principles of democracy and equal rights can long exist in a State that is herself a large property holder.

"The public lands ought to be looked to as a source of wealth belonging to future generations, not on account of the money they will bring, but for the population they will sustain. A steady, industrious, contented and fixed population, are the riches of a country. A provision of the above kind, would, in my opinion, produce that effect; a residence of three years would produce the blessings and attachments of home, while the sale of the freehold, even at an advanced price, would seldom be an inducement to part with it, because a larger quantity of land in most cases could not be purchased elsewhere, and thus contentment would ensue, while the products of the farm would enable the younger branches of the family to provide themselves a home upon the same terms. The next beneficial result would be, to check at once the fearful speculation in public lands that is now in progress, and that ruinous system of borrowing that is resorted to for that purpose; and those now engaged in that business would then turn their attention and means to some other pursuit that would advance the growth, prosperity and permanent wealth of the country. And last, though not least, it would dry up one of those sluices, through which money that is not needed is constantly pouring into the Treasury; and it would preserve for our children and our children's children, even to remote generations, an opportunity of acquiring a freehold on the same terms as was afforded to their fathers. But if we sell this valuable estate now as fast as possible, for the highest price that can be obtained, and make that and not the settlement of the country our object, and then distribute the proceeds among the several States, for the purpose of having it expended, spent, or squandered, we act the part of an improvident spendthrift, who, having acquired by descent a large landed estate, converts it in to money as fast as possible, for the purpose of gratifying his vanity, or acquiring power and influence by corruption and fraud.

"In the next place, I would repeal the entire duties on all articles that are used in any manner or form in the diet of the country; and to show its effects upon that part of the country in which I reside, I would instance the duty on sugar alone, which we now pay into the Treasury or as a bounty to the manufacturer; take the duty off that article, and the price would be reduced at least two cents on the pound. The bill contemplates giving to the State of Ohio about one and a half millions of dollars as her proportion of the spoils for three years; and the profession of the friends of the bill are, that they wish to give this money back to those who paid it, and as they can not do that, they will approximate as nigh as possible, by giving it to the States. Every family in the United States, I presume, uses sugar, and for the argument I will allow one hundred pounds per annum to each family of five persons. In Ohio we have probably three hundred thousand families who pay a tax on sugar of six hundred thousand dollars yearly. In three years we pay one million eight hundred thousand dollars tax on sugar alone; repeal this tax, and you in effect give to each family two dollars per annum—a sum larger than will be distributed to them by the bill, could its friends make its operation as they profess to wish; but if the surplus revenue be so extravagantly large as has been represented, I would go one step further, reduce the duties on articles of wearing apparel of the coarser texture, which are used mostly by the laboring classes, so that the revenue of the Government will not exceed its just wants, and you will relieve the State of Ohio, in one year, from the payment of a much larger amount than is proposed to bestow upon her by the provisions of this bill.

"It has been also said in the course of this debate, as matter of alarming tendency, that it is claimed for the President that he is the representative of the people, and that General Jackson has put up such claim in his own behalf, as the single representative of the whole people of the United States. Whether these assertions be well founded or not, I think it unnecessary to inquire. I have never been alarmed at the cry of danger from Executive power. That power, though extensive in its operations, is held under so many checks and restraints, that I have always viewed it the weakest and least dangerous of the three great powers of this Government. It is in the first place an elective power by the whole people for a short period of years; and being intrusted to a single person, it is watched with the most vigilant attention, and the least departure from correct principles is deeply noted in the public mind. It is a power which can originate no measure, but is the agent, and subject to the orders of the other great powers of the Government. Being in the hands of one man, he is subject to impeachment by the Representatives of the people; and the Senate, with the Chief Justice at its head, are his judges. It would be strange indeed, if the Executive power, thus checked and circumscribed, first by the people, then by the other powers of the Government combined, should ever become dangerous to the liberty of the country. The framers of the Constitution have thrown too many guards around it to excite any such fear. I am myself clearly of opinion, that if the liberties of the people of this country are ever destroyed, it will be the act of an American Congress; and the first scene of the grand drama, constituted as the Senate now is, will take place in this Body."

When Michigan sought admission into the Union, in 1836, a controversy arose between her and the State of Ohio, as to the geographical boundary line between them. The Constitution of Ohio, and that of Michigan, in defining their respective territorial boundaries, came in conflict; Michigan claiming a portion that was included in the geographical limits of Ohio, as described by her Constitution, and established by the Act of Congress, in admitting Ohio into the Union. The Controversy occasioned no little excitement in both States, and each threatened to maintain their rights by force of arms. Governor Lucas, of Ohio, an early legislator and an honest politician and man, called an extra Session of the Legislature, to determine what Ohio would do in the case. The question came before Congress for settlement, when Michigan asked admission into the Union, and was one of grave interest and importance to the National Legislature. In the Senate, a select Committee, of which Mr. Benton was Chairman, was appointed; and many of the Senators participated in the debate, which the controversy originated. Mr. Ewing and Mr. Morris, Senators from Ohio, made lengthy speeches, in defense of the claims of Ohio; the question was settled by an Act of Congress, and in favor of Ohio. Brief extracts from Mr. Morris's able speech, made in the Senate, on the 10th of March 1836, are here recorded:

"Let it be constantly borne in mind, that Ohio, on this question, comes before Congress, as a sovereign State; that she is not soliciting a favor, but demanding a right; that she claims to have the clear grant of the Territory, in dispute between her and Michigan, and appeals to Congress to withdraw the incumbrance they have cast over her title.

"In the year 1806, I first had the honor of a seat in the Legislature of Ohio. No one then doubted the Constitutional boundary of the State; no one thought of a provisional boundary subject to the after control of Congress, or that any assent of Congress then given or withheld, without the consent of the State, could possibly make any alteration of the actual existing boundary. But, as the country in the Northwest part of the State was then unsettled, and its geographical situation not well understood, and as political movements of much importance were then taking place in the United States; the attention of the General Assembly was not turned to this subject during that Session. But the next Session of the General Assembly took up the subject, and after expressing belief that the due east and west line drawn through the Southerly extreme of Lake Michigan would not intersect Lake Erie, or would intersect that Lake east of the Miami River or Lake, they, therefore, instructed their Senators and requested their Representatives in Congress, to obtain a law to ascertain and define the Northern boundary of the State, *and fix the same agreeably to the proviso contained in the Sixth Section, and Seventh Article of the Constitution.* The succeeding session reviewed the request, and also in the Session of 1811. Congress, in 1812, passed an act to authorize the President, to ascertain and define certain boundaries. This act was passed in pursuance of the repeated applications of the General Assembly of Ohio, but, (the war of 1812, intervening) was not carried into effect till 1816. In that year, President Madison directed the Commissioner of the Land Office to authorize the Surveyor General *to run and mark the Northern Boundary of Ohio;* in pursuance of this authority the Surveyor General directed William Harris, to run and mark the line to which Ohio asserted jurisdiction, and which he contends is the true northern boundary. This officer (the Surveyor General) had been President of the Convention that formed the Constitution of Ohio; was the first Governor of the State, and afterward Senator in Congress. As a faithful public officer, he was bound to carry into effect the instruction of the President. Governor Worthington, who had formerly been a member of the United States Senate, from Ohio, in his message to the General Assembly, in 1817, declared that the Northern boundary of the State, had been lately ascertained, *under the authority of the United States.* The message on this subject was referred to a committee who reported 'That the Congress of the United States, fully assented to the proviso in the Constitution of Ohio, by their acceptance of the State into the Union.' A resolution, in accordance with the boundary line, as defined in the Constitution, was reported and adopted.

"Permit me here to pause, and ask the solemn question, how public compacts are to receive construction, action, and validity? We have seen what the compact was, the circumstances under which it was made and the parties to it; and I know of no better source to look for the manner in which it ought to be fulfilled, than public opinion. It was that which laid the foundation of our Government, erected the superstructure, and constantly supports the whole edifice. Let us then test this compact by the public opinion in Ohio. The Constitution of her State was formed when her Territory contained less than fifty thousand inhabitants, and up to the present moment, 1836, when the same Territory is teeming with nearly, if not fully one and a half millions—during all this time, and under every change of circumstances and men, that there has been but one undivided, unbroken opinion in the State, on the question of her northern boundary; and that is, that the northern boundary of the State is established by the Constitution, and is where the line has been lately re-marked by the authority of the Legislature. To this fact, all the public functionaries of the State, have borne ample testimony, as well as the united voice of her citizens. Can it be possible that any portion of the enlightened citizens of this country, acting in the sovereign character of a State, can, in a question of Constitutional right be mistaken, and that mistake persisted in, for more than thirty years; or that a million and a half of our citizens are so unjust, that they ask an alteration in the boundaries of the State, and are willing it should be resolved into a question of mere political expediency. Sir, I can not thus libel the people of Ohio. I can not believe it.

"In January, 1805, Congress passed an act establishing the Michigan Territory, and by the provisions of that act imprudently, if not unwittingly, extended the Southern boundary of that Territory, over the Constitutional limits of Ohio. The authority of Michigan, I think, was not attempted within those limits until 1818, and after the authorities of Ohio had assessed a tax on the people living within that part of the State included in the Michigan Territory, by the act of Congress before mentioned. After this took place, some of the inhabitants applied to the Governor of Michigan for commissions as Justices of the Peace, and other offices, under the authority of that Government, which were readily granted; and thus commenced the jurisdiction of Michigan within the borders of Ohio. After the possession of the disputed territory was thus acquired by Michigan, under color at least of an act of Congress, the application of the military of Ohio would have been unjustifiable in regaining the possession at that time, and would be so still. Congress having cast over our boundary another title, and possession being obtained under that title while we *slept*, the President of the United States, who is bound to take care that the laws of Congress are faithfully executed, would have been required by a faithful discharge of his duty, to have sustained the jurisdiction of Michigan against a military force, until Congress should have withdrawn the jurisdiction of that Territory beyond the boundaries of Ohio; and this is all that Ohio now asks.

"The people of Ohio will not, I know they will not, endanger the peace and safety of the country by an attempt to prevent the operation of an act of Congress by force. They have already had too many evidences of the justice as well as the liberality of Congress, to believe that this will ever be necessary. But this disposition on the part of Ohio, the forbearance of her citizens, will not, I hope, be construed into an abandonment of her rights, or a dulness in comprehending them. Let it be remembered that Ohio has claimed jurisdiction of the country in contest between her and the State of Michigan, as her *undoubted right*, being included in her Constitutional limits; nothing short of a recognition of this principle will satisfy her people; and it would be an act of humiliation to the State, to *give* to her territory to which she has not a Constitutional right, as an act of law, of equity, or political expediency.

"Suppose, Sir, you give Ohio the boundary claimed by the State, on the score of political expediency, will it not be expected that Ohio, under this obligation, will, on the score of political expediency, be bound to favor the political views of the donors, for the favor bestowed. It may be thought that the smallest return she could make would be to act with, or for you in future elections, if it should be at the expense of her honor, as well as Constitutional rights. It will be an entire mistake, if you expect to conciliate the favor of the people of Ohio, by letting them know that the Constitution gave them no such right, but that the same was granted out of your abundant favor and good will, as an act of grace. Is not this the language you hold to Ohio, when you talk of *political* justice and expediency? Ohio, I am fully persuaded, will never so far humble her honor and self-respect, as to acknowledge such a principle.

"We ask for nothing but justice—naked, simple justice; but we ask that, not as an abstract principle, but as our undeniable right. It seems strange, to me at least, that we should feel so much disposed to assail the Constitution of the State, and be constantly looking after some principle, by which we can, with some degree of plausibility, claim the honor of adding to Ohio a strip of territory, which we would make her citizens believe the Constitution of the State had not secured to them; when, if we would look directly to that instrument, and make it the rule of our action, we would find it sufficient for our purpose, and there written all we ask for.

"Are the boundaries of a sovereign State to depend on the fluctuating legislation of Congress? This doctrine of depending exclusively on an act of Congress for their boundary, will not satisfy the people of Ohio. They will require something more permanent; and they will not cease their endeavors until Congress withdraws all jurisdiction foreign to their Constitution and laws, North of a direct line drawn from the most Southerly extreme of Lake Michigan to the most Northerly cape of the Miami bay, and thus recognizing the jurisdiction of the State, under the provisions of their own Constitution, and which they are fully satisfied no power on earth, but themselves, has any right to alter, abridge, or restrain, in a single jot or tittle."

EXPUNGING RESOLUTIONS.

In March, 1834, the Senate of the United States passed a resolution condemnatory of President Jackson, for the removal of the Deposits of the public money from the Bank of the United States. The act of removal created great excitement in Congress and throughout the Union. Mr. Clay offered a resolution of censure, which was passed. Mr. Benton avowed his settled determination to persevere until the resolution of censure was expunged from the Journal of the Senate. After renewing his Expunging Resolutions for several Sessions, it was carried, by a vote of twenty-four to nineteen, on the 16th of January, 1837; and the Secretary of the Senate, in the midst of the silence of the Senate, and a crowded gallery of spectators, proceeded in a formal manner, to draw black lines around the resolutions of censure, and to write in strong letters across the face of it—"EXPUNGED, BY ORDER OF THE SENATE."

Senator Morris received from the State of Ohio, which he in part represented, resolutions instructing her Senators to vote for the Expunging Resolution. These resolutions were passed by the Legislature of Ohio, in January, 1836; and Mr. Morris presented them to the Senate on the 31st of March, 1836, and on their presentation made the following remarks:

Mr. President—It becomes my duty, a duty I owe to the State and the country, to present these resolutions. I take this occasion to say, and I have no doubt of the fact, that these resolutions express the sentiments of a vast majority of the people of Ohio. I venture this opinion without fear of a successful contradiction; for it will be remembered that during the session of Congress, which has so appropriately received the name of the PANIC session, resolutions were passed by the Ohio Legislature, instructing their Senators in Congress to aid in sustaining the President in the removal of the public money from the Bank of the United States, and to oppose a re-charter of that Institution. We were then told with great confidence, that the General Assembly had altogether mistaken the opinion and wishes of their own constituents, and those upon whom resolutions of this kind were designed to operate, took an appeal from the constituent body to the people at large; and to influence the public judgment the people were told, that should the Deposits not be restored and the Bank re-chartered, a most deleterious effect upon the trade, prosperity, and welfare of the country would be the consequence; that in fact it would make our "canals a solitude, and our lakes a desert waste of waters." The long, loud, vehement, and repeated denunciations of the President for his act in removing the Deposits, the fearful forebodings so strongly and eloquently urged on this floor as to the fatal issue of that act, all coming in aid of the means used by the Bank in producing distress in the country, took some effect, and operated for a moment, on the public mind in Ohio. It threw into each branch of the General Assembly for that year, a small majority opposed to the Administration; but even that General Assembly, elected as it was under the full pressure of Bank power and panic speeches, had not the temerity to instruct the Delegation in Congress from Ohio, to vote either for a restoration of the Deposits, or a re-charter of the Bank; they well knew that such instructions would be a violation of the public will, and they still, in appearance at least, paid so much regard to that, that they did not attempt it, but contented themselves with a bare repeal or rescinding of the resolutions passed on that subject at the previous session, and thus in order to save themselves and friends, indirectly denied the right of instruction by the Legislature of their Senators in Congress. The appeal to the people was then perfected, and the issue thus made, fairly presented to the voters of Ohio, to be tried at the election held in October last, and what has been the verdict? A solemn decision that the right of instruction exists in the Legislature, and that Senators are bound to obey. That verdict is recorded, and judgment pronounced in the resolutions I now offer. But, Sir, that judgment has also been reviewed and re-affirmed, and is presented here with a double force, not only as the opinion of the last General Assembly, individually considered, but as required by the people of Ohio at the hands of their Representatives (as the General Assembly has rightfully declared) in the passage of these resolutions. It is hoped and expected, that this high and solemn mandate will not be entirely disregarded, and the requirement of the General Assembly altogether useless. The obligation that a Senator is under to his own State, and the duty he owes, are of too sacred a character to be dispensed with. Disobedience by a Senator to the instructions and requirements of his State as expressed by her Legislature, is a deep and festering wound in the vital principles of our institutions, which if not speedily cured, will soon assume a fatal ulcer. It is, in the first place, a total abrogation of the doctrine that the Legislative Body is the true representation of State sovereignty. And it gives to the Senator, for the time being, all the attributes of despotism, the full and free exercise of his own will and authority, without accountability. But, Sir, could any one for a moment entertain such doctrine, and deny to the Legislature the right of instructing Senators of their States? yet in this case the resolutions offered have another and different support, little inferior to the Legislative Body itself, and probably more conclusive to the real sentiment of the people on this important subject. The Convention which met at Columbus, on the eighth of January last, composed of about five hundred members, representing upward of sixty counties, being nearly the whole number in the State, by a unanimous vote, passed a resolution in the following words:

"*Resolved*, That we regard the right of instruction as the sheet anchor, the main pillar of our freedom, and that we are determined never to surrender it, but to the last to stand by it. Convinced as we thoroughly are, that it is only by the frequent and rigid exercise of this invaluable privilege, that the Democratic character of this Government can be preserved, we believe the agent who disobeys to be unworthy the confidence of his constituents, and that he ought to resign his seat."

"It is true, this Convention was composed of men friendly

to the present Administration; and as a doubt no longer exists, that a majority of the people of Ohio are of the same opinion, the Convention thus re-affirming the principles of the resolutions passed by the General Assembly, must satisfy every man, that Ohio requires her Senators to vote as instructed by the Legislature. But, Sir, this is not all; we had another Convention, a grand Whig Convention, held on the 22d of February last, and they claim that a number of returning prodigals had come into their ranks, and the great ox, instead of the fatted calf, was killed; and they had much rejoicing; and it is hardly necessary to say, that opposition to the Administration was their watchword; and while they boast of having far outnumbered the former Convention, they did not open their lips on the subject of the resolutions of instruction, passed by the General Assembly. In the pride of their strength, they were endeavoring to catch the popular gale, and well knew that opposition to those resolutions would prove their overthrow. I have before me, a paper containing an account of their proceedings, and I find no resolution pro or con on the subject of instruction to Senators here. This silence is evidence of approval by our political opponents in Ohio, or that they well knew that the people of that State strongly disapproved of the condemnatory resolution passed by this Senate. This exciting subject had occupied public attention. Almost every man in Ohio had thought and conversed on the question, and the Whig Convention, no doubt, would have used it to their advantage, if in their power.

Under this highly responsible situation, we are called to act and vote; and the great question is, shall we do our own will, or the will of that sovereign power who sent us here? It is a hopeless warfare to be contending against our States; it is a kind of moral treason, for which, sooner or later, we must expect to suffer the penalty. It is wisdom then, for us to make our submission at once; and when we are called to vote on the resolutions offered by the Senator from Missouri, that we vote in their favor. I have now strong hopes that Ohio will be united in her vote here, on this important question. Her Senators appear to pay the highest respect to the resolutions of her Legislature. I hope the one I now offer will not form an exception to our general conduct. Can we refuse our obedience on the ground that this resolution requires an unconstitutional act? We ought to pause before we make this excuse, and well distrust the correctness of our own opinion, when it comes in contact with the opinion of our State, repeatedly, and I may add almost, if not entirely unanimously expressed, not only of our own State, but of twelve States; while not a single State has expressed a contrary opinion. It is the opinion of the State, and not the individual agent, that ought to be known and felt here. If the agent is unable, from conscientious motives, to express that opinion, his path of duty is plain before him.

These extracts not only give the views of Mr. Morris on the various subjects discussed, and his ability to comprehend and express them in a clear manner, but also show that, as a public Servant, he was faithful to all the interests which he believed were connected with the prosperity and welfare of Ohio, and the Nation.

CHAPTER XXVII.

His Private Life and Personal Characteristics — Liberality to Poor and Honest Young Men—Thomas L. Hamer—His Life and Character—Mr. Morris's Son pronounces his Eulogy in Congress—An interesting fact—His Sense of Justice and Tenderness—Lines on the Death of a Granddaughter—His Dislike to Idler's — Advice to his Youngest Son, on Leaving Home for College—The Editor's Reminiscences—His Religious Faith—The Moral Significance of his life.

THE private life of Thomas Morris, deserves a brief record. In this sphere, where the true nobleness of man is developed, there is an honorable correspondence with the principles that governed him, in his public career and character. Selfishness was not the ruling element of his private, as it was not of his public life. He felt that no one ought to live, without exerting a good and active influence on his fellow-men, and doing his part in the work of humanity and benevolence. In his own way he did his. He was a friend to the poor and oppressed, and no honest person, in want, ever went from his door, without receiving practical sympathy and aid.

His liberality was unbounded and disinterested, toward poor and honest young men, struggling for honorable advancement in life; and he had a pleasurable pride, in witnessing their success in life. Few men, perhaps, were more ready or were, under similar circumstances, more liberal in means and sympathy, to encourage and bring forward men, in the walks of public life, than was Mr. Morris. His influence lives in those who have been, and now are, prominent and influential, in the civil and political history of the country. They have risen to distinction, filled with ability high offices under the Government of Ohio, and of the nation, and gratefully acknowledged their obligations to Mr. Morris for his sympathy and aid.

One such, now sleeps in an honored grave. He rose from obscurity and poverty, to great prominence and influence in the civil and military history of Ohio and his country. In early life, as a young adventurer, he went forth from an humble home, to seek fortune and fame, in the wide world. Friendless, without means, and with only a good common education, he found his way to the village and home of Mr. Morris. He was received into his family, and enjoyed his patronage. Engaging, in the honorable and useful business of a teacher, this young man, pursued it for three years; enjoying during this time, the law Library and Counsels of Mr. Morris, in the bosom of whose family he had found a *home*. In 1821, he was admitted to the legal profession, and soon rose to eminence in his profession. His popularity and abilities soon placed him in the Legislative Halls of his adopted State, over which he presided as Speaker of the House. In 1832, he was elected to represent his District in Congress, to which position he was selected for six consecutive years, when he declined a re-nomination. In 1845, when the war between Mexico and the United States began, he volunteered as a private soldier, was elected Major General of the first Ohio Regiment, and afterward was appointed by President Polk, a Brigadier General in the army. His field of military glory, became his grave. On the 2d of December, 1846, before the city of Monterey, in Mexico, he died with fever. In October, 1846, two months previous to his death, his old District in Ohio, re-elected him to Congress. In 1847, Jonathan D., eldest son of Thomas Morris, was, without opposition, elected to fill the seat in Congress vacated by his death. On the 23d of January 1848, Jonathan D. Morris, in pronouncing in Congress a just eulogy, on his predecessor THOMAS L. HAMER, after a recital of his early life, and political and professional career and character said:

"The intellect of General Hamer was clear and discriminating. He was cautious, energetic, affable, and his colloquial powers were peculiarly fascinating. The purity of his character, in the private and domestic relations of life was never questioned. He was unwearied in his efforts to improve his powers, and though nature had been liberal to him, it is, mainly, to this course on his part, that we are to look for the reason, for his great attainments as a Statesman and a lawyer. His friends being aware of this, claimed that his career would be onward, and that, if he had lived, his final triumph would be the the receiving of the highest honor which men can bestow on man."

His remains were re-interred in Georgetown, Brown County, Ohio, his home, at the expense of the State.

It is a singular and honorable coincidence, that Thomas Morris should be the means of aiding a young man of high talents and ambitious aspirations, and that he, after a brilliant career in the civil and military history of his country, and dying in that service, should have his eulogy pronounced in the Halls of Congress by a son of him, who, thirty years before received him as a friendless youth, and aided him in the achievements which cluster around his active and honorable life. Mr. Hamer, a few years before he died, acknowledged his indebtedness to Thomas Morris, declaring his willingness to aid, if necessary, any child of the friend and patron of his early youth. This liberality of Mr. Morris has been repaid in the success of those to whom he extended practical sympathy and aid.

A sense of justice, equal and exact justice, to all men, independent of circumstances, or conditions, or color, was one of the strong and marked elements in his character.

In professional, political, and private life, this trait had a bold and manly development, and gave executive energy to his acts. His strong sense of justice may not have graced him with a winning *suaviter in modo*, yet it gave him the ardent *fortiter in re*—a purpose to hold on and to carry out the ends of justice everywhere.

And this element was blended with a kind and benevolent heart. Though *seemingly* it was not prominent in outward development, yet his nature had a rich vein of genuine sympathy and kindness running through it. The sorrows and bereavements of life of which he had in his own family a full share, melted his heart into tenderness. He was called to bury four married daughters, from twenty-four to thirty years of age, each leaving a family of small children, some of whom he adopted and educated with parental affection and interest.

The following lines will exhibit the tenderness of his heart in the sorrows of life. They were written after visiting the grave of a pious and accomplished granddaughter, who, after completing her education, fell a victim, at the age of eighteen, to consumption. At the request of her three surviving sisters, he penned these stanzas:

Dearest sister, gone forever
From this scene of care and wo;
The tie that bound us death did sever,
Yet calm and peaceful didst thou go.

April's sun, and vernal flowers,
Saw thee gently pass to rest;
Now the rose which friendship gave thee,
Grows and blossoms on thy breast.

The friendly giver, wan and feeble,
In fond remembrance weeps thy doom,
And kindly asks, if the rose she gave thee,
Is green upon thy early tomb.

Sainted mother — sainted sister,
  Lie side by side in quiet sleep;
Though the grassy hillock hide you,
  Yet our heart your memories keep.

When late we viewed thy graves together,
  Deepest grief our hearts did fill;
Yet resigned we checked our sorrow,
  For 'twas our Maker's holy will.

'Tis flesh that dies, the spirit lives
  Immortal, in a world Divine;
And hope its brightest prospects sheds,
  That now that better world is thine.

Though parted here, we hope to meet you,
  When the toils of life are done;
In a world of light to greet you,
  A world of light without a sun.

The meek example thou hast set us,
  Will, we trust, with us abide,
That our walk in life may fit us
  To die, when called, as thou hast died.

He had an intense hatred for idleness. Himself a hard, practical worker, in his profession or at manual labor, he could not tolerate idleness in others. His motto was:

" Faint not in all the weary strife,
Though every day with toil be rife,
Work is the element of life;
Action is light; —
For man was made to toil and strive,
And only those who labor live."

He left this moral legacy to his children, in the advice he gave to his youngest son, a young man of rare intellectual powers, and purity of moral life, who went to an early and lamented grave, in the autumn of 1842, in Quincy, Illinois. When that son left home to pursue his Collegiate education, the motto that his father put in his memorandum book, as a *souvenir* of parental affection, and a guide to moral conduct, was, "*Idleness is the bane of every enterprise, the downward road to ruin. Let strict morality, untiring industry, rigid economy, and a steady perseverance, be your constant aim and practice.*" A motto that will lead all young men, if adopted, to honor and prosperity.

The editor of this work remembers with gratitude, the many lessons of practical wisdom and morality he received during his five years of College life, at Miami University, Oxford, Ohio; and, as he is indebted to his father, for whatever of influence or good he may have achieved in the Ministry, or in society, he esteems it a privilege that he has been, through a kind Providence, permitted to compile the life and labors of Thomas Morris, and to leave them as a living monument to his country, and his descendants. He was, as a parent, deeply interested in his children, and spared no means to qualify them for usefulness and success in life. "*It is my aim, my wish,*" (said he), "*so to bind together my family, that there may be perfect harmony and mutual assistance given to each other; without this few families can prosper.*

He was not a religious man in the church acceptation of that term. He had an unshaken faith in the Divinity and truth of Christianity, and acknowledged that its obligations were binding upon all men; yet, like too many of our public men, he did not publicly yield his heart and life to its practical power. The general harmony of his political principles with the moral teachings of Christianity, and his frequent reference to the Bible as the fountain of all good, and of the *highest authority*, in *legislation* and in all human conduct, evinces his faith in its Divine origin, and its essential importance to all the interests of men. Nothing afforded him greater pleasure than to witness the members of his family become pious, and join a Christian church.

The record of his life and services here closes, and they have a suggestive and a noble moral significance. They are not surrounded with the halo of a military hero, nor the transient reputation of an ambitious and successful politician, nor the renown of a great statesman; yet they are the record of a moral hero, a true patriot, of a life devoted to freedom, and the true welfare of his country. His memory and services will live in the history of freedom, and the great principles he advocated, undying in their nature, will have universal triumph and a perpetual ascendency in the nation and the world. His life illustrates the great fact, fixed in the moral constitution of things, that truth and right are imperishable, and that true and immutable principles, are the only basis upon which to build solid character, lasting renown, or to gain the final and permanent favor of the world.

That he had his faults, said his friend, Dr. Brisbane, none will deny; that he sometimes erred in practice, as well as in judgment, is but the common lot of humanity.

That he had enemies, is nothing more than the best men have always suffered. That even friends were alienated from him by their misconstruction of his motives and acts, is only proof that they who do not know another's heart, need that charity which covers the multitude of sins. He was a man, not faultless indeed, but who as a husband, as a father, as a friend, as a citizen, was valued most by those who knew him best.

CHAPTER XXVIII.

His Death and Dying Exclamations — Burial — Monument over his Grave — Its Inscription — Notice of his Death by the Friends of Freedom—Dr. Bailey's Notice and Analysis of his character—Meeting of the Liberty Party at Cincinnati—Vote to Erect a Monument to his Memory, in Hamilton County—Final Remarks.

He died suddenly, on the 7th day of December, 1844. In perfect health, with his intellectual powers unimpaired by age, his physical system in vigorous activity, and his heart still warm in the cause of human freedom, he was stricken down by a fatal attack of apoplexy. Engaged in early morning, in making preparation for a visit of affection, to bring the invalid family of his eldest living daughter to the paternal home, he felt the disease coming upon him. He hastily entered his dwelling, sank upon the floor, and, with an audible voice, exclaiming three times, "*Lord have mercy on me,*" expired, in less than five minutes. He died on his homestead farm, four miles from Bethel, Clermont county, Ohio. After the repose of a Sabbath, on the following Monday his remains, surrounded with a vast concourse of neighbors and friends, were entombed in the grave yard of Bethel. Ere the rites of sepulture were completed, his son, a Minister of the Gospel, stepping upon a hillock of dirt beside his grave, about to receive all that was mortal of Thomas Morris, addressed a few brief words, commemorative of his life and the Providence of God, and offered a prayer, and the solemnities of the funeral scene were ended.

The spot of his burial is in a retired rural village, in Clermont county, in the service of which he so long labored, as a Lawyer, and a Legislator. If ever the lover of liberty, or the friend of the slave, should visit that spot, he will find in that cemetery of the dead, a marble monument, which the filial affection of his children has erected to his memory; and on that monument may be read this brief inscription:

THOMAS MORRIS:

BORN JANUARY 3D, 1776. DIED DECEMBER 7TH, 1844.

AGED 69 YEARS.

UNAWED BY POWER, AND UNINFLUENCED BY FLATTERY,

HE WAS, THROUGHOUT LIFE, THE FEARLESS ADVOCATE

OF

HUMAN LIBERTY.

His death was noticed by the friends of freedom, with appropriate tokens of sorrow, and tributes to his memory and services. A public print in the Capital of Ohio, in noticing his death said: "He has possessed the confidence of a very large portion of his countrymen, as a philanthropist and a patriot, and has sacrificed much of political advancement to extend and strengthen Abolitionism in the country."

A friend who knew him well, and a distinguished co-laborer, in the great cause of freedom, Dr. Bailey, present Editor of the *National Era*, said, in noticing his death: "This distinguished citizen is no more; he died suddenly on Saturday last, at his home. On the Thursday before, he was at our house in high spirits, and pressing upon us the importance of soon having a Liberty Convention in Columbus. We little thought it was the last time we were to see his face. During the past six years, we have known him intimately, and we had every reason to respect him for the consistency of his political views, the ardor of his zeal in the cause of human rights, the morality of his sentiments and his respect for the principles and precepts of religion. In our business transactions, we have found him honorable and generous.

"Early education, and a well disciplined judgment would have made him one of the most gifted, as he was one of the most energetic and independent of our politicians. His political integrity has never been questioned; his political consistency, fearlessness, and firmness, have always been admired even by his enemies. He never seemed to seek popular applause. He neither sought to lead, nor would he be led. He was not given to popular arts. If ever there was a politician free from the disposition, and we may add, the ability to play the Demagogue, that man was Thomas Morris. The cause of Human Rights, to which he had consecrated his latter days, has lost one of its most fearless Champions. His views were generally well sustained by sound principle and logic. He was indeed remarkable for the boldness of his propositions, and the force with which he sustained them.

"Thomas Morris will live in the hearts of the friends of freedom throughout the Union. His noble stand in defense of liberty, in the Senate of the United States, can never be forgotten. The mass of the American people may *now* think of him only as a fanatical Abolitionist, but the day is not far distant, when a monument will be erected to Thomas Morris, and posterity will honor him as the first who dared to raise his voice against the despotic acts of a slavery-loving Senate.

"Let his memory be honored. Let the Democracy which disowned him, be ashamed, and hang its head; let the friends of freedom weep over his grave: for when, in coming time, it shall be asked, whose was the ONLY voice that was raised in indignant rebuke of the most eloquent of Senators, when he lifted his hand to crush the cause of freedom and its advocates, the answer will be: '*It was the voice of the* INTREPID *Thomas Morris.*'"

In Cincinnati, the friends of freedom who had labored with Mr. Morris in the cause of human rights, at his death issued a call for a public meeting, in these words:

"The sudden decease of our honored co-laborer in the cause of human freedom, Thomas Morris, has spread a universal sadness among us. It seems to be the unanimous sentiment that those who, in times past, witnessed his courage, disinterestedness, and unshrinking consistency in the cause of human rights, should meet to express their regard for his memory. A pillar in the Temple of Liberty has fallen. There are few of us *now* to mourn over its noble ruins. The patriot heart grows sad when the voice is hushed that rang forth its trumpet tones against National Evil, and the heart ceases to throb whose strongest pulsations were against oppression."

In obedience to this call the friends of freedom met in Wesley Chapel, in Cincinnati, on the 20th of December, 1844, and passed the following resolutions, offered by William Birney:

WHEREAS, it has pleased an all-wise God to remove from among us, by sudden death, our distinguished fellow citizen, Thomas Morris; and as it is becoming to pay a tribute of respect to the memory of departed patriots, who have illustrated by their virtues, the history of their country—

Resolved, That we can never cease to admire the lofty and disinterested patriotism of Thomas Morris, manifested as it was by a consistent public life of nearly forty years.

Resolved, That posterity will honor him as the efficient Legislator, the incorruptible Judge, the able Senator, and above all, the bold and conscientious Advocate of Human Rights.

Resolved, That we shall cherish his memory, because he preferred Truth to party, Humanity to ambition, and his Country to the emoluments of office.

Resolved, That we are encouraged by his noble example to renewed efforts for the abolition of slavery, and will adopt for our motto the closing words of his celebrated Speech in the Federal Senate—"The Negro shall yet be free."

Resolved, That a Committee of three, with power to add to their number, be now appointed to receive contributions, for the purpose of erecting at some point in Hamilton county, a suitable monument to the memory of the deceased.

THE END.

www.ingramcontent.com/pod-product-compliance
Lightning Source LLC
LaVergne TN
LVHW020107110826
845151LV00001B/83

9781425544232